Howard Evans

Our Old Nobility

By Noblesse Oblige, Howard Evans

Howard Evans

Our Old Nobility

By Noblesse Oblige, Howard Evans

ISBN/EAN: 9783337012410

Printed in Europe, USA, Canada, Australia, Japan

Cover: Foto ©ninafisch / pixelio.de

More available books at **www.hansebooks.com**

OUR OLD NOBILITY.

BY
NOBLESSE OBLIGE
(HOWARD EVANS).

(Second Series.)

London:
PUBLISHED FOR THE POLITICAL TRACT SOCIETY,
By E. J. KIBBLEWHITE,
31, TAVISTOCK STREET, COVENT GARDEN, W.C.

1879.

CONTENTS.

CHAP.			PAGE
LIII.	THE ASHLEY-COOPERS		1
LIV.	„ POWLETTS		6
LV.	„ YORKES		11
LVI.	„ BRIDGEMANS		15
LVII.	„ GREYS OF HOWICK		20
LVIII.	„ LOFTUSES		24
LIX.	„ WARDS		28
LX.	„ VILLIERS		32
LXI.	„ GREVILLES		37
LXII.	„ STUARTS OF BLANTYRE AND GALLOWAY		42
LXIII.	„ PERCEVALS		47
LXIV.	„ GORES		51
LXV.	„ NELSONS		55
LXVI.	„ DUNCOMBES		59
LXVII.	„ HEATHCOTES		63
LXVIII.	„ STANLEYS OF KNOWSLEY		67
LXIX.	„ TALBOTS		76
LXX.	„ FITZMAURICES		8.
LXXI.	„ DALRYMPLES		85

CHAP.			PAGE
LXXII.	THE	SOMERSETS	90
LXXIII.	,,	WYNDHAMS	95
LXXIV.	,,	DUNDASES	99
LXXV.	,,	BOYLES	105
LXXVI.	,,	HERBERTS	110
LXXVII.	,,	TRENCHES	115
LXXVIII.	,,	HOWARDS	120
LXXIX.	,,	PRATTS	125
LXXX.	,,	RYDERS	130
LXXXI.	,,	EDENS	135
LXXXII.	,,	THYNNES	140
LXXXIII.	,,	VANES	145
LXXXIV.	,,	WEMYSS-CHARTERIS-DOUGLASES	150
LXXXV.	,,	WALPOLES	154
LXXXVI.	,,	ERSKINES	158
LXXXVII.	,,	VERNONS	163
LXXXVIII.	,,	GREYS	168
LXXXIX.	,,	BRUCES	173
XC.	,,	AGAR-ELLISES	177
XCI.	,,	HAMILTONS	181
XCII.	,,	NEVILLES	186
XCIII.	,,	BUTLERS	190
XCIV.	,,	CAMPBELLS	194
XCV.	,,	ST. MAURS	198
XCVI.	,,	SIDNEYS	202

Contents.

CHAP.			PAGE
XCVII.	,,	FITZGERALDS	207
XCVIII.	,,	MOLYNEUX	211
XCIX.	,,	WELLESLEYS	216
C.	,,	POWER OF THE LANDED	221
CI.		MODERN PEERAGES	225
CII.		THE GROWTH OF THE LANDED INTEREST	230
CIII.		CONCLUSION	235

OUR OLD NOBILITY

LIII.

The Ashley-Coopers.

HE Earl of Shaftesbury, whose seat is at St. Giles's House, near Wimborne, Dorset, owns in

Dorset	. . .	15,579 acres.
Hants	. . .	3,057 ,,
	Total	18,636 ,,

With a rentroll of £14,617.

The Peerage dates from the Restoration, and, though the Ashleys were persons of considerable estate long ere that time, Anthony Ashley-Cooper, first Earl of Shaftesbury, was the real founder of the greatness of the house. The estates seem to have been acquired, for the most part, by purchase or marriage.

In the time of the Plantagenets, Wimborne St. Giles belonged to the Plessy family. It was brought by a Plessy heiress to the Hamelyns, and by a Hamelyn heiress to the Ashleys. Sir Anthony Ashley, who was knighted in the taking of Cadiz, in the reign of Queen Elizabeth, rendered a useful service to his country by introducing cabbages from Holland. He appears to have purchased Hinton Martel, in Dorset, in the reign of James I. It was the heiress of Sir Anthony who brought the Ashley estates into the Cooper family. The Coopers appear to have for a long time settled at Paulet, in the county of Somerset, and Richard Cooper, of Paulet, married Sir Anthony Ashley's heiress, and their son, Sir Anthony Ashley-Cooper, succeeded in 1631 to an ample estate, which has been considerably enlarged at different times. For instance, in 1671 the Earl of Shaftesbury purchased Crichel of Lord Arundel of Wardour, and about the same time he purchased the manor of Berwick and six farms on Cranbourne Chase of the Earl of Salisbury; the latter, however, were afterwards resold. At other times lands at Edmundsham, Fordington, Horton, and other places have also come into the family by purchase.

The character of Anthony Ashley-Cooper, first Earl of Shaftesbury, has been described in two of Dryden's masterly poems, "Absalom and Achitophel," and "The Medal." In the former, describing Shaftesbury under the character of Achitophel, he thus depicts him:—

> "For close designs and crooked counsels fit;
> Sagacious, bold, and turbulent of wit;
> Restless, unfixed in principles and place;
> In power unpleased, impatient of disgrace;
> A fiery soul, which, working out its way,
> Fretted the pigmy body to decay,
> And o'er informed the tenement of clay.
> A daring pilot in extremity;
> Pleased with the danger when the waves went high,
> He sought the storms; but, for a calm unfit,
> Would steer too nigh the sands, to boast his wit."

The censure is qualified by a few lines of praise, eulogising Shaftesbury as an incorruptible Judge in an age when Judges were notoriously venal. But these lines were only inserted in the second edition, and there is too much reason to believe that they were inserted for a handsome consideration at the instance of Shaftesbury himself. Though Dryden was a Court poet, and Shaftesbury Leader of the Opposition, the former was not far wrong in his estimate of the Achitophel of the Restoration, according to Lord Campbell. Macaulay says that he was one of the "men in whom the immorality which was epidemic among the politicians of that age appeared in its most malignant type," and that "he had served and betrayed a succession of Governments, but he had timed all his treacheries so well that through all revolutions his fortunes had been constantly rising." He has the dubious honour of having been a Lord Chancellor with scarcely any knowledge of law.

Royalist, Roundhead, and then Royalist again; Puritan in pretence, Freethinker in reality; one of the notorious Cabal

Ministry, and yet the supporter of most of the good measures passed in the reign of Charles II.; a party to the mercenary alliance of England to France, and yet apparently himself unbribed; at one time a favourite at Court, at another the idol of the City; one whom even Charles II. spoke of as the most wicked of men, and yet who enjoyed the friendship of John Locke; a statesman who fought on the popular side at home, and yet endeavoured to create by legislation an aristocratic republic in Carolina—such was the first Earl of Shaftesbury. It would be fortunate for his memory if everything could be forgotten save the good measures he supported and the bad measures he opposed. He successfully supported the Habeas Corpus Act, by which the power of arbitrary imprisonment without trial was abolished, and he as successfully opposed the abominable Test, as an oath of passive obedience to tyranny, which the Tories of that day would have imposed upon every person holding office in the Kingdom. Unsuccessfully he resisted the oppressive legislation by which the Tories sought to destroy Nonconformity, and supported the Exclusion Bill, by which the calamity of the succession of James II. could have been avoided. Twice he was imprisoned in the Tower, and he died in effect an exile in his old age. On the whole he was a bold, bad man, whom accident and ambition led to render splendid services to the cause of freedom.

Of the son of the first lord there is nothing remarkable to be noticed; the grandson, who was partly educated by the grandfather and partly by Locke, became famous as an author and was spoken of by Voltaire as the boldest of English philosophers. His "Characteristics," in which he deals with ridicule as a test of truth, are little read now, but John Newton tells us that the perusal of that work led him to adopt Deistical opinions in early life. He appears to have looked at everything—even love matters—from a philosophical standpoint, for having been recommended by his friends to take a wife in order to perpetuate the line, he proposed to a young lady, and then wrote to an acquaintance:—" Will it be enough that I take a breeder out of a good family, with little or no fortune, and not in the highest degree of quality neither?"

The fifth Earl married a Wiltshire heiress, and left an only daughter, from whom is descended Lord de Mauley. The sixth Earl, brother of the fifth, for many years held the lucrative position of Chairman of Committees in the House of Lords. His second son, the Honourable William Ashley, was appointed to a rich sinecure as Master of St. Catharine's Hospital, the value of which amounted to several thousands a year, one of those scandalous arrangements by which the rich have been enabled to appropriate the property of the poor. He died only a few months ago. The present Earl married a daughter of the fifth Earl Cowper. This lady's mother afterwards married Lord Palmerston; and thus, by what the Evangelicals doubtless regarded as a special dispensation of Providence, Lord Shaftesbury became son-in-law to a Prime Minister, and for a time Bishop-maker in general.

Probably there is no Peer, who is not a Minister of the Crown, so well known to the mass of the people and so widely respected as the present Earl of Shaftesbury. "One man in his time plays many parts," but few public men have played so many parts as he. Every man with strong convictions who has passed the meridian of life must have found Lord Shaftesbury, at some time or other, on the same platform with himself. Be he Protestant or Catholic, Orthodox or Freethinker, Conservative or Liberal, Aristocrat or Democrat, country gentleman or working-class agitator—he is almost sure to have met Lord Shaftesbury at some time, both as friend and foe. It is not because Lord Shaftesbury is a man of shining abilities—in this country a peer who chooses to take part in any public matter is sure to be placed in the forefront—but he has been a man of immense activity, and his conservative and orthodox convictions have been tempered with such strong humanitarian sympathies that he has often found himself associated with men whose religious and political convictions differed most widely from his own. His family motto is "Love! Serve!" and certainly there is not a peer who has striven so hard to serve the friendless and helpless. The factory child, the Negro slave, the chimney-sweep, the city Arab, have all been the objects of his sympathy. Most provoking, yet most loveable of men! Have we not all seen him shortening the hours of labour, befriending the Negro, patronizing the teetotallers, creating Low Church Bishops, enrolling himself among the noble army of costermongers, savagely denouncing "Ecce Homo," pouring out doleful Jeremiads at religious meetings; converting gutter-children into shoeblacks and sailors; renouncing the S.P.C.K., because Mr. Brownlow Maitland, in defending Christianity, has conceded too much; inveighing in turn against Turkish and Russian atrocities; presenting a Bible to a labourers' agitator, and uttering unproved calumnies against the miners; standing on the same platform with High Churchmen against political dissenters, and again on the same platform with those wicked dissenters against High Churchmen—but everywhere the same warm-hearted, opiniative, impulsive, narrow, provoking, loveable spirit. I suppose if I came in his way he would denounce me with the same reckless extravagance of language with which I have heard him denounce Ritualists, Rationalists, and Radicals; but none the less should I regard with respect, and almost with affection, a man who, throughout a long life, has striven, according to his light, to serve, not so much his own order, as the outcast and the wretched.

Lord Shaftesbury's second surviving son, the Member for Poole, has already done good service as a Liberal in the House of Commons, and given fair promise of yet better things. His fourth son—who has yet his spurs to win—is spoken of as a Liberal candidate for a Northern borough. The heir to the peerage is never likely to be anything else but a lord; and, judging by a speech which not long ago he attempted to make in the City, I should think he is hardly likely to add much lustre to the house of Shaftesbury.

LIV.

The Powletts.

WHEN I was a lad, at the time I first became interested in the history of my own country, especially of the period prior to the Reformation, I used to wonder what had become of many of those old families whose names are never heard now, but which used to be always prominent in the days of the Plantagenets, the Yorkists, and the Lancastrians. Their names may have disappeared, like the African rivers that are said to lose themselves in the sands, but their lands of course still remain, and somebody must be in possession of them. Take for instance the family of Scrope, one of the strongest houses in the North, which was so prominent in the reigns of Edward III. and Richard II.—what has become of it? Well, the greater part of its possessions are now in the hands of the descendants of a placeman in the reign of George III., whose patent of nobility dates no later back than 1797.

Paulet, Marquis of Winchester; Powlett, Lord Bolton; Powlett, Duke of Cleveland; and Poulett, Earl Poulett, are all different branches of the same common stock; but Earl Poulett's line has a lengthy history of its own, and the Duke of Cleveland is only a Powlett through the marriage of one of his ancestors with a Powlett heiress. Let us confine ourselves, therefore, at present, to the Winchester line. The Powletts are a family whose history is interesting, for the Marquis of Winchester is the premier Marquis in England, and his ancestors once held the higher title of Duke of Bolton. The first Powlett who was ennobled played no inconsiderable part in four successive reigns, and the story of the siege and sack of Basing House, one of the most widely-known episodes of the Civil War, has become familiar to Londoners from the fresco in the corridor of the House of Lords.

The Paulets, were originally a Somersetshire family, who were seated at a place of that name in the same county. Their

The Powlettes.

early history I must leave till I come to Earl Poulett; the Winchester line was descended from a younger son, who was the founder of his own fortunes. This younger son married a sister of Lord St. John of Basing, who ultimately became heiress of that nobleman, and brought Basing House into the family. Their great-grandson was Sir William Paulet, a favourite of Henry VIII. I don't often quote Cobbett, preferring more accurate authorities; but in this case I am quite safe in doing so, though, of course, I do not endorse anything beyond that which refers to Paulet himself.

In his "Rural Rides," Cobbett says, speaking of Netley Abbey, "Its revenues when suppressed amounted to £3,200 a year of our present money. The possessions of the monks were, by the wife-killing founder of the Church of England, given away (though they belonged to the public) to one of his court sycophants, Sir William Powlett, a man the most famous in the whole world for sycophancy, time-serving, and all those qualities which usually distinguished the favourites of such kings as the Wife-killer. This Powlett changed from the Popish to Henry VIII.'s religion, and was a great actor in finishing the Papists. When Edward VI. came to the throne, this Powlett turned Protestant, and was a great actor in punishing those who adhered to Henry the Eighth's religion. When Queen Mary came to the throne, this Powlett turned back to Papist, and was one of the great actors in sending Protestants to be burnt at Smithfield. When old Bess came to the throne this Powlett turned Protestant again, and was, until the day of his death, one of the great actors in persecuting, in fining, in mulcting, and in putting to death those who still had the virtue and the courage to adhere to the religion in which he and they had been born and bred." Powlett was created Marquis of Winchester in the reign of Edward VI., and in that reign and in those of Mary and Elizabeth, he held the office of Lord Treasurer. On being asked how he could retain his office during three such reigns, he made the ignoble reply, "By being a willow, and not an oak." It is not to willows like Powlett, but to oaks like Tyndale and Bradford, and Latimer and Penry that England owes a debt of gratitude. To those her monarchs gave the martyr's stake and faggots; to these they gave the broad acres they had confiscated.

The son, grandson, and great-grandson of the first Marquis

successively inherited the title and estates. The fifth Marquis had the mortification of seeing his house stormed and burnt by the Roundheads at a loss of £200,000 to himself. A great deal of maudlin pity has been expended upon him, but for my part I have none to give. The Cavalier soldiery, whom he harboured, pitilessly robbed the traders of London, and he only suffered a righteous retribution. Says Carlyle, " Basing House had long infested the Parliament in those quarters; and been especially a great eyesorrow to the Trade of London with the Western Parts. With Dennington Castle at Newbury and this Basing House at Basingstoke, there was no travelling the Western roads except with escort or on sufferance." It had stood siege after siege for four years, and at last Cromwell was sent to dispose of it, and dispose of it he did most effectually. Let me quote Hugh Peters' account thereof:— " Lieutenant-General Cromwell had spent much time with God in prayer the night before the storm, and seldom fights without some text of Scripture to support him. This time he rested upon that blessed word of God written in the 115th Psalm, 8th verse—'They that make them are like unto them; so is every one that trusteth in them.' 'Which, with some verses going before,' says the sturdy old Roundhead, 'was now accomplished.'" A mile or two from Basing House the Paulets had in the days of Queen Elizabeth a hunting-lodge called Hackwood, and after the destruction of Basing House the Marquis altered and enlarged it in order to make it suitable for a residence. The first Duke of Bolton erected the present mansion at Hackwood Park, now a seat of the present Lord Bolton.

The next Marquis was created Duke of Bolton the year after the Restoration—I presume rather on account of his son's merits than of his own. His eccentricity almost reached the point of derangement, and, according to Burnet, "he was a man of most profuse expenditure, and of a most ravenous appetite to support that." By his first wife he had no issue, but by his second he had a large family. This lady was an heiress who brought considerable property into the family, at Bolton, in Wensleydale, and elsewhere. At Bolton, in the North Riding of Yorkshire, stands an ancient castle, formerly the seat of the Scropes, a family which for hundreds of years held land here, in unbroken descent from the time of the Conqueror. Sir Henry Le Scrope was in 1317 Chief

The Powlettes. 9

Justice of the King's Bench, and subsequently Chief Baron of the Exchequer. Burke, in his "Visitation of Seats and Arms," says that "the vast estates he died possessed of, show how profitable a use he had made through a long life of Court favour and professional emolument." His younger son, who was subsequently his heir, was Lord High Treasurer in the reign of Edward III., and Chancellor of England in that of Richard II. He it was who built Bolton Castle, where the ninth Lord Scrope held captive Mary Queen of Scots for a short time. The eleventh lord was created Earl of Sunderland by Charles I., but, dying without legitimate issue, his estates were divided between illegitimate daughters, one of whom married the Marquis of Winchester who became the first Duke of Bolton. It was owing to his possession of Bolton that he chose that place for his ducal title. The castle still remains, but the Powletts have built a mansion, Bolton House, in a more favourable situation not far off.

The second Duke, when Earl of Wiltshire, took an active part in the Revolution of 1688. He was one of those who assembled at the Hague and came over with William, and when James had fled he was the man who proposed a Speaker of the House of Commons favourable to William's assumption of royal power. He afterwards became Lord-Lieutenant of Ireland. His youngest brother was appointed to a lucrative sinecure as Teller of the Exchequer. He sat for a family borough, and was Chairman of Committees in the House of Commons. Walpole tells some comical anecdotes of him, one of which will suffice to estimate his abilities. A pamphlet called "The Snake in the Grass" being reported, probably in joke, to have been written by his Lordship, a gentleman abused in it sent him a challenge. Lord William professed his innocence, but the gentleman would not be satisfied without a denial under his own hand. Lord William took up and began—"This is to seratify that the buk called the Snak"—"Oh, my lord, said the person, "I am satisfied; your lordship has clearly convinced me that you did not write the book."

The third Duke married an actress, by whom he had previously had three illegitimate sons, and, dying without any legitimate issue, the title passed to his brother, who left two sons, each of whom successively inherited the dukedom. The fifth Duke had an illegitimate daughter, of whom more hereafter, and the sixth Duke had one legitimate daughter, who married the Duke of Cleveland. At his death the dukedom expired, but the Marquisate of Winchester passed to a distant relative descended from a younger brother of the Marquis who defended Basing House against Cromwell. His son, the thirteenth and late Marquis, being poor, provided for his sons in the services; the second became Prebend of Salisbury and Rector of Wellesbourne, the third became an Admiral, and the fourth and fifth Generals in the Army.

We pass now to the Bolton branch. Lord Bolton owns in

Hampshire	.	.	.	13,808 acres.
Yorkshire	.	.	.	15,418 ,,
			Total	29,226 ,,

With a rentroll of £27,553.

The fifth Duke of Bolton, as I have already stated, had an illegitimate daughter, and upon her he entailed the greater part of his estates, in default of his brother, the sixth Duke, having any legitimate male issue. She married a Mr. Orde, who was Secretary of the Treasury in 1782, and who, having been useful to William Pitt, was by him rewarded with a peerage, being created Baron Bolton in 1797. The late Peer appointed his nephew to the family living of Wensley, in Yorkshire, value £1,337 and a house, another example of that beautiful provision for younger sons which the Church of England affords.

LV.

The Yorkes.

THE Earl of Hardwicke has lately been making a speech at a Conservative banquet in Cambridgeshire. I don't suppose anyone cares what he says; but the appearance of his name reminds me that the Yorkes are another brilliant example of disinterested Conservatism. The Earl himself was Controller of the Household from 1866 to 1868 (salary £904), and since 1874 he has drawn £1,700 per annum as Master of the Buckhounds, the duties of which office, I believe, consist in now and then hunting a poor tame stag with fierce dogs, who sometimes worry it to death. When Bill Sykes sets his bullpup to worry a wretched cat he is called a brute and sent to hard labour for a month or two; but there is a great deal of difference between a cat and a buck, at least I presume the Royal Society for the Prevention of Cruelty to Animals think so. But I am digressing. The Earl, as I said, receives a modest £1,700 a year. The Hon. and Rev. Grantham Yorke was for thirty years Prebendary of Lichfield and Rector of St. Philip's, Birmingham, and is now Dean of Worcester (£1,200 and a house). The Hon. Eliot C. Yorke, late M.P. for Cambridgeshire, who married a daughter of Sir Anthony Rothschild, was Equerry to the Duke of Edinburgh. The Hon. J. M. Yorke is a Captain in the Navy. The Hon. A. G. Yorke is Equerry to Prince Leopold. General Sir C. Yorke, G.C.B., has filled a large number of military offices, and is Lieutenant of the Tower of London. Major-General F. A. Yorke has retired on full-pay as Colonel. Lieut.-General John Yorke is Colonel of the 19th Hussars, and has filled a number of military offices. Joseph A. Yorke filled an office in the Bankrupcy Court, at a salary of £1,000 per annum, and when it was abolished eight years ago he received a compensation allowance of £666 13s. 4d. per annum. The Yorkes, I am inclined to think, have good reason to be satisfied with things as they are. They have always been a race of voracious tax-eaters from the first, as we shall see.

Philip Yorke, first Earl of Hardwicke, was the son of a Dissenting attorney at Dover, who sent him up to London, where he became a lawyer's clerk, in Brooke-street, Holborn. Philip seems to have studied hard, and having eaten his terms and been called to the Bar, he was fortunate enough to be appointed law tutor to the sons of Chief-Justice Parker, afterwards Earl of Macclesfield. Parker became his patron, and when he had only been in practice four years, and was but twenty-nine years old, secured him the post of Solicitor-General, much to the disgust of the Bar. Four years after, Parker contrived to advance him to the Attorney-Generalship, an office which he held for thirteen years. Although he owed so much to Lord Macclesfield, when that nobleman was disgraced and condemned for malpractices in the Court of Chancery, Yorke was not generous enough to say or do anything in his defence. In 1733 he was made Lord Chief Justice, at a salary of £2,000 a year more than any of his predecessors. In 1737 he was offered the post of Lord Chancellor, and took care to bargain for a rich sinecure Tellership in the Exchequer for his son beforehand. At his elevation he was created Baron, and subsequently Earl of Hardwicke. He held the Chancellorship for nearly twenty years. As a man he was heartless, selfish, and avaricious; but Lord Campbell says that he is universally considered the most consummate judge who ever sat in the Court of Chancery. His wife bears the reputation of having been more stingy and rapacious than himself.

He began with nothing, he did not marry a great heiress, he was only twenty years at the Bar, but he died worth a million of money. Well might Dunning declare in the House of Commons that he "uniformly throughout his life pursued his own private interests, and raised the greatest fortune and provided the most amply for his family of any lawyer that ever lived." It is said that even George II. was somewhat disgusted by his greediness. On one occasion, when Hardwicke was begging for a place for a distant relative, the King said, " My Lord, you have been a frequent solicitor, but I have observed that it has always been for some of your family or within the circle of your relations." Lord Campbell, who had a high regard for the Earl of Hardwicke, as a Chancellor, is compelled to admit that "he had no retired allowance, but, beside his own immense fortune, not only his sons, but all his kith and kin and dependents were saturated with places, pensions, and reversions." Lord Stanhope defends Hardwicke from the charge of personal avarice on the ground that "the head of the Law must endeavour to found a family and earn an estate, and not leave his son a poor peer, a burthen on his country." The first Earl of Hardwicke certainly did obtain an estate, and he did not leave his son a poor peer; but a considerable number of the Yorkes have been a burthen upon the country notwithstanding, from the time of the first Earl down to that of the present. As to the sons of the first Earl, the eldest had, as I have said before, an Exchequer Tellership; the second, conjointly with one of his brothers, the lucrative post of Clerk of the Crown; a third was a general in the Army, and, for more than a quarter of a century, Ambassador to Holland; a fourth "had several lucrative sinecures conferred upon him by his father"; and a fifth became Bishop of Ely.

The Earl owns 19,049 acres, of which all but 71 are situated in Cambridgeshire, rental £26,417. Wimpole House, a mansion which has a deer-park of 250 acres, was built in 1632 by the Chicheleys; it subsequently passed by purchase to Holles, Duke of Newcastle, and thence by marriage to the Earl of Oxford, who added two wings to it. Wimpole and other manors were purchased in 1739 by the first Earl of Hardwicke. He and succeeding Earls have at various times added to the estate by purchase of lands at Kingston, Guilden Morden, Steeple Morden, Haddenham, Foulmire, West Wickham, and other places.

Charles Yorke, the second son of the first Earl, was born with a silver spoon in his mouth. He was called to the Bar before he was twenty-one, and, practising in the Court of Chancery where his father presided, he soon attracted a good share of business from the solicitors. His cousin owned the pocket borough of Reigate, and thus he was provided with a cheap and safe seat in Parliament. He married a Hertfordshire heiress, a Miss Freeman, of Aspeden. At twenty-five he was appointed Solicitor-General to the Prince of Wales, at twenty-six counsel to the East India Company, at thirty-seven he was Solicitor-General, and on the accession of Lord Bute to power he became Attorney-General. When Bute retired he resigned office, but resumed it on the accession of the Rockingham Ministry. When Lord Camden broke away from the Grafton Ministry he was much pressed to take the Seals, but he had promised his friends, the Rockingham Whigs, and his brother especially, that he would not do so. At last he allowed himself to be over-persuaded by George III., and was bitterly reproached by his former associates, who upbraided him with a breach of honour. His patent of nobility was made out, but before the Great Seal had been affixed he was dead. According to popular report he died by his own hand, but his relatives denied the statement. Lord Campbell leaves the matter somewhat in doubt, but Lord Stanhope considers the evidence too strong to be disputed, and I cannot but think that the conclusion to which he comes is correct.

Charles Yorke had three sons. The eldest, who for some years was Lord-Lieutenant of Ireland, succeeded his uncle as third Earl. The second held various Government offices, and a sinecure Tellership of the Exchequer, which alone was worth £2,700 a year. The third was an Admiral in the Navy. The eldest son of this last, who was also an Admiral in the Navy, ultimately succeeded to the Peerage. One of his brothers held the family living of Wimpole (£470 and a house), the Rectory of Aspeden, also at that time a family living (£357 and a house), and a Canonry of Ely, worth now £800, but probably worth considerably more when he held it. Another brother is the present Dean of Worcester before mentioned, an appointment which he owes to the present Tory Ministry.

I have now shown that the first Earl of Hardwicke not only succeeded in amassing a million of money, and in obtaining for his sons enormous sums in the way of out-door relief from the tax-payers of the country, but that the descendants of the first Earl have faithfully followed in their father's footsteps, and have with uniform regularity lived to the utmost of their power upon the national exchequer. Truly a magnificent example of disinterested Conservatism! The family motto is "*Nec cupias nec metuas*" (Neither desire nor fear). By this I suppose that the Yorkes mean that they have no desire to live by their own exertions, and no fear of putting their hands in the pocket of John Bull.

LVI.

The Bridgemans.

TURNING over Horace Walpole's letters to verify my recollection of a statement made by him concerning the first Earl of Hardwicke, I came upon the following passage:—"By the way, you know the reverend head of the Law (Hardwicke) is frequently shut up here [at Twickenham] with my Lady Mountrath, who is as rich and tipsy as Cacafogo in the comedy. What a jumble of avarice, lewdness, dignity—and claret!" Lady Mountrath, *née* Newport, reminds me of an extinct Peerage which has been revived in the descendants of the female heir of the estates, the Earldom of Bradford. The Earl of Bradford is to me an object of some little interest. He is descended from Sir Orlando Bridgeman, who, I have somewhere read, had much to do with building up that elaborate system of legal chicanery by which landed estates are tied up so that they never come into the market. Moreover, he is one of those mighty Midland lords who, because they draw some thousands annually from the industry of the Midland towns and manufacturing villages, consider themselves under an obligation to win the obstinate Midlanders back to Toryism. We have already seen what a noble and unselfish thing is the Conservatism of the Marquis of Hertford and the Earl of Dartmouth; the Earl of Bradford is an equally splendid example of disinterested Conservatism.

I am unable to judge of his lordship's abilities, because I do not recollect ever reading a single speech from him in the House of Lords' debates; but he has held office in different Tory Administrations as Vice-Chamberlain of the Household and Lord Chamberlain, and he now draws £2,500 annually for doing nothing as Master of the Horse, a post which fortunately does not require much mental ability. The Earl, however, is a man of large acres, for he owns in

Shropshire	. . . .	10,515 acres
Stafford	. . . .	6,689 ,,
Warwick	. . . .	1,860 ,,
Montgomery	. . . .	34 ,,
Leicester	. . . .	6 ,,
	Total	19,104 ,,

With a rentroll of £31,934.

Although the Earldom of the present creation only dates from 1815—the Bradford in question is an obscure little place in Shropshire—on the female side the Earl is descended from several ancient noble houses. His eldest son, Viscount Newport, sits for the 10,515 acres in Shropshire; a younger son, a captain in the Guards, recently contested Tamworth in the Conservative interest, and was soundly beaten.

The founder of the house was Dr. Bridgeman, who was Bishop of Chester and Rector of Wigan from 1615 to 1645, when he was ejected by the Long Parliament. His long occupation of bishopric and rectory enabled him to purchase an estate at Great Lever, near Bolton; and the rectory of Wigan itself, by what means I cannot ascertain, ultimately came into the possession of the Bridgemans. The living is put down as worth £1,600 a year and a residence, but it is no doubt worth much more, and the connection of the Bridgemans therewith is noteworthy. Let us take the history of the rectory for the last 140 years. During this period there have been seven rectors, four of them Bridgemans, and a Bridgeman is in possession of it now. Another Bridgeman is rectory of Weston-under-Lizard, Shropshire (£503 and a house), of which living the Earl of Bradford is also patron. These are the two richest livings out of the twelve in the possession of the Bridgemans, and so they keep them as much as possible to themselves. In the year 1823 I find that a Bridgeman held both these livings, besides a third, which was in the gift of another member of the family; and at the same period another Bridgeman held two other livings, presented to him by noble patrons who were connected with him by marriage. There are not a few flunkey souls who would prefer being preached to by the son of a Lord, but my sympathies go with the hard-working servants of the Church who have plenty of merit but no family influence, and whose

only reward for their faithful labours is to see the prizes of
the Church snapped up by the younger sons of the aristocracy.
The son of the Bishop, Orlando Bridgeman, was a lawyer,
who in the reign of Charles I. was returned to Parliament for
Wigan, probably by his father's influence. His sympathies
were entirely with the Tyrant, but he had not courage enough
to meet such men as Pym in debate, and contented himself
with silently voting against the abolition of the Court of Star
Chamber and other useful reforms. He was one of the King's
Commissioners in the abortive negotiations at Uxbridge; he
encouraged the citizens of Chester to fight against the Parliament, but he was too timorous to take up arms himself;
and when the Royalist cause collapsed he came back to
London and remained in sulky retirement till the Restoration.
Then he was appointed Lord Chief Baron, and presided at
the trial of Harrison and the other members of the High
Court of Justice who had sat in judgment on the King. He
had his reward, being created a baronet and Lord Chief
Justice, and at the fall of Clarendon he became Lord Keeper.
Roger North says "he was timorous to impotence, and
affixed the Great Seal to grants to Lady Castlemaine and
others, which Clarendon had stopped." Lord Campbell
pronounces him to be "a most execrably bad Equity judge."
Like many other Tories of that age, he lacked consistency,
for, after having strenuously maintained the dispensing power
of the King to over-ride the Law, he denied it when Charles
II. wished to use it to give religious freedom to Catholics and
Nonconformists. The difficulty was for the time arranged by
exempting Catholics from the advantages of the exercise of
the dispensing power. But soon after Bridgeman was dismissed. The King and his Ministers were bent on an
iniquitous war against Holland in the interests of Romanism.
They could get no money in a legitimate way, so they shut up
the Exchequer for twelve months, and thus had £1,300,000
at their disposal. The bankers, unable to obtain from the
Exchequer the money they had lent it, were unable to repay
to their customers the sums they had advanced, and were in
consequence threatened with bankruptcy. The Government
recommended the bankers to apply to the Lord Keeper for an
injunction to stay legal proceedings, and the King sent the
Lord Keeper a message directing him to give the injunction
needed. But the illegality was so flagrant, that, slavishly

submissive as Bridgeman was, he dared not comply, and yet he had not the manliness to refuse. He therefore said he would take the papers home with him, and give judgment another day. The judgment was never delivered by him, for the King and his Ministers, who wanted a bolder and more unscrupulous man, took the Great Seal from him, and Shaftesbury became Lord Chancellor. Sir Orlando married the heiress of a Shropshire squire, John Kynaston of Morton.

His son, who also married an heiress, purchased the property now held by the Bridgemans, at Castle Bromwich, in Warwickshire. The son of this last also married a Shropshire heiress, daughter of Roger Matthews of Blodwell, who had inherited a portion of the estates of an ancient Welsh Prince, from whom she was descended. But his son, the fourth baronet, made a still more fortunate marriage, through which Weston Hall, the principal seat of the family, came into possession of the Bridgemans.

He married Lady Anne Newport, sister of the Lady Mountrath before mentioned, and at the death of the last Earl of Bradford of the first creation, who was uncle to these ladies, the Newport estates were divided between them. The Newports had been landowners in Shropshire from the days of Edward I., which makes it probable that they had come into possession of the confiscated lands of some Welsh Prince, and they increased their possessions in Salop by marriage at various times. Sir Richard Newport, espousing the Royalist cause, was created a baron in 1642. This Lord Newport had married a sister and co-heir of Sir Richard Leveson, of Trentham. James Leveson of Trentham was one of those who were enriched by the plunder of the monasteries, Wombridge, Lilleshall, and a priory at Stafford falling to his share. Another Newport had married the heiress of the Wilbraham family, whose ancestors had obtained considerable lands at Walsall, which also were part of the spoil of the monastic houses. What a fortunate thing it was for some of our great houses that there was a rich Church to plunder.

At the Restoration the elder of the sons of Lord Newport was appointed Comptroller, and afterwards Treasurer, of the Household, and was also created a Viscount; the younger obtained the post of Commissioner of the Customs. The elder, by the way, being a supporter of William III., was ultimately created Earl of Bradford, and one of his sons

The Bridgemans.

obtained the lucrative sinecure of a Tellership in the Exchequer. A little later on I find another Bridgeman who was for many years Comptroller of the Board of Green Cloth and Surveyor of the Royal Gardens.

The son of the baronet who married the Newport heiress was created Baron Bradford in 1794, and his son was created Earl of Bradford in 1815. Of the four sons of the latter, the second was provided for in the Navy, the third in the Army, the fourth in the Church. The second Earl had three sons, of whom the second and third were provided for in the Church. I fear that some of my readers will find this a dry and dreary record of Masterships, Comptrollerships, Treasurerships, Tellerships, and Rectorships; however, that is not my fault, but that of the Bridgemans. To me it is but a misfortune to have to deal with a family almost the sole landmarks of whose history are the rich places they occupied.

LVII.

The Greys of Howick.

I SHOULD be sorry to convey the impression, from the recent examples of disinterested Conservatism which I have given, that the place-hunting families are to be found only in one political party. Therefore, from the Tories let us turn to the Whigs, where we shall find examples of rapacity equal to, if not surpassing, any which I have yet given. Probably it would be difficult to find a more glaring case than that of the Greys. It is a long, dreary record of shameless greed and official nepotism; and I fear that the story will be but imperfectly told, for it is difficult at the present time to discover what was done for cousins and brothers-in-law, and other connections who did not bear the Grey patronymic. But the story must be told, in order that we may understand the bitter hatred which Cobbett and other popular leaders a generation or two ago entertained to what they called Whiggery. Earl Grey is the owner of 17,599 acres in Northumberland, the gross annual rental of which is put down at £23,724.

For more than five hundred years the Greys have flourished in Northumberland. In the reign of Edward III. a Sir Thomas de Grey is said to have held Howick and other manors in that county. How the Greys came there it is impossible to say, but they were a Norman House, and Tankerville, though a modern title, is really the revival of an old Norman peerage held by one branch of the family. Sir John Grey was a distinguished soldier in the reign of Henry V. The descendant of his younger brother in the reign of Henry VIII. possessed a moiety of the Manor of Howick. A grandson of this latter, the first Lord Grey of Warke, fought for the Parliament in the Civil War, and was Speaker of the House of Lords. His great-grandson was the first Earl of Tankerville. But our present business is with the Howick line.

The father of the first Lord Grey of Warke married the daughter and heiress of a kinsman, Sir Thomas Grey, of

Horton, in Northumberland. One of his younger sons was Sir Edward Grey, who appears to have inherited Howick. His son increased the estates by a marriage with another Northumberland heiress. One of their descendants, Henry Grey, was created a Baronet in the year 1746. The eldest son of the first Baronet died unmarried, and the second fell in a duel. The third son became a General in the Army, and in 1801 was advanced to the Peerage as Baron Grey, and in 1806 as Earl Grey. His eldest son was the Earl Grey of the Reform Ministry. His second son was a General in the Army and Colonel of the 13th Dragoons, with £1,057 per annum. His third son was a Naval Captain, Marshal in Barbadoes, and Resident Commissioner of Portsmouth Harbour. The fourth was a Colonel in the Army. The fifth had the Rectory of Bishopsgate (£1,650 and a house) and Prebendary of Westminster, and when his brother became Prime Minister he also held the Deanery of Hereford (present value £1,000). Subsequently he became Bishop of the same diocese. In the short-lived Whig Ministry of 1806, lasting less than a year, the second Earl Grey, then Lord Howick, held successively the offices of First Lord of the Admiralty and Foreign Secretary. At that time it was that the second brother and four other Greys received lucrative appointments. The brother in question was sent out to the Cape of Good Hope as Commander-in-Chief and Lieutenant-Governor, with a salary of £4,000 per annum attached to each office.

In 1807 Lord Howick succeeded as second Earl Grey on the death of his father. At 22 years of age he had been elected member for Northumberland, and he at once ranged himself with Fox and the Whig party. The Whigs then had an extended programme, which embraced the Reform of Parliament, the abolition of the slave trade, the repeal of the Test and Corporation Acts, Catholic Emancipation, and other great reforms. Save for a few months in 1806-7, Lord Grey had to be content with a prolonged exile from office. At length, when he was long past 60 years of age, the time was ripe for the first Reform Bill, and Earl Grey, the acknowledged leader of the Whigs, became Premier. It would be impossible here to discuss at length the various questions that have been raised in regard to the policy of the first Reform Bill. It may be fairly claimed on behalf of the Earl that, by his firmness and perseverance in insisting upon the passage of the Bill, he saved his country from the horrors of Civil War. It would be both ungrateful and unjust to undervalue the services which the first Earl Grey rendered to his country at one of the most perilous crises in the present century. The first Reform Bill was undoubtedly defective in many respects; I should be inclined even to say purposely defective. The man who "stood by his order" could not fully trust the people, and no doubt saw much more clearly than they did that the Bill itself would leave a large, if not a preponderant, power in the hands of the great houses. But, after all, the first Reform Bill was a great step forward, and its chief merit was that it made all other reforms possible. The Whig Ministry of which Earl Grey was Premier somewhat disappointed the high expectations which had been formed by ardent and hopeful spirits, though it really accomplished much useful work. But its nepotism was scandalous. The emoluments given to his family connections by Earl Grey very soon after his appointment as First Lord of the Treasury, including his own, were estimated to be of the value of £60,000 per annum.

We will glance simply at the sons of the Earl Grey of Reform Bill days. The eldest, the present Earl, was Under-Secretary of the Colonies in his father's Ministry, then Under-Secretary in the Home Department, then War Secretary, and subsequently Secretary for the Colonies, his official career lasting on and off from 1830 to 1852. The second was the late General Grey, who, after a series of rapid promotions in the Army, became Colonel of the 71st Regiment, Private Secretary to the late Prince Consort, and afterwards Private Secretary (£1,000) and Equerry (£750) to the Queen. The third and fourth sons when quite young men were Post Captains in the Navy, and in due time became Admirals. The fifth son, soon after coming of age, was presented with the vicarage of Wooler (£478 and a house), and a few years after obtained the Rectory of Houghton-le-Spring (£1,600 and a house). The sixth son, at 29 years of age, obtained the rectory of Morpeth (£1,611 and a house). These two reverend Greys must have had from the Church in the course of their lives more than £100,000 between them. The seventh son became a Captain in the Army; the eighth was Secretary of Legation at Paris. I doubt not some pretty little additions could be added to the list if I had space and time to look into the career of the grandsons.

The Greys of Howick.

It would be an unpardonable omission if I were to forget that veteran placeman, Sir George Grey, Bart., who sat for the family borough of Morpeth till the Reform Bill of 1867 passed, when he had to stand on one side for that genuine and able son of toil, Thomas Burt, the miner. Nothing gave me more delight at the elections of 1868 than to see the jailor of Ernest Jones replaced by a man who not long before had worked in the pit. There have been men, who called themselves gentlemen, mean enough to sneer at the modest allowance made to the present member for Morpeth by the Northumberland Miners' Union; suppose we consider what political life meant to the former member. Sir George was the son of a younger son of the first Earl Grey. This younger son, a veteran placeman, was not only a Captain in the Navy, but Marshal in the Island of Barbadoes, and Resident Commissioner of Portsmouth Dockyard. Sir George's younger brother was Paymaster of the Civil Services in Ireland. Sir George himself, for sixteen years, held various first-class offices in successive Whig Governments, and when he was not in office, of late years, he drew an annual pension of £2,000. In all, he must have received not far short of £100,000 for his political services, and, with all due respect to the Greys, I cannot but think that he was dear at the money.

LVIII.

The Loftuses.

RENDS MOI TEL QUE JE SUIS—"Take me as I am"—says the motto upon the crest of the Marquis of Ely. Let us accept the invitation. The Marquis owns in

Fermanagh	. . . .	34,416 acres.
Wexford .	. . . .	12,660 ,,
Dublin	. . . .	484 ,.
	Total	47,560 ,,

The annual rental of these properties is put down at £22,556. The Loftus family are English adventurers who have by various means acquired their extensive Irish Estates within the last three hundred years. The name was formerly written Lofthouse, and is of Saxon origin, the Lofthouses claiming to have held lands in Yorkshire long before the coming of the Norman Conqueror.

The real founder of the family was the Rev. Adam Lofthouse, who, having accompanied the Earl of Sussex, Viceroy of Ireland, as private chaplain, to Dublin, played his cards so well that in 1562 he was consecrated Archbishop of Armagh, from which see he was in a few years translated to that of Dublin. In 1578 he was elevated to the dignity of Lord Chancellor of Ireland, and he held that office till his death. In the reigns of Elizabeth and James I. a man who held the Great Seal of Ireland for more than thirty years could hardly help laying the foundation of a great family. Wholesale confiscations and lavish grants were the order of the day, and a man must have had almost superhuman virtue not to take a portion of the plunder when it might be had for the asking. The elder son of the Archbishop being well provided for, the younger obtained grants of the estates of Killyan and Clonard, and the office of Constable of Wicklow Castle. The elder son, Sir Dudley Loftus, of Rathfarnham, in due time succeeded his father; and his grandson, Lord Lisburne, had a daughter and heir, who carried the estates of the elder branch of the family to Lord Wharton on her marriage. The second son of Sir Dudley Loftus enjoyed lucrative offices as joint clerk of the Pells and of the Irish Treasury. He also advanced his fortunes by a marriage with an Irish heiress. In this latter particular his example was imitated by his son, whose eldest son was elevated to the Irish Peerage as Viscount Loftus. The second Viscount married the heiress of Sir Gustavus Hume, Bart., of County Fermanagh, and gained a step in the Peerage, being created Earl of Ely. At the death of the second Earl, his uncle succeeded; but, he dying without heirs, the titles expired—the estates passed to Charles Tottenham, of Tottenham Green, whose mother was a Loftus. This gentleman, who married another Irish heiress, changed his name to Loftus, and soon after coming into the Loftus estates he was created Baron Loftus. This was in 1785. Four years after he was a Viscount, five years after that he became an Earl, and six years later, in 1800—the date is ominous—he was created Marquis of Ely. By the way, this Ely is not Ely in Cambridgeshire, nor this Tottenham Green in Middlesex; the former place is in Fermanagh, and the latter in Wexford. The estates of the Tottenhams have passed away from the Marquis of Ely, having been devised to a younger son of the first Marquis, who once more assumed the name of Tottenham.

The first Marquis of Ely was one of those Irish noblemen who were bribed into supporting the Act of Union. It is hardly my province here to discuss the merits or demerits of the Act. Some of the Acts of the Irish Parliament towards the close of its existence, particularly the Act by which "Flogging Fitzgerald" obtained an indemnity for his inhuman crimes, were so outrageously unjust and oppressive, that one is almost tempted to declare that anything was better than such an assembly as that. Presupposing that the Union was absolutely necessary, it must be allowed, on behalf of Pitt, that a profligate distribution of money and titles was the only possible road to success. "The flag of prostitution and corruption" was hoisted accordingly. But what can be said on behalf of the men whose consent to the Act of Union could only be obtained by wholesale bribery, save that they were men who all their lives had fattened on corruption? As Mr. Massey says—"When an Irish gentleman gave £20,000 for a borough he invested his money in a speculation from which he had reason to expect a safe return. The commoner wanted a peerage; he had two votes at the service of the Minister, and Irish Peerages were held in higher estimation by the Irish commoners than by the British Premier." Castlereagh, the Irish Secretary, was the chief agent in this disgraceful business. To quote Mr. Massey again :—" The foremost men in Ireland—men whose abilities would have raised them to eminence in any country, whose eloquence would have moved any assembly, ancient or modern, whose patriotism was sincere—had first been tempted, but had refused every offer to betray the independence of their country. Another class of leading persons was then tried, and from them, for the most part, evasive answers were received. The Minister understood the meaning of these dubious utterances. Bribery of every kind must be employed without hesitation and without stint." It was so used. The first £5,000 that Castlereagh drew from the Secret Service Money melted away at once, and he then drew up a scheme by which, under the name of compensation, £1,500,000 was to be distributed among the owners of boroughs, part owners of counties, and members of the Irish Parliament.

We have it on the authority of a letter of the Duke of Portland that the King had authorised assurances to be given to Lord Ely that he should be made a Peer of Great Britain as a reward for the part he had in the transaction, and he was accordingly created an Irish Marquis and a Baron of the United Kingdom. In this respect he presented a pitiable contrast to Lord Gosford, who, though by conviction favourable to the Union, refused to accept an Earldom, on the ground that he did not think he was entitled to a reward for his vote in Parliament. But Lord Ely was not alone; no less than twenty Irish peers were advanced to higher titles as a reward for the votes they gave. The money needed for systematic corruption was raised by taxation of the wretched people of Ireland, and the Marquis of Ely was not ashamed to take £45,000 thereof as " compensation" for the loss of his Parliamentary interest. It must be admitted that political morality at the time was at a very low ebb, but that does not alter the fact that the descendants of the first Marquis of Ely sit in the House of Lords in virtue of a transaction which, if imitated by a Parliamentary voter of the present day, subjects him to condign punishment as a criminal. "Take me as I am," said the first Marquis; and Pitt accordingly took him as a creature who, though possessed of enormous wealth—the Tottenham as well as the Loftus estates—was ready to sell himself and his country for £45,000 and an additional title.

Let us turn from him to his sons. The elder, afterwards second Marquis, was made Irish Postmaster-General, Teller of the Irish Exchequer, and a Commissioner of the Treasury. The younger was appointed Bishop of Clogher, a diocese which possessed 27,000 acres of land; while a cousin, General Loftus, had a sinecure Colonelcy worth £1,579 a-year, and the Lieutenancy of the Tower, £745 a-year. Of the sons of the Bishop of Clogher I note that three were provided for in the Church, two in the Army, two in the Navy, and one in the Civil Service. Of the sons of the third Marquis one went into the Army, another into the Church, and a third was, till very recently, our Ambassador at St. Petersburg.

LIX.

The Wards.

THE history of the Wards presents no features of striking interest, inasmuch as they are but a line of illustrious obscurities, whose names are conspicuous by their absence in our national annals, and whose only merit has been to achieve a succession of lucky marriages, with the result of accumulating a large amount of landed property in the Midland Counties. Nevertheless, as the Earl of Dudley is immensely rich, and draws a very large part of his wealth from the labour of the district around Birmingham, he must not pass unnoticed. According to the landowners' return he possesses in

Staffordshire	4,730 acres	£68,460 rental.
Worcestershire	14,698 ,,	48,545 ,,
Merioneth	4,472 ,,	3,115 ,,
Roxburgh	1,086 ,,	2,825 ,,
Salop	568 ,,	233 ,,
Total	25,554	£123,178 ,,

As the Earl is also a great colliery proprietor in South Staffordshire these figures by no means represent his real income. Everyone knows that the Earl of Dudley is the owner of Dudley Castle, and those who have caught a hasty glimpse of that ancient fortress from the railway would naturally suppose that the Wards are an ancient house; they are, however, descended from a London tradesman who flourished in the reign of Charles I.

William Ward was the sixth son of a Norfolk squire, whose family had been for generations seated at Bixley in that county. He came up to London when a lad, was bound apprentice to a City goldsmith, and subsequently set up in business for himself in Lombard Street. Not long after he had opened his shop, a sailor, who had just landed from his ship, came in and offered to sell him what proved to be a lot of rough diamonds. Ward bought them at an immense advantage to himself, and the same night treated the whole of the ship's crew to a carouse at a neighbouring tavern. The next day another lot was brought him, which he bought up at an equally low price as the first. This lucky stroke of fortune proved to be but the first step up the ladder, and in time Ward became jeweller to Queen Henrietta Maria, wife of Charles I., and was one of the most opulent bankers and goldsmiths in the City. Among the improvident nobles of that time who came to him for monetary accommodation was the last of the Suttons, Lords of Dudley. He had squandered his means on harlots, but he had yet a splendid estate—ample security for the £20,000 loan which he wished Ward to advance him. Ward replied that Lord Dudley might do better than that. He himself had a son, Humble by name, and his Lordship had a grand-daughter. If his Lordship would marry the young lady to his son Humble Ward he should be well satisfied with that security. The bargain was struck, and thus the Wards and the Suttons of Dudley became united. We must now go back some centuries, and trace the history of Dudley Castle and the surrounding lands.

Dudley Castle is supposed to have been built by a Saxon named Dodo. Soon after the Norman Conquest we find it in the possession of Fitz-Ansculph. Shortly afterwards Paganel obtained possession of it, possibly through a marriage with FitzAnsculph's daughter. The sister and heir of his grandson, Gervase Paganel, married John de Somerie, who rebuilt the castle. Henceforth the Someries were barons of Dudley. One of them married a sister and co-heir of D'Albini, Earl of Arundel. In time the male line of the Someries was exhausted and a sister and co-heir of the last Somerie baron of Dudley married John de Sutton, and brought with her the town and castle of Dudley, with the manor of Sedgley, chase of Pensnett, manor of New Swynford, &c. In the reign of that amiable weakling, Henry VI., John de Sutton obtained grants of divers additional lordships, as well as the stewardship of several others for life. He was Treasurer to Henry VI., but ultimately Edward IV. purchased his support by relieving him of all liability for any debts he owed the former monarch. A subsequent Lord Dudley, who was nicknamed "Lord Quondam," from his practice of sponging upon his friends in his adversity, became entangled in debt, and lost nearly all his property to John Dudley, Duke of Northumberland, who took advantage of his folly and weakness to drive some very hard bargains with him.

The said John Dudley, Duke of Northumberland, in the reign of Edward VI., claimed to be descended from the Sutton Dudleys; but his father, Dudley, the extortioner of Henry VII., seems to have been a lad of obscure birth, who was educated by the charity of a Sussex monastery. At Northumberland's execution his property reverted to the Crown, but the Dudley estates which he had acquired were re-granted by Queen Mary to the heir of the Sutton Dudleys, so that the ancient property of this family now possessed by the Earl of Dudley is derived from a Crown grant a little more than 300 years old. In 1600, an old writer informs us that Lord Dudley hath Dudley, Sedgley, Swinford, Clent, Mere, Enfield, Bushbury, Amilcote, Morfe, Over and Nether Penn, Hagley, Molesley, Overton Wimbourne, Oxeley, Tresell, Seisdon, Himely, Hondesworth, Sandshall, Cocorton, and several other places. Not a few of these appear in Domesday Book as held by FitzAnsculph. Rowley was the King's till the reign of Edward II., when Somerie obtained a grant of it. Old Swinford was purchased in the same reign of Bernard de Bruys.

The Sutton Dudleys deserve some credit for increasing the trade of the district. In 1619 Dud Dudley left the University to manage his father's ironworks in the Chase of Pensnett. Wood becoming scarce, he began to use pit-coal, and obtained a patent from James I. for the process. He continued to struggle against many difficulties. Rival manufacturers injured him by their narrow jealousy, ignorant workmen cut his bellows, a flood swept away his works, and, finally, his property was confiscated by the Commonwealth as a punishment for the aid he afforded to the Royalist cause.

After this lengthy, but necessary, digression, let us return to Humble Ward and his descendants. Humble was created Baron Ward of Birmingham. His eldest son married the heiress of Sir William Brereton, of Handford, Cheshire. At the death of the fifth Baron of this line the ancient Barony of Dudley passed to Fernandino Lea, whose grandmother was a Ward, and at his death it fell into abeyance. The estates and the Ward Barony passed to John Ward, who was descended from a younger son of Humble. This younger son had married the granddaughter and heiress of Thomas Parkes, who in 1600 had purchased Willingsworth and Sedgeley of the then Lord Dudley, and thus, after a long lapse of years, these manors were again united with the Dudley estates. John was created Viscount Dudley and Ward. The fourth Viscount was advanced to an Earldom, but, dying unmarried, all the honours expired save the Ward Barony, which was inherited by his second cousin, a clergyman, whose son, the present Peer, was created an Earl in 1860.

It may be worth while to glance at the Church livings in the hands of the Earl of Dudley. Of these there are thirteen, whose united annual value is nearly £7,000 beside the residences. The patronage of several of these has always gone with the ancient manors of the old Dudley estates. Dudley, Kingswinford, St. Mary's, Pensnett, Kidderminster, Stourbridge, and Sedgley, are all vicarages, so in all probability Lord Dudley receives the great tithes from most of these places, which must amount to a very large sum. The vicarage of Dudley is not only worth £1,080 and a house, but carries with it the patronage of four other livings, whose united value is £1,300, with a house to each. It cost the Wards nothing to obtain it. I find that in the year 1342 the Bishop of Worcester summoned the Prior and Convent of Dudley to show title to the appropriation of the Church of Dudley, and their title was allowed. It continued in their hands till the dissolution of the monasteries, when it was granted to John Dudley, Duke of Northumberland. At his execution it was given by the Crown to Sutton, Lord Dudley, and has remained in the family ever since. The rectory of Kingswinford (£950 and a house), carries with it the patronage of Brierly Hill (£300 and a house). Sedgley Vicarage (£503 and a house) carries with it the patronage of Upper Gornal (£215 and a house). The Vicarage of Kidderminster (£1,000 and a house) carries with it the patronage of four other livings, value in all £820 with residences. The Kidderminster living, until a comparatively recent date, was in the possession of Lord Foley. I presume that it has been purchased of the Foleys by Lord Dudley, who has also purchased of them his present seat at Witley Court, in Worcestershire.

LX.
The Villiers.

THE name of Villiers will be for ever associated with the worthless favourite of the two first Stuart Kings who fell beneath the knife of Felton; and though the holders of the Jersey and Clarendon peerages are not descended from him, they owe to his influence the first advancement of their common ancestor. The Villiers family appear to have come over from Normandy at the Conquest, and for centuries they were comparatively obscure landowners in Lincolnshire, and afterwards in Leicestershire. George Villiers, a younger son of Sir George Villiers, of Brooksby, at the age of twenty-two attracted the notice of James I. by his personal beauty. Shortly after he was made a Gentleman of the Bedchamber, and was presented with a pension of £1,000 per annum. A year or two later he was made Master of the Horse, and elevated to the peerage as a Viscount. Then he was presented with the Lordship of Whaddon, in Bucks, worth £80,000. Then he became Earl, and then Marquis, of Buckingham. Offices were showered upon him in profusion. He was Lord High Admiral, Chief Justice in Eyre, Master of the King's Bench, Constable of Windsor Castle, High Steward of Westminster, and I know not what else—all in five or six years. In his private life an abandoned profligate, in his public life a greedy, unscrupulous, and insolent Minister, he was, perhaps, the worst man who ever held the destinies of England in his hands. The extent to which he profited by the favour of James I. and Charles I. may be partly estimated from the fact that his son, on obtaining his father's estates back at the Restoration, had a fortune, so Pepys tells us, of £19,600 a-year, a very large sum in those times. This son married the daughter of Fairfax, by whom he derived great property in Yorkshire. During the reign of Charles II. he held a number of lucrative appointments, and he was one of the principal members of the Cabal Ministry. Macaulay describes him as a man "in whom the

The Villiers.

immorality which was epidemic among the politicians of that age appeared in its most malignant type." Before his career was finished he had dissipated most of the splendid fortune which he inherited.

His cousin, Barbara Palmer, *née* Villiers, daughter of Viscount Grandison, and wife of Roger Palmer, Earl of Castlemaine, "the most profuse, imperious, and shameless of harlots," according to Macaulay, was, for her "personal virtues," according to Dugdale, created Baroness Nonsuch (!), Countess of Southampton, and Duchess of Cleveland, by Charles II., by whom she had three sons and a daughter. The eldest became Duke of Cleveland, of whom more in a subsequent article; the second was created Duke of Grafton, with hereditary claims upon the revenue, of which I have already spoken when dealing with that family.

Let us turn now to Edward Villiers, half-brother of the first Duke of Buckingham. As the younger son of a Leicestershire commoner, we may safely assume that he began the world with next to nothing, especially as his brother, the Duke, only started with £50 a-year. That was 260 years ago. At the present time, his descendant, the Earl of Jersey, owns in

Glamorganshire	7,110 acres	£36,929 rental.
Middlesex	1,982 ,,	7,588 ,,
Oxfordshire	7,042 ,,	7,477 ,,
Warwickshire	1,090 ,,	1,966 ,,
Kent	1,713 ,,	1,813 ,,
Total	18,937 ,,	£55,773 ,,

How has all this been acquired? The Villiers have not earned the purchase-money of these estates, or acquired it by successful trading. How have they acquired these 19,000 acres? Partly by pursuing the profession of courtiers, and partly by marriage. In 1622 the Duke of Buckingham obtained from James I. for his brother Edward, the presidency of the province of Munster, and subsequently a peerage. We have seen by what nefarious means lands were acquired by English adventurers in Ireland in those times, so we need not inquire particularly into the Grandison estates. Suffice it to say that the daughter and heir of the last Earl of Grandison married a son of the Marquis of Bute, and that their son, who was created a peer, with the title of Lord Stuart de Decies, has an Irish estate of 37,793 acres, with a rental of £16,368.

The youngest son of the first Viscount Grandison, Edward Villiers, fought in the Royalist cause, and became a courtier after the Restoration. He obtained first of all a grant of the Manor and Palace of Richmond for two lives, and his wife was appointed Governess to the Princesses Mary and Anne. Afterwards he was made Knight Marshal of the Household, Colonel of a regiment, and Governor of Tynemouth Castle. In the reign of James II. he gave up Richmond, which had cost him nothing, to the King, for a valuable consideration. At his death his second son, who also had a Colonelcy, succeeded him in the Governorship of Tynemouth, as also did that son's son in turn.

Let us turn now to his other children. He had a daughter, Elizabeth, who, through her mother's interest, went over to Holland as Maid of Honour to the Princess Mary, and who, notwithstanding her uncomely appearance, became the mistress of William III. This circumstance was of great importance to the family. Elizabeth herself obtained from her Royal lover a large grant of the old hereditary domains of the Crown in Ireland, estimated by the supporters of the Resumption Bill to be worth £26,000 per annum, but, by Macaulay, at only £4,000. Mr. Froude says that "these lands consisted of 100,000 acres of the finest land in Munster. The rental was £6,000 a-year. The selling value at the time of the grant was £332,000." This monstrous grant was cancelled afterwards by a Resumption Bill. Elizabeth Villiers married Lord George Hamilton, who was created Earl of Orkney by William, and whose descendant owns 11,489 acres in Ireland, with a rental of £5,789. The sister of Elizabeth Villiers was provided with a residence at Richmond Palace; for the Duchess of Marlborough (on such a matter the best authority) says that Queen Anne, when Princess of Denmark, desired the use of Richmond Palace, where she had lived in her childhood, but it was refused because a sister of Lady Orkney lived there.

Elizabeth's eldest brother had also gone over to Holland, and accompanied William and Mary to this country in 1688. His father dying a few months after, he succeeded to the office of Knight Marshal of the Household, was appointed Master of the Horse to Queen Mary, and shortly after was created Viscount Villiers of Dartford. Next he was sent as Ambassador to Holland; then was appointed a Lord Justice in Ireland; then was one of the English Plenipotentiaries at the Peace of Ryswick; then gained a step in the Peerage, being created Earl of Jersey; then became Ambassador to France; then a Secretary of State; then Lord Chamberlain, which last office he held during a portion of the reign of Queen Anne. In 1700 he was also appointed Keeper of Hyde Park. His sister's connection with King William seems to have been almost as fortunate for him as Arabella Churchill's connection with James II. was to the Duke of Marlborough.

Of his son, the second Earl, there is nothing remarkable to be said, save that his younger son married the granddaughter of the last Earl of Clarendon, of the old line, and was himself created Earl of Clarendon. The estates of this branch of the Villiers family are but small; consequently they have had to be provided for in other ways. The first Earl was a Postmaster-General, Chancellor of the Duchy of Lancaster, and Ambassador at Berlin. His two elder sons successively inherited the title, but left no male issue. The latter held the sinecure offices of Chief Justice in Eyre, North of Trent (£2,250), and of Prothonotary County Palatine of Durham, £450 a year. His third son had several children, the eldest of whom was the late Lord Clarendon, who was early in life provided with a Commissionership in the Customs (£1,400 a-year), and ably filled high offices in several Liberal Governments. One of the late Earl's brothers is that honoured friend of the people, Charles Pelham Villiers, M.P. for Wolverhampton, whose exertions in the Repeal of the Corn Laws deserve to be held in lasting remembrance. Another was the Bishop of Durham, who made himself notorious by the presentation of the rich living of Haughton-le-Skerne (£1,000 and a house) to his son-in-law, Mr. Cheese. The Bishop's son obtained the living of Addisham (£750 and a house), at the early age of 25, just after his marriage with the daughter of Earl Russell.

We must now return to the Jerseys. The third Earl, who married the daughter of the first Earl of Bridgwater, who was descended from Henry VIII., purchased the manor and mansion of Middleton Stoney, in Oxfordshire. The latter he afterwards rebuilt. He was a Gentleman of the Bedchamber to Frederick, Prince of Wales, and for many years held the sinecure office of Chief Justice in Eyre, value £2,250 a year. The fourth Earl followed in his father's footsteps, being successively a Lord of the Admiralty, Lord Chamberlain, Master of the Buckhounds, Captain of the Gentlemen Pensioners (!), and a Lord of the Bedchamber, all of course well-paid offices. The fifth Earl married a granddaughter of Robert Child, the banker, whose ancestors were wealthy London citizens, two of them having filled the office of Lord Mayor. By this marriage Osterley Park, Middlesex, a mansion with a park of 350 acres, came into the family, it having been purchased many years before by Sir Thomas Child. His Countess was the Countess of Jersey to whom Byron wrote a poem on the Prince Regent's returning her picture. The Countess was a leader in both fashion and politics; the Earl was simply a placeman who was twice Master of the Horse and twice Lord Chamberlain. The next Earl only survived his father a few days, and was succeeded by the present Earl of Jersey, who, treading in the steps of his ancestors, draws £702 per annum as a Lord-in-Waiting. Both in Wales and Oxfordshire he is well spoken of by those who would be the first to find out faults. I believe that the Earls of Jersey still retain their ancestral partnership in the Child banking-house at Temple Bar.

LXI.

The Grevilles.

A YANKEE tourist, as he gazes upon the ancient pile of Warwick Castle, would imagine that the Grevilles held one of the oldest peerages in England. As a matter of fact, however, the modern Earldom of Warwick is little more than a hundred years old, dating from 1759. There have been so many Earls of Warwick, of so many different families, that they become somewhat confusing. Briefly, therefore, let us dispose of the extinct peerages of that name. Passing by the famous Guy, Earl of Warwick, whose existence is hardly more than a vague tradition, we first come upon Henry de Newburgh, a Norman, who received a grant of the Earldom and lands from William Rufus. After a time, they were carried by an heiress on her marriage to John De Plessetis, the Newburgh line having no male descendants, and again by a De Plessetis heiress to the Mauduits, and again by a Mauduit heiress to the Beauchamps, and again by a Beauchamp heiress to the Nevilles, and again by a Neville heiress to a Plantagenet, the Duke of Clarence who was drowned in a butt of malmsey in the Tower of London. The son of this Duke was beheaded, simply because he was a Plantagenet, by Henry VII. The castle and lands adjoining then reverted of course to the Crown. Next they were obtained by John Dudley, Duke of Northumberland, who was beheaded by Mary. His son obtained the Earldom of Warwick, and his grandson, Queen Elizabeth's Earl of Leicester, founded in Warwick the Charity which is known as the Earl of Leicester's Hospital.

We must now go back some two hundred years. The last Lord Beauchamp of Powyk left three daughters co-heiresses, among whom his lands were divided; the eldest of these married Robert Lord Brooke. They left a daughter, the wardship of whom was conferred on Sir Edward Greville. The Grevilles, judging from their name, were of Norman descent, but the real founder of the family is supposed to have been a wealthy woolstapler. They were seated for some generations at Milcote, in Warwickshire, and Campden, in Gloucestershire. Sir Edward desired his ward to marry his eldest son, but she preferred his second son, who was a captain in the Navy in the reign of Henry VIII. The lady had her own way, and thus "the manor of Alcester, with many fair lordships and lands, came in right of his wife to Sir Fulke Greville," who further augmented his estate by purchases. A generation or two later another Sir Fulke, who was Chancellor of the Exchequer and Treasurer of the Navy to James I., and who was created Lord Brooke, obtained from that Monarch a grant of the Castle of Warwick and the lands adjoining. But what of the Dudleys? Had Elizabeth's Earl of Leicester left no heir? Yes. He had a son, Robert Dudley, to whose wife was granted the title of Duchess of Dudley by Charles I., and in this grant the following facts are recited:—That the Earl of Leicester had left a son, Robert, whose legitimacy was contested, but proved by his mother and other witnesses; that the Star Chamber made a special order that the depositions should be sealed up, and no copies taken; that thereupon Robert Dudley left the kingdom and refused to return; and that on his refusal to return his lands were seized by James I. Warwick Castle was granted to Fulke Greville, and the Earldom of Warwick to Lord Rich, and they were still retained although the Crown admitted Robert Dudley's legitimacy, and made his wife some small pecuniary compensation for the loss of Kenilworth out of the revenue. Thus we see that the stately domain of Warwick Castle came into the possession of the Grevilles by a direct grant from the Crown less than three hundred years ago, to the exclusion of the rightful owners. Well might the Grevilles adopt for their motto—" I can scarcely call all these things our own."

The second Lord Brooke was a distinguished member of the Puritan party, eminent alike for his piety and his patriotism. He fought under Essex at Edgehill, and defended Warwick Castle against the Cavaliers; but, like Hampden, he was slain early in the Civil War, being killed by a shot from Lichfield Cathedral, when he was making an attack upon that place. Henceforth the history of the Grevilles is uneventful. The Puritan lord was succeeded by his three sons, one after the other, the last of whom was succeeded by his two grand-

The Grevilles. 39

sons. The last of these was advanced to the dignity of Earl of Warwick on the death of Edward Rich, last Earl of that creation. The founder of the Rich family was one of those courtiers who had grown wealthy out of the plunder of the monasteries, whose grandson was created Earl of Warwick by James I. Since the Grevilles obtained the Earldom their history has been as uneventful as before. There is simply nothing of any interest to be noted in regard to any of them till we come to the fourth Earl.

The fourth Earl's connection with Warwick was the subject of warm debates in the House of Commons in 1834-5. A Committee having been appointed to investigate the charges of bribery and intimidation relative to the Warwick election after the return of the Earl of Warwick's brother, the following facts were brought out. It was proved that Lord Warwick, who was Recorder of the Borough, as well as Lord-Lieutenant of the County, was the nominator of the Town Clerk, who had been the agent in all the corrupt transactions; that, in 1831, a system of fraudulent rating had been commenced by Lord Warwick's land agent, who had made a number of faggot-voters and supplied them with fictitious receipts at the Warwick Arms; that a cheque for £8,000 was signed by Lord Warwick's agent just before the election, and presented at the bank, and that the money had found its way into the hands of the persons who distributed the bribes; and, further, that bands of rioters, armed with bludgeons, had been imported into the town to overawe the electors. The Earl himself, in a sort of *Salisbury* fashion, denied knowledge of these transactions; but so little was he believed that Sir De Lacy Evans and Mr. Cobbett proposed in the House of Commons that he should be prosecuted, and, but for the interference of the House of Lords, Warwick would at that time have been united with Leamington for electoral purposes.

And now, having glanced at the head of the house, let us turn our attention to his relatives. We shall see that the Grevilles were voracious tax-eaters. First comes C. C. F. Greville (author of the "Greville Memoirs"), with £500 as *late* Naval Officer at Demerara, with £2,000 more as Clerk of the Privy Council, and with yet £3,000 more as Secretary and Clerk of the Enrolments at Jamaica. How he could attend to his duties both at Jamaica and St. James's I cannot explain; I only know that in the same year his name is down for both the £3,000 and the £2,000. There was another ubiquitous Greville, Charles by name, who drew £600 per annum as Comptroller of Cash in the Excise at London, £600 more as Receiver of Taxes at Nottingham, £350 more as Secretary of the Island of Tobago, and yet again £572 allowance as Naval Officer at Trinidad. I suppose the Grevilles must have come of the same stock as the Spaniard of whom it was said,

> "His body is in Segovia,
> His soul is in Madrid."

Next comes A. F. Greville, with a modest £90 as Bath King-at-Arms, £150 as a Commissioner of the Alienation Office, and a pension of £250 as late private secretary to the Duke of Wellington. Next comes Sir C. J. Greville, a Major-General, with a sinecure Colonelcy of something over a thousand a year. Beside these there are two other Grevilles in the Army, and yet another, an Admiral in the Navy. In the Church, E. C. Greville had two livings, annual value £292 and £420, with a house; J. Greville had also two livings, value £800 and £159, with two houses; and R. Greville had also two livings, each worth £210 and a house. Thus, the head of the family was generously relieved by the nation of any care for his relatives.

A descendant of the fifth Lord Brooke married the daughter and heiress of the late Marquis of Westmeath, and was created Baron Greville in 1869. He owns in Ireland 20,611 acres, with a rental of £14,169. The lands of the Nugents were obtained by successive confiscations, the first of the family who went to Ireland obtaining large grants of land in Westmeath about the year 1200, and another obtaining further grants in Cavan and Longford in the reigns of Elizabeth and James I. It is in these counties that most of Lord Greville's lands are situated.

The magnificent baronial pile of Warwick Castle was partly destroyed by fire a few years ago, and its noble owner condescended to allow it to be restored by public subscription. How are the mighty fallen! The Chief of the great house of Warwick rebuilds his baronial castle by voluntary subscriptions, just as if it were a hospital or a charity-school, although his lordship owns in Warwickshire 8,262 acres, and in Somersetshire 1,840 acres, with a rental af £18,337 per annum. To make the matter worse, I am told by people who have visited the place that you have to give half a dozen tips to different domestics before you can see all that is to be seen in this historic pile. The Earl owns a large part of Warwick, and the shadow of the castle seems to cast a blight over the place. The capital of one of the finest counties in England looks as if it had been to sleep for a century. Shops and streets and market-place all appear mildewed. The last time I was there, I was struck with the number of houses to let, and, remarking on the fact to an inhabitant, I was told that some years ago some low manufacturer wanted to start a big factory there, but the Earl would not grant him a lease, so he had to take his capital elsewhere, and the serene atmosphere of Warwick Castle remains undisturbed by the proximity of industry. Why such a place should still continue to send two members to the House of Commons is a question which will have to be answered when a redistribution of seats occurs. I spent a day in a polling booth at Warwick once, and was struck with the large number of illiterate electors, who, of course, invariably voted for the Tory candidates. The borough in which I live, which has a very large population of middle-class houses and 38,096 electors, has but equal voting power with Warwick, which has but 1,680 electors.

LXII.

The Stuarts of Blantyre and Galloway.

IT is probable, my Lord Blantyre, that I should not have thought it worth while to devote a column to the long line of mediocrities of which you are one of the living representatives, but for a letter of yours which has just been made public. In that letter you remark :—" It is surprising how much is done for our poorer classes from their birth to the grave. Parliament provides for registrations, schools, churches, aliment and clothing, medical attendance, house-room, &c., besides voluntary institutions." To me it is surprising that a noble lord, presumably of good education, should write such nonsense. How much truth and how much error there may be in these statements I have not space now to point out. But they lead to other considerations. If you begin to talk of obligations, we are quite ready to take up the discussion. As a matter of fact, any worn-out labourer on your lordship's estates, who, after working fifty years, is now in receipt of relief, has produced far more wealth than he has ever received or will receive. The world is all the richer that he has lived in it. Can we say the same of you? Have you ever earned a sixpence by productive industry? Have any of your ancestors? In the language of St. Paul—"Who art thou, that differest from another, and what hast thou which thou didst not receive?" I thought that all the wealth in the world, save that which comes from the natural productiveness of the soil, came from labour. From the style in which you write, it appears as if you thought otherwise. Did landowners create land? Do noblemen make crops? Do Parliaments build up schools and churches, and manufacture aliment and clothing? I always thought that God created the land; that ploughmen and reapers produced crops; that bricklayers and stonemasons built schools; that bakers made bread; and that tailors made clothes. If you, and the like of you, made all these things,

The Stuarts of Blantyre and Galloway. 43

and can prove that you did, then those who belong to the industrious classes will not only acknowledge their immense obligations to you, but beg you to still further exercise your creative powers during this present distress. However, till you have proved these powers, they must remain sceptical.

As you have reminded us of our obligations in that we of the industrious classes receive that we pay for in local and imperial taxes, suppose we remind you of your obligations. I see, in the landowners' return, that you are the owner of large estates :—

Berwickshire	2,878	acres.
Dumbarton	2,946	,,
Haddington	2,953	,,
Renfrew	4,449	,,
Lanark	835	,,
		,,
Total	14,061	,,

from which you derive an annual rental of £20,558. The Earl of Galloway, who is descended from a common ancestor with yourself, owns in Wigtonshire, Kirkcudbright, and Cornwall 79,346 acres, with a rental of £32,368. Pray, whence did you and he get all this? Did you purchase it? Did your fathers purchase it, or did they make it? I am no Communist. However these lands were gotten, I fully recognise your prescriptive right, so long as the exercise of it does not militate against the well-being of the nation. But we are talking of obligations just now; and as you think that the obligations of the poor are so great, I want to draw your attention to your own.

Your ancestors are said to be of the royal blood of Scotland, and in 1293 one of them received a grant of the lands of Garlies, in Wigtonshire, from the King. His grandson received a charter of Garlies, and was presented with the barony and lands of Dalswinton by Robert Bruce. Subsequently another Stewart obtained the estate of Minto, in 1429, "after much opposition from the Turnbulls, the former possessors." Thomas, the second son of this Sir William Stewart, was the founder of the house of Blantyre. He obtained, from his father, Minto and other lands in Roxburghshire, which descended to the posterity of his eldest son, whose female descendants, I presume, hold them still. The Blantyres are descended from a younger son. The younger son of an English squire is not usually very wealthy now; what must have been the position of the younger son of a Scottish knight three hundred years ago? At Court he filled various offices—Gentleman of the Bedchamber, Keeper of the Privy Seal, Lord of the Session, and finally Lord High Treasurer. I know that James VI. was a very impecunious monarch till his accession to the English Throne; but then his poverty mainly arose from the folly with which he lavished gifts upon his favourites, of whom the first Lord Blantyre was one.

I open "Hamilton's National Gazetteer" and I read this: —" Blantyre is the site of a priory of the Augustine Order. At the Reformation it was given by James VI. to Walter Stewart [your ancestor], who was shortly afterwards made a baron with the title of Lord Blantyre. The barony is still held by his descendants. The cotton manufacture is carried on here, and gives employment to nine hundred persons. The district contains ironstone and limestone." So, then, it seems that your ancestor got it for nothing, simply by a gift from the Head of the State. "No," you would say, "that is not correct. If you will turn to the Statistical Account of Scotland you will find it stated that he was presented with the benefice of Blantyre, but he purchased the barony." It was only a part that was given him. Can you tell us how much he gave for the rest? He was a younger son at Court, who had to make his own fortune somehow or other. He was the Treasurer of a King who was so desperately hard up that his own nobles had to club together to pay the expenses of his daughter's christening. We can imagine how small was the price he had to pay for Crown lands. Do you think it is at all likely that he gave a sum equal to the present annual rental of the land in question? And from that time forward no man could farm, or spin cotton (cotton was not spun in Scotland at all till 1700), or dig ironstone or limestone, without paying tithe and toll to the Lords of Blantyre. Pray tell us, my lord, which lay under the greatest obligations—the men who took the rents of Blantyre, or the men who, by their industry, made Blantyre prosperous? It is you, not I, remember, that have opened this question. By the way, let me remark that forty years ago the rental of the parish of Blantyre was £2,579, and the cotton-spinners of Blantyre, not its lords, supported their own poor. Can you tell us what is

The Stuarts of Blantyre and Galloway. 45

the rental now, and, if there is any increase, what the Lords of Blantyre have done towards creating it? By the way, there used to be an extensive common of 600 acres, called Blantyre Moor; what has become of it? It is nearly all in cultivation now, but who takes the rent from it? Certain it is that, if that land is reclaimed from barrenness, it was not your ancestors who drained and ploughed it.

The Bolton and Lethington estates were sold to the Stewarts in 1702. The necessary funds for the purchase were bequeathed by Frances, granddaughter of the first Lord Blantyre—"La Belle Stuart," of whom Charles II. was enamoured, and who married the last Duke of Richmond and Lennox. It matters little how she obtained the money; certain it is that neither she nor her husband, nor their ancestors, ever earned it. They had had extensive royal grants which compelled industrious people to all generations, who lived upon certain lands, to pay an annual tax for the right to live and work, and out of the savings thus obtained Bolton and Lethington, or Lennoxlove, as it is now called, were bought. Erskine and Bishopton, in Renfrew, were, I believe, purchased out of the savings from the rentals of the older estates. Possibly some military members of the family may have made something in war time, but the business of a soldier does not exactly come under the category of productive industries.

Now, my Lord, I have no doubt you are a most estimable nobleman. I understand you have shown your enthusiastic devotion to the Turkish cause by supplying surgeons and medical appliances at your own expense to the Turkish soldiers. As I presume your chief motive was pity for suffering, though it may have been mixed with political sympathy, I do not doubt that you are a humane and considerate landlord. I take all that for granted; but pray do not talk any more about the obligations of the industrial classes. It is they who have produced everything you possess, save land in its natural state; and it is a pity that your class so often forget this fact. Napoleon Bonaparte once was walking along a narrow path when an elegantly-dressed lady met a labourer carrying a heavy load. The lady stood her ground as if expecting the labourer to turn on one side, but the great Head of the Army said to her, " Respect the burden, Madam!" It was the best thing Napoleon ever uttered.

Respect the burden, my Lord. The creators of wealth, for the most part, have but a hard time of it. Their lot is generally to toil hard for very scanty reward. They are the first to suffer when any calamity falls upon a nation, and they usually suffer with uncomplaining patience. You may think that Parliaments have done very much for them, but they think otherwise. At any rate they do not consider themselves under any particular obligations to the class to which you belong. Your obligations are far greater than theirs. My Lord, I pray you, "Respect the burden." You and I have been relieved of the burden of the rough work of the world, and Parliaments have done far more for landowners than for the industrial classes. We ought to be rather astonished that Parliament has done so little for them than that it has done so much.

LXIII.

The Percebals.

HE name of Egmont seems an out-of-place title for a British nobleman. It at once calls to mind the Count Egmont, whose love for Clärchen was the theme of one of Goethe's most pathetic tragedies. However, Goethe's Egmont was a Fleming, who was executed by Philip II., and the Earldom of Egmont was not created till 1733. The Earl owns in

Cork	.	.	.	. .	16,626 acres
Sussex	.	.	.	.	14,021 ,,
Surrey	.	.	.	.	3,297 ,,
Bucks	.	.	.	.	540 ,,
				Total	34,484 ,,

with a rent-roll of £19,784. I am surprised to find that he has not more. If it were possible to sum up the total value of the public lands and the total amount of public money received by the Percevals, the figures would look altogether beyond credibility. The task, however, is an impossible one; and I must content myself with giving an outline of the history of this fortunate race of place-holders.

The Percevals claim to have come over with the Conqueror, from whom they derived grants of confiscated lands in Somerset, on which they seem to have vegetated for centuries, till at last one Richard Perceval quarrelled with his father, and went on the Continent. After staying four years in Spain, and acquiring a good knowledge of the Spanish language, he was, through the interest of a relative, who had married Lord Burghley's sister, taken into the service of that statesman. Having succeeded in deciphering some secret despatches which had been captured in a Spanish ship, by which means the projected expedition of the Spanish Armada became known to the English Government, he was rewarded by Elizabeth with a place of

£400 a year and an annual pension of 800 marks for life. Subsequently he was promoted to the Secretaryship of the Court of Wards, worth £2,000 a year, and afterwards he was made a Commissioner in the same Court, which brought his annual official income up to £4,000. On the death of the younger Cecil he was dismissed from all his places, but afterwards was sent to Ireland as Registrar of the Irish Court of Wards, with a salary of 1,000 marks. He then sold the greater part of his ancestral property in Somerset, and invested the proceeds in Irish land and mortgages. Of course, like other English adventurers, he obtained some grants of forfeited lands, and before his death he contrived to secure the reversion of his offices to his two sons.

His son, Sir P. Perceval, was still more fortunate. Beside holding his father's office, he was Keeper of the Rolls in the Irish House of Lords, Joint Clerk of the Crown in the King's Bench, Clerk of Common Pleas and Keeper of the Records, Joint Customer and Collector of the Port of Dublin, and holder of a monopoly of ale and spirit licenses. In 1627 he obtained a grant of Crown lands; in 1630 a second grant of lands, with special exemption from the payment of all taxes thereon; in 1634 a further grant of forfeited lands; in 1637 yet another grant of lands, so that his territorial estates in Ireland swelled to 100,000 acres. Besides this, his houses, &c., were valued at £60,000, and his offices brought him in at least £2,000 per annum. This Perceval was at first a Royalist, but drifted gradually to the side of the Parliament, and became a member of the Presbyterian party. He seems to have had heavy losses during the Irish Rebellion of 1641-2.

His son, who allied himself with the Independents, then rising into power, like his father found it profitable to swim with the stream. Beside offices held by his father and grandfather, he obtained others. He was prothonotary of the Court of Common Pleas, Keeper of the Public Accounts, Registrar of the Court of Claims, and I know not what else beside. At the Restoration he again swam with the stream, and was created a baronet. Some little time after the Restoration the Percevals obtained a decision of the Court of Claims, in which they held office, which gave them possession of Kanturk Castle, Co. Cork, which had been mortgaged by the McCarthys, of the race of the ancient Kings of Desmond, to Sir Philip Perceval.

The third baronet and his brother had a grant in reversion, or rather a grant for three lives of all the various lucrative offices held by the first baronet. The fifth baronet was created Baron Perceval, Viscount Perceval, and finally Earl of Egmont, with, strange to say, a grant of twenty marks out of the Irish Treasury to enable him to support the honour. I need hardly say that the younger sons of this voracious family were almost invariably well provided for either in Church or State.

The second Earl, who filled various offices at Court, and was Postmaster-General and First Lord of the Admiralty, was created an English as well as an Irish peer, under the title of Lord Lovell. He was not the Lord Lovel of the old ballad, "out of whose bosom there grew a red rose," for he married two wives and begat sons and daughters. His descendants by the son of the first marriage have died out, so we will turn our attention to the children of the second marriage. His second wife was created Baroness Arden, with remainder to her heirs male. Her eldest son Lord Arden, like many of his predecessors, held a number of offices. He was Steward to Queen Charlotte, Lord of the Bedchamber to George III., Master of the Mint, and last and best of all, Registrar to the Court of Admiralty. During one year of the great French War he admitted that his gross receipts therefrom amounted to £38,574, less £26,012 deductions, making his net income from the office £12,562, or more than two and a half times the present salary of a Prime Minister. No wonder he could afford to purchase a mansion at Banstead. One of his sons he provided for in the Navy, and two others in the Church. One of the descendants is the present Earl of Egmont.

The younger son was Spencer Perceval, who was brought up to the law. He became Solicitor-General, and then Attorney-General, and on accepting office as Chancellor of the Exchequer he wanted to bargain that he should have the Chancellorship of the Duchy of Lancaster for life at a salary of £2,000 a year, but in this he was defeated. He ultimately became Prime Minister, and a few months afterwards was shot in the lobby of the House of Commons, from motives of private revenge by one Bellingham. His widow was voted an annuity of £2,000 a year for life. She married again not long afterwards, and lived to enjoy her pension for 32 years.

A lump sum of £50,000 was also voted for the benefit of her children. One of the sons obtained a sinecure Tellership in the Exchequer worth £2,700 a year and a Commissionership of Lunacy, value unknown. Another obtained a clerkship in the Tellers' Office, £529 a-year, and another a Church living, value £527 a-year and a house. Altogether Spencer Perceval's family must have received from public money at least a quarter of a million. If the Percevals have been officials of but moderate abilities, they have at least received by no means moderate payment for their services.

Nork House, Surrey, appears to have been purchased by Lord Arden, whose office in the Court of Admiralty produced him such enormous profits. The Earl of Egmont's seat in Sussex is Cowdray Park, Midhurst, which for some generations was the home of the Montagus. Less than half a century ago it was in the possession of the Poyntz family, who derived it by inheritance. It thence passed, I suppose by purchase, to the Earl of Egmont. The owner of Cowdray Park is also Lord of the Manor of the diminutive borough of Midhurst, which contains a population of less than 7,000 persons. Midhurst has been occasionally used as a family borough, the present Earl having sat for it prior to his succession to the Peerage.

LXIV.

The Gores.

IT was with some concern that I learned the other day that Viscount Sudley had become one of the directors of a shop in the general provision trade (see prospectus of the Universities' Co-operative Stores). Unlike Mawworm in "The Hypocrite," I do not think it is a sin to keep a shop, but I am quite aware that shopkeeping is a social sin which, in the estimation of the Upper Ten Thousand, places the sinner outside the pale of "Society." Many a man who, in education and intellect and wealth, would compare not unfavourably with half the honourables and naval and military officers in London, would be blackballed in any second-rate club simply because he is in trade. I don't object to the line being drawn, but the rule has ceased to have any consistency in it. The lord has a right to taboo the shopkeeper, but when the lord himself becomes a shopkeeper it is quite time he ceased to regard shopkeepers as anything less than equals. Where the distinction lies between a shopkeeper and a shop director I fail to see. Both are occupied in business for pecuniary gain, both deal in the same articles, both supply the same class of people; and neither, if in a large way of business, personally serves across the counter. Why should Mr. Attenborough, the pawnbroker, or Mr. Melton, the hatter, or Mr. Medwin, the bootmaker, be excluded from White's and Brookes's when directors of co-operative shops are admitted? I am not a West-end tradesmen, but if I were I should think it particularly hard, when the Government was screwing out of me as much Income Tax as possible, to know that one of the Income Tax Commissioners was a rival in trade in one of those shops where they contrive to dispense with the Tax-gatherer. As Income Tax Commissioner Lord Sudley has a salary of £600, apparently with no very onerous duties, since he can find time to devote to Co-operative Stores. I at first supposed that the Gores must be in somewhat straitened circumstances, but I am

happy to say that that is not the case. The Earl of Arran
—of Arran Isles off the coast of Galway, not of Arran in Scotland—is the father of Viscount Sudley, and owns 37,229
acres in Donegal and Mayo, with a rent-roll of £9,279. Sir
St. George Gore, who died very recently, owned a few thousand
acres in Cavan, Galway, Dublin, King's County, and Limerick.
Sir Charles Gore has 8,569 acres in Sligo. Major Gore has
8,562 acres in Clare. Sir F. A. K. Gore has 30,818 acres in
Sligo and Mayo. Lord Harlech has 55,418 acres in Ireland,
England, and Wales. In Ireland alone the Gores hold more
than 150,000 acres, although no member of the family set foot
in that country till the days of Queen Elizabeth. It is hardly
necessary to say that these enormous possessions were chiefly
derived through confiscation.

In the reign of Queen Elizabeth there lived in London a
certain Alderman Gore, a Merchant Taylor, who had a
numerous family, the youngest of whom went over to Ireland
as captain of a troop of horse. This officer, Sir Paul Gore,
obtained a grant of the barony of Boylagh and Barnagh, in
Donegal; but, after the accession of James I., he was compelled to relinquish it in favour of the Earl of Annandale, one
of James's Scotch favourites, and to be content to take, in
exchange, 1,348 acres of forfeited lands in the same county,
which were created into a manor, under the title of Manor
Gore, and for which he had to pay an annual rent to the
Crown of £10 16s. This property, with others, subsequently
obtained, was inherited by the descendants of his eldest son,
who obtained a baronetcy, and subsequently the now extinct
Earldom of Ross. The third baronet greatly increased the
fortunes of the family by marrying the heiress of James
Hamilton, of Castle Hamilton, by whom he derived that estate
and extensive lands in Fermanagh. These Hamiltons were
also adventurers who had gone over to Ireland in the time of
Elizabeth, one of whose descendants had obtained a grant of
the Barony of Manor Hamilton from Charles I. This barony
is, or was till lately, in the possession of the Earl of Leitrim.
The head of this branch of the family was subsequently
created Earl of Ross, the ancient Irish Earldom of that ilk,
held by the Parsons family, having become extinct. In time
the second Earldom also became extinct for want of direct
male heirs, but most of the estates are held by one of the
Gores above mentioned.

The second son of Sir Paul Gore, from whom the Earl of Arran is descended, obtained a grant of the lands of Newtown, in Mayo, created into the Manor of Castle Gore in 1666. The third son also obtained in 1661 a grant of divers lands in Kilkenny, Sligo, and Galway. The old Irish Earldom of Arran held by the Butlers having become extinct, one of the descendants of the second son of Sir Paul obtained a new peerage with that title. Henceforth the various branches of the family pursued a quiet and inglorious course of self-aggrandisement, marrying heiresses whenever they had the opportunity, and securing for their younger sons a share in the Church's feast of fat things, such as deaneries, prebends, and rectories, or else quartering them upon the services, where, as examiners of customs, ornamental clerks, &c., they ceased to be a burden upon their wealthier relatives. Since the union of the two countries there is very little to be said of them. Even in the days of George IV. I can only find one solitary Gore with a comfortable sinecure of £1,000 a year.

For many years past the Hon. C. A. Gore, brother of the Earl of Arran, has been a Commissioner of Woods and Forests at a salary of £1,200. During the thirty-nine years that he has been in office he has received nearly £47,000 for his services. Even now the present expenses of the Woods and Forests are 22 per cent. of the receipts, and of the manner in which the property is treated we had a striking illustration in the case of Epping Forest, where the Crown rights were almost given away to a set of rapacious landowners. Be it remembered that not a rood of this land could be built upon or even enclosed so long as the Crown rights existed. A committee of the House of Commons having, in 1848, reported in favour of the sale of the Crown rights to the lords of the manors, they were, accordingly, sold by the Woods and Forests Commissioners, to the extent of about 3,000 acres, for the paltry sum of £6 per acre, the land being actually worth from £300 to £1,000 per acre for building purposes. Fortunately for the people of London, these astounding bargains have only brought to their purchasers prolonged litigation and ultimate defeat. But looking at that diminutive figure of £6 per acre, I cannot think that the country has derived any great advantages from the Hon. C. A. Gore's prolonged tenure of office. Another brother of the Earl of Arran is Rector of Withcall, in Lincolnshire

(£516 and a house). There are five other Gores in the Church, with livings of the value of £244, £427, £426, £202, and £300 respectively, with a house to each. There is another Gore a major-general, and yet another a retired captain in the Navy.

The Ormsby-Gores still remain to be noticed, the head of this branch of the family being Lord Harlech, who has a seat at Brogyntyn, or Porkington, in Shropshire, on the Welsh border. The Welsh property has been derived by successive marriages. Porkington and other lands had descended to the Owens through a matrimonial alliance with one of the Maurices, who had in the same way obtained it from an ancient Welsh house. The last male descendant of Sir John Owen, a gallant Cavalier who narrowly escaped execution in the time of the Commonwealth, through the personal influence of Ireton, married the sister of the last Lord Godolphin, and, through her, acquired such of the Godolphin property as was not entailed on the Duke of Leeds. His daughter and heiress married Owen Ormsby, a large Irish landowner. An ancestor of the Ormsbys, like the Gores and Hamiltons, had gone over to Ireland as an adventurer, in the time of Queen Elizabeth, and obtained considerable grants of forfeited lands in Roscommon, Sligo, and Mayo. This Owen Ormsby had an only daughter, who married a certain William Gore, whose descendants henceforth bore the double name of Ormsby-Gore. The present Lord Harlech is brother of the first lord of that ilk, who, while a commoner, drew for many years £335 annually as a Groom-in-waiting to the Queen, and was advanced to the peerage in 1875. As Moore says:

" 'Tis pleasant, while nothing but mercantile fractures,
  Some simple, some compound, is dinned in our ears,
To think that, though robbed of all coarse manufactures,
  We keep up our fine manufacture of peers."

LXV.

The Nelsons.

T is not often that a statesman delivers such a suggestive speech as that of Lord Derby at Rochdale. I am anxious that the lessons therein taught should not be forgotten, especially the lessons which bear upon our national expenditure. I shall take for my text in this chapter a few sentences from Lord Derby's speech, and endeavour to drive the lesson home. Lord Derby said :—

"We all profess to wish for peace; I hope most of us do so sincerely; but do not let us forget that in a country like this there are various interests which tend steadily and constantly in an opposite direction. In the first place, we have a more numerous and more highly trained military class than we ever had before. There is a natural, not discreditable, desire among them to test the value of what they have been learning, and to acquire the professional distinction which can only come with actual service. They are much more a writing class than they were; they have learned to work the press instead of treating it with contempt, and when you recollect that there is in what are called the upper classes scarcely a family that has not some connection with the Army, there is a social influence which tells powerfully when questions of war or peace are in the balance. It is a mere delusion to say, as people are continually saying, that everybody is against war if it can be honourably avoided. On the contrary, there are a good many persons who either think that they will make a very good thing out of a war, or that they will serve to keep off something that they dislike even more; and in either case we must not be surprised if they act under their convictions."

Of course, all this has been said before in the *Echo* and other journals, but probably it will obtain more attention now that it is re-stated by so eminent a statesman. I pass by, for the present, the references made by Lord Derby to the growing influence of the fighting class, and for the present confine myself to the rewards of the successful warrior, more especially for the successful warrior who happens to be in command. These rewards must have a highly stimulating effect upon those who have any hopes of obtaining glory of that description. They are rewards which the people generally think little about, but which it is impossible for those most interested to ignore. Already I have given a striking instance in the case of the Marlborough Peerage; but the first Duke of Marlborough owed his first successes to the favour of one of the mistresses of Charles II., and he was assisted in no small degree afterwards by the position held by the Duchess as the favourite of Queen Anne. It is well, then, that we should take a peerage whose existence is owing solely to the distinguished services of him who first held it, and I purposely select the Nelson Peerage because it is one of a purely professional character.

It is not my province here to discuss whether the Great French War was necessary to us or not; or, supposing it was a war which in the end we could hardly avoid, when our responsibility for it would properly have commenced. The name of Lord Nelson is dear to the hearts of Englishmen, and of all our fighting heroes his biography is probably the best known. So long as England is a great naval power the memories of the Nile, Copenhagen, and Trafalgar will be cherished. Even those who have an innate horror of war cannot but feel a certain amount of admiration for the hero whose dauntless courage in the face of desperate odds has won for him such world-wide renown.

The Nelsons were an old Lancashire family. One of them appears to have followed the fortunes of the youngest son of the first Earl of Derby, who, in the reign of Henry VII., was created Bishop of Ely. The See of Ely had considerable possessions in Norfolk, and from that time forward the Nelsons were established in that county. The grandfather and father of Lord Nelson were Norfolk clergymen. It is quite needless for me to dwell upon the career of the great naval commander, whose death at Trafalgar, in the very hour of victory, prevented him from a full enjoyment of the nation's gratitude. I should indignantly repudiate any charge that I have herein insinuated that Nelson was actuated by any low motives of obtaining pecuniary reward; rather would I echo the words of our Poet Laureate—

"Mighty Seaman, tender and true,
And pure from taint of craven guile."

But I remember that when the debate arose in the House of Commons on the Nelson Grant and Pension, William Wilberforce said he viewed the matter as a pledge of national liberality to encourage imitation. And it is from that point of view that I wish to look at the gains of the Nelson family, still bearing in mind the wise and weighty words of Lord Derby quoted above.

Let us put on one side the ordinary pay of a naval officer, and the prize-money, which at the battle of the Nile alone amounted to over £3,000, and the grant by the King of Naples of the Brontë estate, whose annual value was £3,000. In 1797 Nelson was awarded a pension of £1,000 per annum. In the following year he was awarded further pensions of £1,000 by the Irish Parliament, and £2,000 by the English. At his death the £2,000 pension was continued to his childless widow. The East India Company presented him with £10,000. Soon after Nelson's death, in 1806, Lord Henry Petty, afterwards Marquis of Lansdowne, proposed, on behalf of the Government, that a sum of £120,000 should be vested in trustees, of which £10,000 was to be given to each of Nelson's two sisters; £10,000 to Nelson's brother (a clergyman, who was created an Earl), or his brother's daughter; and £90,000 to be expended in the purchase of an estate for the holders of the Nelson Peerage. Further, a perpetual pension of £5,000 per annum was annexed to the peerage to enable its holder to support the dignity of an Earl. It was objected that these rewards would be received " by collateral relatives, personally unknown to the public, who could have no claim but what they derived from the accidental honour of bearing Nelson's name"; but of course the Bill passed with little difficulty. Let us proceed to sum up these grants and pensions :—

£1,000 pension 1797—1805 . . .	£8,000
£1,000 „ 1798—1805 . . .	7,000
£2,000 „ 1798—1831, received by Lady Nelson after Lord Nelson's death . .	66,000
Grant by East India Company. . .	10,000
Grants to two Sisters	20,000
Grant to Brother (1st Earl) . . .	10,000
Purchase of Estate	90,000
£5,000 pension for 72 years to be continued in perpetuity.	360,000
Total	£571,000

With the £90,000 above alluded to an estate was purchased near Downton, in Wiltshire. The manor and mansion of Standlynch (the latter is now known as Trafalgar House) have been at various times in the possession of a number of different families. In the reigns of Henry VI. and VII. the estate belonging to Lord St. Amand, who bequeathed it to an illegitimate son. In the reign of Elizabeth it belonged to a family of the name of Greene, from whom it passed to the Bocklands. The male line of the Bocklands died out, and it was then purchased by the Vanderputs, who resold it to Sir Peter Young, who sold it again to Mr. Henry Dawkins, from whose executors it was purchased by the trustees appointed by the Act of 1806. Trafalgar House is a comparatively modern erection, the old manor house having been taken down and the present mansion erected by Sir Peter Vanderput in 1733. A subsequent possessor of the estate, Mr. Dawkins, greatly enlarged it.

The only son of the first Earl Nelson died young, and while his daughter, who married Lord Bridport, inherited the Brontë estate, the Nelson Peerage, with its estates and pension, passed to a son of Mrs. Bolton, the great Lord Nelson's sister. At his death the earldom was inherited by his eldest son, the present Earl.

LXVI.

The Duncombes.

VERY recently, the magnificent mansion of the Earl of Feversham, at Duncombe Park, near Helmsley, in the North Riding, was unfortunately destroyed by fire. I am all the more pleased to know that it was insured, as it is said to have been a popular place of resort for the people of the North Riding in the summer months. The familiar names of Helmsley and Duncombe, however, remind me that I have not yet sketched the history of the house to which this great mansion belonged.

The Earl of Feversham owns 39,312 acres in the North Riding of Yorkshire, with a rent-roll of £34,329. Two hundred years ago his ancestor did not own a foot of land in that or any other county. The wealth of the family is due almost entirely to one man, its founder; and what manner of man he was we shall see hereafter. For many generations the castle and manor of Helmsley had been in the possession of the De Roos family, most of whose property was derived by marriage with the Albinis. At the confiscation of the monastic property, the far-famed Abbey of Rievaulx, near to Helmsley, with the lands appertaining, was granted to De Roos, Earl of Rutland, whose descendants, the Manners family, still hold many of his ecclesiastical confiscations. The heiress of the sixth Earl of Rutland, however, married Villiers, Duke of Buckingham. The Villiers estates in Yorkshire were given by the Long Parliament to Fairfax, whose daughter married the second Villiers, Duke of Buckingham. The career of this profligate nobleman, who wasted his substance in riotous living, has been immortalised in a few lines by one of our great poets. In 1695 his trustees sold the estate in question to Charles Duncombe.

The Duncombes till then had been obscure Buckinghamshire squires. Charles, who was the son of a younger son, early in life started in business as a goldsmith in the City of London. From small beginnings he rose to be one of the wealthiest men in the country. Swift, in his Journal to Stella, under date April 5, 1711, makes a note of his death as follows:—" Duncombe, the rich Alderman, died to-day, and, I hear, has left the Duke of Argyll, who married his niece, £200,000." The first mention I can find of him is that, though a Tory in politics, he was one of a deputation from the City appointed to present an address to William of Orange when he arrived in London, and that he offered to place his purse at the disposal of that Prince. A year or two after the Revolution he purchased of the Chaplins the estate of Barford, near the rotten borough of Downton, in Wilts, by which means he and his nephew after him obtained a safe and snug seat in Parliament. Later in the reign of William, as we are informed by Macaulay, he laid down nearly £90,000 for Helmsley " at the moment when the trade of the Kingdom was depressed to the lowest point." How was his enormous wealth obtained ? Mainly through the prevalence of a crime which no longer is known—the clipping of the coin. All students of the history of the Revolution period know what grievous injury was inflicted upon the people generally by the state of the coinage, and with what brilliant success Charles Montague, who had among his advisers Newton and Locke, grappled with the difficulty. A mill had been set up in the Tower, which turned out a new and improved coinage ; but as fast as the milled money came out it disappeared, while the old coins, which could be easily clipped, were clipped more than ever, till at last the weight of many of the coins did not exceed half their nominal value. The clipped money was a daily grievance to the traders and workers, inflicting upon them continual and heavy deductions from their labonr and profits ; but it will at once be perceived that there was one class to whom a debased coinage brought immense profit. What was the poison of labour was the meat of the banker ; and of all the bankers of that time Charles Duncombe appears to have profited most largely by a condition of affairs which involved the people generally in disastrous loss. Of course, Duncombe was not responsible in any way for the crimes of the clippers ; and that he made the utmost use of the opportunities which were placed in his way, in the eyes of many would simply prove him to have been a smart man of business, who always did the best he could for his own interest. I only wish to emphasise the fact that, though Helmsley was obtained by purchase, the gains of him who bought it were largely derived, not from beneficent trading, but from accidental circumstances which enabled him to grow rich as other people grew poor.

But Charles Duncombe had other means of increasing his wealth; he held one of those offices connected with the Revenue which enabled him to add largely to his gains. Macaulay says:—"Possessed of a private fortune equal to that of any Duke, he had not thought it beneath him to accept the place of Cashier of the Excise, and had perfectly understood how to make that place lucrative; but he had recently (1698) been ejected from office by Montague, who thought, with good reason, that he was not a man to be trusted." Enraged by his dismissal from his post, Duncombe, who was a strong Tory, sought an opportunity for revenge; and, charging Montague with malversation of office as Chancellor of the Exchequer, instigated a Parliamentary inquiry. It was a repetition of the old story—"The wicked diggeth a pit, and falleth himself therein," for Montague not only passed scatheless through the ordeal, but had the satisfaction of seeing his enemy put to confusion. To quote Macaulay once more, Duncombe "made one unguarded admission after another, and was at length compelled to confess, on the floor of the House, that he had been guilty of an infamous fraud, which, but for his own confession, it would have been scarcely possible to bring home to him." The same historian adds:— "That Duncombe was guilty of shameful dishonesty was acknowledged by all men of sense and honour in the party to which he belonged." The fraud was that, being ordered to pay £10,000 into the Exchequer, when he had in hand double that sum in cash, he bought Exchequer bills, which were receivable at par by the Treasury, at a considerable discount, and paid them into the Treasury; while, in order to make it appear that these Bills had been received by him in payment of taxes, he had employed "a knavish Jew" to forge endorsements of names.

A Bill of Pains and Penalties to deprive him of two-thirds of his property, which then amounted to considerably more than £400,000, was carried by a considerable majority in the Commons, but was rejected in the Lords by the casting-vote of the Duke of Leeds, who, as we have already seen, was very much tarred with the same brush, and to whom, according to popular rumour, Duncombe had made a golden sacrifice. The following year he was tried in the King's Bench, but acquitted, apparently because the Lord Chief Justice directed the jury that, although he had committed a fault in appropriating a large sum of money to his own uses, it was not the fault set out in the indictment. In 1700 there came a turn in the tide of his fortunes. He was chosen Sheriff, and received the honour of Knighthood; and in 1709 he became Lord Mayor of London. As he had been a good party man, fraud and forgery did not stand in the way of his advancement when his own political friends were in power.

At the death of Sir Charles Duncombe, who was never married, his property was divided between his nephew and his sister or niece. The former sat for many years for the pocket borough of Downton, and in 1747 was created Baron Feversham. He left no male issue, and the title expired with him; but Mary Duncombe married a Mr. Thomas Brown, who assumed his wife's name. Their son Thomas married the daughter of Sir Thomas Slingsby, and he left only a daughter, who married Mr. Robert Shafto, of Whitworth, Durham. The Yorkshire property then passed to a younger son of Thomas Duncombe, who had two sons. The younger was the father of Tom Duncombe, the Radical M.P. for Finsbury. The elder, who sat in the House of Commons for the rotten borough of Aldborough, was rewarded with a peerage, as Baron Feversham, by Lord Liverpool in 1826. Of the next Lord Feversham there is nothing noteworthy to record. The present Peer, who had previously sat as a Conservative M.P. for the North Riding, succeeded his father in 1867, and was advanced to an earldom by Mr. Disraeli in 1868. One of his uncles, an Admiral, was for some years a groom in waiting, and afterwards a Lord of the Admiralty. Another uncle is Dean of York, with a salary of £2,000 per annum and a residence.

LXVII.

The Heathcotes.

HIS family is a curious mixture of the old and the new. Lord Aveland's title—derived from a Wapentake in South Lincolnshire—only dates from 1856, and the Heathcote baronetcy only from 1732. It would at first sight appear odd to include the Heathcotes among Our Old Nobility; but it happens that through his mother Lord Aveland is descended from more than one ancient noble house. The Marquises of Lindsey and Dukes of Ancaster are now represented by him. Lord Aveland owns in

Lincolnshire	. . . .	17,637 acres
Rutland	. . . . .	3,638 ,,
Derby and Hants	. . . .	5 ,,
	Total	21,280 ,,

with a rent-roll of £46,800. Lord Aveland's mother, Lady Willoughby D'Eresby, owns in

Lincolnshire	. . . .	24,696 acres
Denbigh	. . . . .	396 ,,
Carnarvon	. . . .	30,391 ,,
Perth	. . . . ,	76,837 ,,
	Total	132,320 ,,

with a rent-roll of £74,005. As Lord Aveland is an only son, I suppose he will some day inherit her property, and then the grand total will be 163,600 acres; annual value, £120,805. I am informed that his Lordship has recently become a Conservative, but till recently he ranked as a Liberal, and the Heathcotes have, for the most part, been steady and consistent Whigs. Lord Aveland, if not formally allied to the Tories, at any rate voted with the Government on the Afghan War.

The father of Gilbert Heathcote was an Alderman of

Chesterfield; Gilbert Heathcote himself was a London merchant, who, in the reign of William III., Anne, and George I., amassed a large fortune, and became successively Alderman, Lord Mayor, and M.P. for the City of London. He was an ardent supporter of the Whig party, and did not a little to break down the monopoly of the East India Company at the time when that corporation claimed the exclusive right of trading with India. He was also one of the founders of the Bank of England. Gilbert Heathcote was created a baronet in 1732, and towards the close of his life purchased a large estate in Rutlandshire. Normanton-park had been for several generations the property of the Mackworths, but, one member of that family having lost heavily by the Civil War, and another having deeply involved himself by a ruinous election contest in Rutlandshire, the manors of Normanton and Empingham were sold for £39,000. Six years after the new purchaser resold the estate, including—beside the above-mentioned—lands at Weston, Ketton, and Whitwell, to Heathcote, who built a new mansion at Normanton-park, the stone for which is said to have cost no less than £10,000. From that time forward the Heathcotes seem to have sat for Rutlandshire pretty regularly. The fifth baronet, who was a prominent member of the Whig party, was created Lord Aveland in 1856. He married one of the two daughters of the nineteenth Lord Willoughby D'Eresby.

It is necessary now to trace back the history of the Willoughby D'Eresbys, which is not a little complicated. To begin with the Berties, they were a Saxon family, who had some property at Busted, in Kent. One of them having been killed in a quarrel about tithes with the monks of Canterbury, his father solicited Sweyn of Denmark to invade the kingdom, and had the satisfaction of murdering every tenth monk in the archiepiscopal city. Treason and murder, however, met their due reward in the expatriation of the Berties till 1154, when they once more returned, and obtained from the King a new grant of their ancient lands. In the reign of Henry VIII. the heir of the Berties married the daughter and heiress of Lord Willoughby D'Eresby, and their son was summoned to Parliament by that title in the reign of Elizabeth, having inherited the estates of his mother. The son of that nobleman was created Earl of Lindsey by Charles I., and fell in the Royalist cause at Edgehill. The third Earl

was created Marquis of Lindsey in 1706. The second
Marquis, who was created Duke of Ancaster, married the
daughter and heiress of Sir Richard Wynne, of Gwydyr, in
Carnarvonshire. The Gwydyr estate is situated in the
loveliest part of North Wales, as all who have visited Bettws-
y-Coed, Llanrwst, and Trefriew can bear witness. It is rich
in minerals as well as in natural beauty, especially in slate,
zinc, and lead. Edenham, in Lincolnshire (6,300 acres), was,
I believe, part of the ancient property of the Willoughby
d'Eresbys; but the Lincolnshire estates were further increased
by the marriage of the next heir to the daughter and co-
heiress of Sir John Brownlow. The fourth Duke of Ancaster
died childless, and the estates, as well as the barony of
Willoughby d'Eresby, passed to his sister.

We now come to the Burrells. The Burrells had long been
small landowners in Kent and Sussex, and a younger son of
that family, who was engaged in trade in the City, was
created a baronet in 1766, while another held the lucrative
office of Surveyor of Crown Lands. The grand-nephew of
the first baronet succeeded to the baronetcy and estates, and
married the sister of the Duke of Ancaster. On the death of
the latter without issue, she succeeded to the property, and
her husband was created Lord Gwydyr. On the death of his
mother the second Lord Gwydyr inherited the ancient barony
of Willoughby d'Eresby. The next and twentieth Lord
Willoughby d'Eresby, of whose extraordinary escapades the
less said the better, left no male heirs. The Gwydyr estates
passed to a cousin, but the ancient barony and estates to his
two sisters, the survivor of whom is the present Lady
Willoughby d'Eresby, who married the first Lord Aveland.

The nineteenth Lord Willoughby d'Eresby married the
daughter and heiress of James Drummond, Lord Perth,
through whom were derived the large estates in Perthshire.
These included, and I suppose still include, an extensive
deer-forest, and the far-famed Loch Katrine, the scene of Sir
Walter Scott's "Lady of the Lake." The Drummonds have
been settled in Scotland about 800 years, and are supposed
to derive their name from the lands of Drymen, in Stirling-
shire. One of the race declared that it was a name given to
them by the King, derived from *drum*, a height, and *onde*, a
wave—in allusion to the storm through which the first Drummond safely brought a Saxon Princess who was afterwards

Queen of Scotland—a rather far-fetched derivation. However, it is stated that the Drummonds are descended from a Hungarian nobleman who accompanied Edgar Atheling and his sisters to Scotland, and on the elevation of one of the latter to the throne he received large grants of lands from the King. One of his descendants added largely to them by marriage with an heiress. About 400 years ago the head of the house was created Lord Drummond, and in the reign of James I. the holder of the barony was advanced to an earldom, with the title of Earl of Perth. The fourth Earl, who was Lord High Chancellor of Scotland under James II., followed the exiled monarch to France, and was rewarded with the barren honour of a Dukedom which he could not claim. It is remarkable that the Drummonds, though implicated in both the Jacobite rebellions, contrived to keep the estates in the family. The first titular Duke of Perth resided at the Court of the Pretender till his death. His eldest son was engaged in the Rebellion of 1715, and was attainted accordingly; but he had taken care in 1713 to convey his estates to his infant son. The second titular Duke of Perth died in 1730, and in 1745 his heir took part in the second Jacobite Rebellion, and was mortally wounded at Culloden. His younger brother also took part in the Rebellion. Both were included in the attainder and forfeiture that followed; but after the death of the younger brother his heirs obtained an Act of Parliament authorising the Crown to grant them the forfeited estates on payment of £52,547. This was paid by James Drummond, afterwards created Lord Perth, whose sister, as I have said, married the nineteenth Lord Willoughby d'Eresby.

I read somewhere recently that Lord Aveland was entertaining a distinguished party at Normanton Park, and that about 1,000 head of game per day fell to their guns. If this be true, I should hardly like to be one of the unfortunate tenants whose crops fed the game in question. However, there are plenty of other landowners to keep Lord Aveland company in that respect.

I ought not to omit to say that the Barony of Willoughby d'Eresby carries with it the hereditary title of Great Chamberlain of England

LXVIII.

The Stanleys of Knowsley.

"WHOM are you going to vote for?" asked a friend of mine at a Lancashire election some years ago. "Oh, I vote for Stanley," was the reply; "it's the Stanleys that made Lancashire." "Nonsense," my friend retorted, "you mean that Lancashire made the Stanleys." That Lancashire mill-hand only gave expression to one of the most prevalent of absurd popular delusions—a delusion which is constantly repeated, simply because people never pause to think. I propose to examine it in the light of facts.

I must say that I approach the Stanleys with some reluctance. From the respect, and even gratitude, with which I regard the present Earl of Derby, I should have preferred to pass over the family in silence; but the prominence of the Stanleys, both in history and in the new Domesday Book, requires that their story should not be left untold. Well, at least, that story will serve as a foil to the rectitude, the conscientiousness, the fidelity to principle, the hatred of bloodshed, which has been so nobly manifested by the present heir of Knowsley. Alike on account of their ancient lineage, their romantic history, their electoral influence, and their vast wealth, the Stanleys occupy a foremost position. Among the Earls the Earldom of Derby occupies the second place in the order of precedence, the Earldom of Shrewsbury alone coming before it. Lord Derby owns in

Lancashire	47,269 acres
Cheshire	9,202 ,,
Tipperary	6,531 ,,
Limerick	740 ,,
Flint	92 ,,
Total	63,834 ,,

With a rent-roll of £170,268,

although these figures, of course, do not convey an approximate idea of his annual income, for, while Lord Derby owns one-eighth of the great county of Lancaster, it must be remembered that his property is situated in the southern and richest portion of that county.

The Stanleys claim to be descended from Adam de Audley, who was settled in Cumberland in the reign of Henry I. The patronymic they now bear was assumed somewhat later, when one of the family acquired the Manor of Stanleigh, in Staffordshire. Afterwards one of them acquired by marriage the Manor of Stourton and bailiwick of Wyrrel Forest, in Cheshire. Their rise into power and fame is contemporaneous with the Wars of the Roses. The motto of the family, "*Sans changer*," is diametrically opposite to the truth, for no family ever trimmed its sails more cleverly with the rising or falling winds, or to greater personal advantage.

With Sir John Stanley the greatness of the house may be said to have commenced. He was a younger son, who inherited a modest estate at Newton, in Macclesfield. Sir John was appointed Lord Deputy of Ireland by Richard II., and from the same monarch he received a grant of the estate of Castle Blake in that island. He was afterwards successively Lord Justice and Lord Lieutenant. Sir John, like his still more famous grandson, showed a remarkable faculty for discerning, just in time, the winning side in a dispute; and at last, foreseeing the downfall of Richard, he joined himself to Henry of Bolingbroke, and, on that Prince's accession as Henry IV., Stanley was reappointed Lord Lieutenant of Ireland. When the Percys revolted, Stanley made himself useful in suppressing the rebellion, and was rewarded with a grant of the sovereignty of the Isle of Man—*i.e.*, with a gift of 170,000 acres of land—which remained in the possession of his male and female descendants till about 100 years ago, when, as I have already stated in the sketch of the Athol family, it was repurchased, at enormous cost, by the nation. Under Henry IV., Sir John Stanley held a number of lucrative offices.

Sir John Stanley also contracted a marriage which greatly conduced to the advancement of his fortunes. His wife was Isabella, daughter and heiress of Sir Thomas Lathom. The Lathoms were a Norman family, whose original patronymic was FitzHenry; but they afterwards assumed the name of Lathom, from the manor of Lathom, of which they obtained a grant. One of them had married a Knowsley heiress, and

The Stanleys of Knowsley. 69

had thus acquired the estate bearing that name. Henceforth the names of Knowsley and Lathom became indissolubly connected with the Stanleys. Lathom House, which was so gallantly defended by the Countess of Derby during the Civil War, was destroyed by order of the Parliament. The ninth Earl rebuilt it, but left it in an unfinished state; and one of his co-heiresses sold it about 150 years ago. It is now the property of Lord Skelmersdale. Knowsley, near Prescot which has a park between nine and ten miles in circumference, is still the principal seat of the Earls of Derby. The father-in-law of Sir John Stanley presented him, on his marriage, with a house at Liverpool; and, soon after, Sir John obtained a license to fortify this house, which he had rebuilt or enlarged. Thus commenced the connection of the Stanleys with Liverpool. It is worthy of mention that this old house was sold in 1737, and afterwards converted into a gaol. It was finally pulled down in 1819.

At the fall of the Lancastrian dynasty, the Stanleys were once more on the winning side, and received from the conqueror, Edward IV., as their reward, large estates formerly belonging to the Duchy of Lancaster. This transaction brings us to Sir Thomas Stanley, grandson of the last-named, who was Lord-Lieutenant of Ireland and Lord Chamberlain to Henry VI. During the Wars of the Roses he also acted a most treacherous part; but, like his grandfather, he had the knack of making his treasons profitable, and of always appearing on the winning side. By turn he was Yorkist, Lancastrian, and neutral. While still nominally a Yorkist, he married the Countess of Richmond, mother of Henry Tudor, afterwards Henry VII. From Richard III. he received a large pension, and extensive grants of manors, lordships, castles, and farms, as also did his brother, Sir William Stanley. He was also appointed Steward of the Household to Richard III., and was commissioned by that King to raise forces to oppose Henry as soon as he landed in England; but all the time he was in league with Richard's enemy, and furnished him with secret information of Richard's plans. How he and his brother turned upon Richard at Bosworth Field, and how one or other of them (it is not quite certain which) set the crown upon Henry's head when the battle was over, is known to every reader of English history. The gains of both brothers were enormous. Sir William was executed not very long after by Henry. As for Sir Thomas, almost all the confiscated lands of the vanquished Yorkists in the North fell to his share, including the estates of Sir James Harrington of Hornby, Sir Thomas Broughton of Broughton, Lord Lovel, Sir Thomas Pilkington of Chetham, Bythom of Bythom, Pooton of Pooton, Newby of Kirkby, "with at least twenty gentlemen's estates more." From the despoiled Pilkingtons alone Stanley had no less than seven manors. Of these confiscations I shall have something more to say hereafter. Sir Thomas had been created Lord Stanley in the reign of Henry VI.; by Henry VII. he was created Earl of Derby, Knowsley being situated in the hundred of West Derby.

The third Earl, who lived during the Reformation period, was renowned for his hospitality and lavish expenditure—his housekeeping expenses are said to have amounted to £4,000 per annum, an immense sum in those times. His political career, however, was a most inglorious one. Under Edward VI. he acted as a Commissioner for the Advancement of the Reformation; under Mary he delivered Protestants to be burnt at the stake, and had to endure their reproaches for his inconsistency; under Elizabeth he hunted Catholics to the death. Thus he contrived to keep all he had and to acquire still more. For instance, in the reign of Edward he increased his Knowsley estates by exchanging Derby Place, afterwards the Heralds' College, for lands belonging to the Crown in the vicinity of Knowsley. Like all such bargains in that reign, the exchange was doubtless greatly to the advantage of the subject at the expense of the Crown. He also obtained, in the reign of Edward VI., a grant of the lands belonging to the Collegiate Church of Manchester, whose annual value in 1649 was reckoned at £1,355. Subsequently the College was reconstituted, and the Stanleys had to disgorge. His son appears to have acquired three small monastic houses in Lincolnshire; what has become of them I am unable to trace. Ormskirk, in South Lancashire, formerly belonged to a monastic house, but at the suppression of the religious houses it was granted to Lord Derby, and, with the advowson of the Vicarage, is still in the possession of his descendants.

The seventh Earl, down to the outbreak of the Civil War, was regarded as an adherent of the Puritan Party, but he afterwards joined the Royalists. After the relief of Lathom

House by Prince Rupert, the Earl and the Prince attacked Bolton, and took it by storm. After the fighting was ended, a wholesale massacre of the townspeople took place, for which the Earl, rightly or wrongly, was held in part responsible. On the collapse of the Royalist cause, the Earl retired to the Isle of Man; but, having taken part in the Battle of Worcester, he was captured, and sent to Bolton to be executed. At the Restoration, his son, who had risked his life in one of the later Royalist risings, obtained a large part of the family estates once more, but the Stanleys lost heavily by the Civil War. Lathom had been destroyed, Knowsley was little bettter than a heap of ruins, and, as Ormerod says in his History of Cheshire, "half the estates were sold or sequestered, and the Bill to effect their redemption, which justice had induced both Houses of Parliament to pass unanimously, was rejected by the son of that King for whom the Earl's father had risked his fortunes and laid his head upon the block." His successor asserted that "he possessed no estate in Lancashire, Cumberland, Westmoreland, Yorkshire, Cheshire, Warwick, and Wales whence he could not see another of equal or greater value lost by his grandfather for his loyalty and his service to his king and country." The strong feeling which he held in this respect he permanently recorded by the inscription on Knowsley;—" James Earl of Derby and Lord of Man and the Isles, grandson of James Earl of Derby, and of Charlotte, daughter of Claude Duke of Tremouille, whose husband James was beheaded at Bolton, 15 Oct., 1652, for strenuously adhering to Charles II., who refused a Bill passed unanimously by both Houses of Parliament for restoring to the family the estates lost by his loyalty to him. 1732."

This Earl and his brother both died without issue, and while a portion of the Stanley property went to co-heiresses, the Earldom of Derby and the major part of the estates reverted to the Stanleys of Bickerstaffe, who were descended from a younger son of the son of the first Lord Derby. The manor of Bickerstaffe they had acquired by marriage. The present Earl has no children, and the heir presumptive is his brother, Colonel Stanley, the present Secretary of State for War.

We have seen how the Stanleys acquired most of their property; let us now proceed to glance at the state of that property at the present. I believe that Lord Derby is as liberal and enlightened a landowner as anyone would judge him to be simply from reading his speeches. He understands that a rural landowner's first duty is to refrain from doing any mischief, and has said so in almost those identical words. I wish that all the landowners in England had as clear an understanding of the limits of their rights, and of the way to subserve their real interests, as Lord Derby. But our inquiry is not whether Lord Derby is or is not a good landlord, but whether the Stanleys made Lancashire, or Lancashire the Stanleys.

The North of England at the present time is great in wealth, enterprise, and power; but its preponderance is quite of modern growth. That growth has been one of immense rapidity. In 1692 the real property of Lancashire assessed for the Land Tax amounted to £97,242; in 1860 it amounted to £11,453,851. Take another fact. In 1590 Chorlton Hall and Estate at Manchester was sold by Edmond Trafford for £320; at the close of the last century the same property fetched £60,000; its present value would have to be reckoned by hundreds of thousands. Whence the enormous increase in prosperity? Take the Land Tax. In the time of William III. it was 4s. in the pound; the poundage of Lancashire at the present time is one-eighth of a penny. Have the Stanleys made this difference, or in any appreciable degree contributed to bring it about? I suppose that no one, whatever interest he may find in the Wars of the Roses, will contend that the dethronement of Richard II. or the accession of Richard III., or the establishment of Henry VII. upon the throne, had much to do with the prosperity of modern Lancashire. The Stanleys profited greatly, as we have seen, by each of these transactions; but Lancashire did not grow rich till a very much later date. It is the cotton manufacture which has made Lancashire what it is, and the cotton manufacture is quite of modern growth. In 1760 the whole amount of its production was £200,000; in 1860 it had grown to £85,000,000. Was this, or any considerable proportion of this, owing to the Stanleys? No. They had, by betraying certain kings and fighting for others, obtained the right to say to the industrious and enterprising men of Lancashire, "Before you build your mills and your warehouses and docks, before you shall live near enough to those mills, warehouses, and docks to work in them, you must agree to pay us out of your profits or earnings so much per annum, you taking all

The Stanleys of Knowsley. 73

risks." And it must be borne in mind that the right to impose such conditions involved the duty of taking a proportionate share in the defence of the country. It is on record that once in time of peril a Stanley mustered 20,000 armed men on a Lancashire heath; I wonder how many men Lord Derby's Land Tax would keep at the present time. It was not the mere accidental possession of the soil of Lancashire by any particular families that made it strong and rich and prosperous, but the inventive skill of Hargreaves, Arkwright, and Crompton, the capital and enterprise of the Peels and Philipses and Potters and Cheethams; the industry of her myriads of operatives.

Let us take Bury as a sample. It formerly belonged to the Pilkingtons, who had seven manors in Lancashire, all of which were confiscated and granted to the Stanleys after the Battle of Bosworth. The comparative smallness of its value, down to within the last hundred years, may be gathered from the fact that, in 1793, the population was less than 3,000. In 1831 it had grown to 15,000, in 1861 to 37,563, and in 1871 to 41,517. The latter figures apply to the borough area, thus swelling the total by about 10,000; but we shall be within the mark in stating that Bury has grown tenfold in population since 1793. According to Baine's "History of Lancashire," with the exception of a few small freeholds, one-half of the town is glebe, belonging to the rectory (Bury being a family living of the Stanleys); the other is leasehold under Lord Derby. As to the rectory, I note that in 1764, a Stanley being rector, an Act of Parliament was passed empowering the Rector of Bury to grant building leases for ninety-nine years of the glebe lands. In 1834 the annual value of the living was estimated at £1,937. What it is at the present time I am unable to state, as Bury is one of those livings the value of which is not given in Clergy reference books. Several district churches are now in existence, and, as the patronage is in the hands of the Rector, probably a large portion of the endowments came out of the funds of the mother church. Considering the actual value of the patronage appendant to it, the living of Bury must be almost a small bishopric, the property be it remembered, of the Stanleys. In 1867 the rateable property in Bury was £362,300. How much of this was actually in the hands of the Stanleys of course I cannot say, but if the authority I have previously quoted is right in stating that, with the exception of a few small freeholds, Bury is the freehold property of the Stanleys and their family living, at some time or other, as the leases fall in, we know to whom nearly all this vast property will belong. The Stanleys sign leases, and silly people fancy that in writing their names the Stanleys have made Lancashire.

Had I space I might pass in review other properties held by the Stanleys in the Cotton Districts. The Manor of Bolton, for instance, belonged to the Harrington family, one of whom was attainted for his devotion to the cause of Richard III. One fourth of the manor is still the property of the descendant of the first Earl of Derby, who obtained a grant thereof from Henry VII. Some of the Stanley confiscations were, like Broughton-in-Furness, sold in the time of the Great Rebellion; others, like Upholland, near Wigan, were sold by the daughters of the ninth Earl; others, like Broughton, in South Lancashire, were alienated to make provision for a bastard son; but the most valuable still remain in the possession of the heir of Knowsley.

Down to the early part of the last century the Stanleys held but little property in and around Liverpool, the most important being the old tower already described. But about the year 1710 the extensive estates of the Moores, of Bank Hall, in Liverpool, Bootle, and Kirkdale, who had long held a prominent position in the town, were sold to the Earl of Derby for the sum of £12,000. The Manor of West Derby, indeed, was once the property of the Stanleys, but it was long since sold by them, and, after passing through various hands, it came into the possession of the Salisbury Cecils by the marriage of a former Marquis of Salisbury with an heiress of the Gascoynes. The Moore estate cost £12,000 in 1710. Now let us pursue our inquiry whether Lancashire made the Stanleys or the Stanleys made Lancashire. I presume no one will be bold enough to affirm that the accidental and quiescent possession of land by one particular man in itself caused the development of the Liverpool trade. The cotton manufacture made Liverpool what it is; and I have yet to learn that the Stanleys made the cotton trade. Had Liverpool remained a fifth-rate seaport, the greater part of the Stanley estates would have produced no more than an agricultural rent, and on the coast line nothing at all. But as Liverpool grew it began to construct docks; as it grew bigger it enlarged them. Most of the land upon which the docks were constructed belonged to the Corporation; but in 1843 further extension was necessary, and one thousand linear yards of frontage to the river in the township of Kirkdale were bought of Lord Derby for £17,500. Liverpool alone made that land valuable, and Liverpool bought it at a high figure.

But the time arrived when it was necessary to enlarge the Dock accommodation. Lord Derby had yet an enormous frontage to the sea which only the Dock authorities could utilise. In 1847 the whole of the foreshore to the extremity of the township of Bootle was acquired by the Dock Trustees. The price was that the excavations made should be used in making land for Lord Derby, at the expense of the Dock Trust. When the land, which had before produced next door to nothing, was duly made, it was purchased by the Dock authorities. The quantity was 270,000 square yards, and the price was £90,000. I very much doubt whether that particular slice of land at the time when Mr. Moore sold it with his other property would have fetched as many pence.

I have dealt with the Stanley family at such a length that I must refrain from drawing any conclusions from the facts which I have adduced. Indeed, to the thoughtful reader, comment is unnecessary. Viscount Halifax once said that, even including local rates, and including what they pay of the general taxation of the country, the landed proprietors pay a less amount of taxation, in proportion to the whole amount raised, than any other people in Europe. Richard Cobden warned the same class "not to force the middle and industrious classes of England to understand how they have been cheated, robbed, and bamboozled upon the subject of taxation." In the present state of the country, is it not high time that the middle and industrious classes should inquire how and by whom they have been " cheated and bamboozled " ?

LXIX.

The Talbots.

"AS the heaven is rendered ornate and bright by the stars, so not only realms, but royal diadems, shine by the light of dignities, and the more noble and brave be he who is exalted to the fasces of honour, so much the more valorous doth he become; when, as gifts increase, the motives for confirming them increase, and from him to whom more is committed a more perfect order of conversation and polity is expected. Hence it is that we, considering the strenuous probity and circumspect foresight, and begemmed splendour of manners and lineage, of our most dear Cousin John, Baron of Talbot," &c. So runs the preamble of the patent of nobility held by the Earl of Shrewsbury, the Premier Earl of England. The first sentence is a rather tangled one; but I quote it in order respectfully to commend the last clause of it to the Earl of Aylesford and other inheritors of titles:—"To whom more is committed a more perfect order of conversation and polity is expected." The patent in question was only granted in 1442, but the Talbots were ennobled long before.

The Talbots have claimed to have been settled in England before the Conquest; but the probability is that they came over with the Conqueror or shortly afterwards, and obtained a small estate in Bedfordshire as under-tenants of the Earl of Buckingham. Somewhat later a Talbot obtained an extensive grant of lands in Herefordshire. The great-grandson of this Talbot was engaged in a good deal of fighting on the Welsh border, and married a daughter of Rhys ap Griffith, Prince of South Wales. One of his descendants married an heiress, by whom other property in Herefordshire and South Wales was acquired. This same Talbot, who married a second Welsh heiress, also had lands in Oxon, Berks, and Kent. One of his descendants died possessed also of lands in Gloucester and Wilts. Another Talbot, of whom more hereafter, married an heiress whose chief possessions were in Yorkshire. Strange to say, the present head of the house has no estates either in

The Talbots.

Bedfordshire, Hereford, Glamorgan, Oxon, Berks, Kent, Gloucester, Wilts, or Yorkshire. The present Earl owns in

Staffordshire	18,954 acres.
Cheshire	8,640 ,,
Worcester	3,608 ,.
Shropshire	2,186 ,,
Derby	1,348 ,,
Total	34,736 ,,

With a rentroll of £58,335.

Mr. C. Talbot has 33,920 acres in Glamorgan, and Mr. John Talbot 6,026 acres in Roscommon.

Sir John Talbot, who made his family one of the foremost in England, inherited from his father estates in Herefordshire, and from his mother the inheritance of the Le Stranges of Blakemere, near Whitchurch, in Salop. By a marriage with the heiress of Lord Furnivall, he succeeded to large estates in and around Sheffield, which have descended by marriage to the Dukes of Norfolk. He also in the same manner became possessed of the estate of Alveton, or Alton, on which is erected the far-famed seat of Alton Towers. Alton was in the possession of the Crown soon after the Conquest. It is not certain to whom it was granted, but shortly afterwards the De Verdons acquired it by marriage; in the same way it passed to the Furnivalls, through whom it passed to the Talbots. Ingestre, in the same county, from whence the Earl of Shrewsbury derives a secondary title of Viscount, was derived later on by the marriage of another Talbot with an heiress of the Chetwynds, who in turn had obtained it by a marriage with an heiress of the Mittons, who had probably obtained a grant of it not long after the Conquest. Thus it may safely be said of the greater part of the Staffordshire estates that they have been inherited by the descendant, either on the male or female side, of the very persons who originally obtained grants of them from the Norman Kings.

It is worthy of notice that the Earls of Shrewsbury derived considerable benefit from the confiscation of monastic property. Among their grants I find Worksop Priory, Notts; a small religious house at Derby; the site of another small house at Knaresborough; Tickhill Collegiate Church, Yorkshire; Rufford Abbey, Notts; Flanesford Priory, Hereford, and lands belonging to Rocester Abbey, Staffordshire. All these appear to have passed away; even the land in Rocester, Blore, Mayfield, and Swincoe, in Staffordshire, belonging to Rocester Abbey, in the time of Elizabeth had passed to a younger son.

Sir John Talbot, Lord Talbot, and subsequently Earl of Shrewsbury, played an important part in his time, was for some years Lord Lieutenant of Ireland, and was one of the most conspicuous figures in the French wars of Henry V. and Henry VI. Though we may lament that so much English blood and treasure were spent in these unprofitable struggles, the prophecy which Shakespeare put into the mouth of Henry V. on the eve of Agincourt has been amply fulfilled—

> "Then shall our names,
> Familiar in their mouths as household words,
> Harry the King, Bedford and Exeter,
> Warwick and Talbot, Salisbury and Glo'ster,
> Be in their flowing cups freshly remembered."

In the following reign Talbot was taken prisoner by Joan of Arc, and, after three years' captivity, was ransomed. It was for his valour and conduct in the subsequent French wars that he was created Earl of Shrewsbury. In 1453 the hero of no less than forty-seven battles and skirmishes was killed by a cannon-ball. I suppose, as an Englishman, I ought to feel grateful to him for all this fighting; but, if I ought, I don't. To me the net result of it all appears to be simply that he was conspicuous enough to be immortalised by Shakespeare as

> "The Talbot so much feared abroad,
> That with his name the mothers still their babes."

The first Earl of Shrewsbury had grown grey in the service of the House of Lancaster, but the house of Talbot was secured from any possible danger of taking the losing side at Bosworth from the fact that the heir was but a child. In his after years he stood stoutly by Henry VII. and Henry VIII., and, as we have seen, had some share in the spoil of the monasteries. His son was for fifteen years the gaoler of Mary, Queen of Scots. *His* second wife was the famous Bess of Hardwicke, whose daughter, Mary Cavendish, his heir married. The latter had no children, and was succeeded by his brother, who also died childless.

The title and estates then passed to a distant kinsman

descended from the third grandson of the first Earl. This grandson, Gilbert Talbot, had obtained from Henry VII. grants of the manors of Grafton and Upton Warren, in Worcestershire, with divers other lands in that county which had been forfeited by the attainder of Stafford, Duke of Buckingham. In the Civil War the Talbots fought on the Royalist side, and their castle at Alton was destroyed. The Earl who was in possession at the time of the Revolution of 1688 had been bred a Catholic, but abjured Romanism, and is said to have mortgaged his estate in order to raise money to assist the expedition of the Prince of Orange. Like several other vacillating statesmen of that period, though he more than once held office under William, he had secret relations with the exiled King. He was elevated by William to the Dukedom of Shrewsbury. The double part he played was, however, redeemed at last by the energy and decision he showed at the death of Anne. Unsummoned he attended the Council, and uniting with Argyll and Somerset, he prevailed over Bolingbroke and the other Jacobite intriguers. Inconsistent and unfaithful as he was, England owes gratitude to the man who, at the Revolution of 1688 and the accession of the House of Hanover, placed his great influence at the service of Constitutional Government when the cause was trembling in the balance.

The Duke of Shrewsbury left no children, and the dukedom expired; but the earldom passed to a distant kinsman, a Catholic priest. From him it passed thrice from nephew to nephew. At length it passed to one who, having no issue, bequeathed the estates to the Howards, in spite of the Family Act which the Duke of Shrewsbury had obtained, entailing his estates for ever. The case was fought out in the Law Courts, and decided against the Howards, and title and estates passed to a descendant of the third son of the second Earl. One of the Talbots of this line had risen to be Lord Chancellor, and acquired by marriage with a Welsh heiress considerable property in Glamorgan. His son was created Earl Talbot and Baron Dynevor—the latter peerage passing to his daughter, who married George Rice, a Welsh landowner. The Dynevor peerage is still held by their descendants. Earl Talbot left no sons, and was succeeded by a nephew who had married a Chetwynd heiress, and from whom the present Earl of Shrewsbury is descended.

The Earl who was living at the time of the passage of the first Reform Bill ought not to be passed by unnoticed. He was a Roman Catholic, but he was a staunch supporter of "the Bill." In one of the debates in 1832, he declared that he was at a loss to know from what evils the Constitution (as it was then) had saved the country. We had had expensive wars; we had £800,000,000 of debt; we had had rebellion and revolution, great and frequent commercial embarrassments, and the strange picture of an intelligent and active population idle and starving in the midst of abundance. The only way to test the value of the Constitution was to pass a measure to give its merits fair-play. They must either consent to right the people, or the people would right themselves. The Clergy, who had too frequently been the willing ministers of the worst forms of tyranny, and participators in all acts of extravagance, spoliation, and corruption, ought to be the first to come forward to discharge their duty to the country. He further declared that "if the House of Commons needed reform, so likewise would the House of Lords, to prevent the danger of continual collision, and to secure that unity of action essential to the management of the affairs of a great nation." It would be rather difficult to find such an outspoken peer now.

LXX.
The Fitzmaurices.

THE Fitzmaurices have been for more than a century among the most distinguished of the great Whig houses. Politically, the house is now represented by Lord Edmond Fitzmaurice, M.P. for the little family borough of Calne, who is certainly something more than a Whig, and who occasionally contributes political articles to the magazines. In Wiltshire he is a tower of strength to the Liberal party. On the rare occasions when he addresses the House, though he is not the man to command a large audience, he shows a thorough knowledge of his subject, and possibly in the future, with the family advantages which he possesses, he may become a much more prominent politician than he is now. His elder brother, the Marquis of Lansdowne, does not take a very active part in public affairs, but fulfils the duties of a liberal and enlightened landowner. I know something of the condition of Wiltshire, where for the most part the agricultural labourers are in a low condition, and if I were asked to point out the district in which they obtain the highest wages and occupy the best cottages, I should certainly give the palm to the estates of the Marquis of Lansdowne. Indeed, some time back, when there was a dispute between the farmers and the men, in which the Marquis endeavoured to play the part of a mediator, the men were divided, because a considerable number of them lived in the cottages of the Marquis, and had a very strong sense of the advantage of being his tenants.

The Marquis of Lansdowne owns in Wilts 11,145 acres, and in Hants four acres. The greater part of his property is in Ireland, where he owns in Dublin, Kerry, Kilkenny, King's County, Meath, Limerick, and Queen's County 124,368 acres, making a total in England and Ireland of 135,517 acres, with a rent-roll of £53,465. Besides this, the Dowager Marchioness his mother, who claims the Barony of Nairne, has 9,070 acres in Perth and 134 in Kinross, with a rental of £8,812.

The Fitzmaurices derive their ancient lineage from the family by whose name they are now known, but most of their wealth from the Pettys, whose name they used to bear alone. The third Marquis, who for some years before his death was the Nestor of the Whig party, was prominent in the politics of the opening years of the present century as Lord Henry Petty. Petty is certainly not so pretty as Fitzmaurice, but it happens that Sir William Petty is one of the most distinguished of the ancestors which the family can boast.

Sir William Petty was the son of a Hampshire clothier, and as a boy giving evidence of great ability, he was sent to Oxford, where he made the best use of his advantages. Subsequently he went on the Continent, and continued his studies at Leyden, Paris, and other Universities. Returning to England about the close of the Civil War, he took up his residence at Oxford as a Physician, and became a Professor at the University. The man who had studied under Thomas Hobbes, and who was associated in university work with John Owen, though he had made a great reputation, had yet to make a great fortune. The opportunity, however, arrived in 1651, when he was appointed Physician-General to the Irish Army. The allowance was but £1 per day, but Ireland was then to adventurous spirits what India became a hundred years later. He practised as a physician in Ireland for a time, but he also obtained the offices of Clerk of the Council and Secretary to the Lord-Lieutenant. The division of confiscated lands among the English soldiers afforded a fine opportunity for using his scientific attainments, and he was appointed to make a careful survey of the island. He was paid by a percentage on the redistributed lands, and his profits were so enormous that he acquired about 50,000 acres of land in Kerry, his Irish estates being estimated at a value of nearly £6,000 per annum. Though high in office under Cromwell, he had not taken such a decided part in political affairs as to preclude him from making his submission to Charles II. at the Restoration, and having his newly-acquired property settled upon him by special order of the King, together with considerable additions thereto. He was knighted by Charles II., was one of the founders of the Royal Society, and in his old age still pursued his career of invention and scientific research. Of all the men who profited by the Cromwellian confiscations, he was apparently the worthiest. He is said to have expended

£10,000 in planting an English colony at Kenmare, in the county of Kerry, where he established fisheries and ironworks. In 1685 the colonists were driven away by the natives, but they returned when William III. had accomplished the subjection of Ireland. In modern times the Fitzmaurices have liberally expended their money in roads and piers in the neighbourhood. Sir William lived almost till the Revolution of 1688, and was succeeded by his son, who was created Baron Shelburne, and, agreeably with family traditions, sided with William. His younger brother succeeded, and obtained a re-grant of the Kerry estates, then 80,000 acres, and two steps in the Peerage as Earl of Shelburne. He purchased an estate at Wycombe, Bucks, which included that pocket borough, which was afterwards sold (shall we not say borough as well as estate?) to the Carringtons. He died without issue, and bequeathed his estates to John Fitzmaurice, his nephew (second son of the Earl of Kerry), one of whose descendants ultimately succeeded to the title and estates of the latter nobleman. The second Earl of Shelburne obtained by purchase the estate of Bowood, Wilts.

We must now turn to the Fitzmaurices. It is probable that the first of this family who set foot in England was one of the foreign favourites of Edward the Confessor. From him are descended the Fitzgeralds and the Fitzmaurices. One of his descendants, William Fitzwalter by name, assisted Earl Strongbow in the conquest of Ireland in the reign of Henry II. He returned to England; but his second son, Raymond, remained, and obtained as his reward a considerable grant of land in Kerry. His eldest son (illegitimate) succeeded him, and from him the name of Fitzmaurice is probably derived. It is unnecessary to go into details as to the part played by the Fitzmaurices in the stormy history of Ireland; suffice it to say that they largely profited by the confiscation of the Abbey lands in the reign of Henry VIII., though these did not long remain in the possession of the family. In the reign of Elizabeth the Fitzmaurices had, by repeated rebellions, forfeited their lands; but from James I. the head of the house obtained pardon and restoration. The twenty-first Lord Kerry married the daughter of Sir William Petty above mentioned, and at the death of the twenty-fourth Lord Kerry the estates of both families became united.

The first Marquis of Lansdowne is better known to fame

as the Earl of Shelburne, the friend of Chatham, Fox, and Lord Holland. Few statesmen of his time had more liberal and enlightened views. When all the Jingoism of that age supported the Tory Government in the disastrous struggle with the revolted Colonies, the voice of Shelburne was raised with that of Chatham and other true patriots in denouncing the war. In 1784 he was created Marquis of Lansdowne, and withdrew from political life. At the outbreak of the French Revolution he emerged from his retirement to denounce the war made by England upon the new Republic. Faithful in his maintenance of the Whig policy of peace and retrenchment, he continued to oppose the great war with France down to his death, soon after the opening of the present century.

The career of the second Marquis was, happily, a short one; and he was succeeded, in 1809, by his younger brother, Lord Henry Petty, who was already looked upon as one of the rising statesmen of the Whig party. It was the third Marquis who inherited the Kerry estates and title, and who thereupon reassumed the ancient family name of Fitzmaurice in addition to that of Petty. A supporter of Catholic Emancipation twenty years before that measure was carried; an avowed Free-trader a quarter of a century before Peel abolished the Bread-tax; a member of the Reform Cabinet of Earl Grey; and, in later years, the trusted and confidential adviser of the Queen, the Marquis of Lansdowne fairly earned the gratitude of his countrymen during his long and useful life. His grandson is the present Marquis.

The name of Fitzmaurice is also borne by the Earl of Orkney, who owns 11,489 acres in Tipperary, Queen's County, and Kerry, with a rent-roll of £5,789. He is descended from Lord George Hamilton, afterwards Earl of Orkney, who was a prominent figure in the Irish War of William III. One of his descendants, the third Countess of Orkney, married a Fitzmaurice, the brother of the first Marquis of Lansdowne.

LXXI.

The Dalrymples.

PRESUME that the narrow Protestants who used to accuse me of hostility to the Reformation because I did not shrink from exposing the deeds of the time-serving Protestants in the reigns of Henry and Edward have long since found out their mistake. It may be that because I have endeavoured to do justice to such great Whig houses as the Cavendishes, Fitzwilliams, and Fitzmaurices, some may yet be disposed to think that I am actuated by party prejudice in favour of the Whigs. Perhaps, in dealing with the Dalrymples, I may be able to remove such an impression. I know that men are sometimes actuated by an unconscious bias; but because I am aware of that fact, I believe I have spoken favourably of the great Whig houses only in so far as they have really aided the popular cause by honest and disinterested service.

So far as the landed possessions of the Dalrymples are concerned, they are exclusively a Scottish family. In the new Domesday Book the Earl of Stair is credited with the possession of 83,872 acres, with a rent-roll or £44,640. The Countess of Stair has also 19,266 acres, with a rent-roll of £13,616; and the trustees of the eighth Earl have 13,201 acres, with a rent-roll of £10,701. In all, the Dalrymple family have, in Wigtonshire alone, 82,666 acres, the total acreage of which county is but 288,960; so that they hold two-sevenths of the whole county.

The origin of the Dalrymples is somewhat obscure. According to Burke, a certain William de Dalrymple acquired the lands of Stair Montgomery, in Ayrshire, by his marriage with an heiress of the Kennedys. These Dalrymples were among the first families of importance in Scotland who accepted the Protestant faith, for we find that as early as 1494 the wife of the son of this William de Dalrymple was accused before the Council of James IV. of holding heretical doctrines. The charge was, however, dismissed. The great-grandson of this lady was one of the first who, about 1544, openly professed the doctrines of the Reformation.

The Dalrymples still hold considerable property in Ayrshire, at Stair, from which place they take their title, and elsewhere. Forty years ago the estates of Bargany, which derived additional value from its coalpits and ironworks, was the property of Henrietta Dalrymple Hamilton, Duchess of Coigny, but the present Earl married the daughter of that lady, and thus has consolidated the property.

The real founder of the family was James Dalrymple, a lawyer, who was a Lord of Session under Cromwell. He retained the office under Charles II., ultimately becoming President of the Court. Burnet describes him as "a man of very mild deportment, but a false and cunning man; a great perverter of justice, in which he had a very particular dexterity of giving some plausible colours to the greatest injustice." It was this Dalrymple who was first seated in Wigtonshire. Early in life he married a lady by whom he became possessed of certain lands in the parish of Old Luce in that county. A much larger portion of his acquisitions in Wigtonshire, however, was purely ecclesiastical property, which for a time was in the possession of the Earl of Cassilis. Mr. Burton's account of the way in which Gilbert, Earl of Cassilis, became possessed of the lands of Glenluce Abbey is worth quoting. According to the family historian, Gilbert was "ane particular man and ane greedy man, and cared not how he gat land so that he could come by the same." He had his eye on a few of the estates of the Abbey of Glenluce, and had dealings with the Abbot about them. That Abbot, however, died before the writs were signed, "and then he dealt with ane monk of the same abbacy, wha could counterfeit the Abbot's hand writ and all the haill convent, and gat him to counterfeit their subscriptions. When this was done, fearing that the monk might make unpleasant revelations, he got a certain carl to 'stick' (stab) him, and then he got ane to accuse the carl of theft and hung him in Cronsgate, and so the lands of Glenluce were conquest." A pretty story of forgery and murder, is it not? I dare say not a few such tales would have been told if historians had been always faithful. The Earl did not, however, permanently profit by this villainy, for some half-century after I find that Glenluce was erected into a barony by James VI. And

The Dalrymples. 87

then, according to the "Statistical Account of Scotland," it "was afterwards annexed to the See of Galloway, the revenues of which had been much reduced, and towards the end of the 17th century it was again erected into a barony, and became the property of the noble family of Stair," or in other words Charles II. robbed the Church, and enriched the Dalrymples with the plunder.

This is not the only piece of ecclesiastical plunder now held by the Dalrymples. They hold a considerable estate in Midlothian, viz., the Oxenford Castle property. The barony of Cranston was formerly the property of the Macgills, who acquired the Church of Cranston, which anciently belonged to the monks of Kelso. These estates were brought by a Macgill heiress into the Dalrymple family. The Manor and the Chapelry of Cousland, too, were annexed to the Barony of Cranston at the Reformation. Thus, these lands, with their then unknown wealth of coal-pits and stone-quarries, passed out of the hands of the Church to swell the possessions of the House of Dalrymple.

Whatever his faults, the natural bias of Sir James Dalrymple seems to have been towards Presbyterianism and liberty; and he, therefore, was unfitted to be the tool of a Government so abominable as that which ruled Scotland at the close of the reign of Charles II. He accordingly quitted office, and retired to Holland. We have seen already, in the history of other Scotch families, how cleverly they contrived to hold with the hare and run with the hounds—father and son, brother and brother, taking different sides, the one as Whig, the other as Jacobite. The Dalrymples were the first to teach the Scottish aristocracy the lesson. When Sir James retired to Holland, his son remained behind, became Lord Advocate, and assisted in the evil work of the last few years of the reign of Charles II. As Macaulay remarks, "The Revolution brought a large increase of wealth and honours to the House of Stair." The younger Dalrymple was quite ready to desert James for William. The father was raised to the peerage; the son was reappointed Lord Advocate, and soon afterwards Secretary of State for Scotland, in which capacity he left behind, to quote the words of Lord Stanhope, "a memory on which a load of infamy rests." The story of the Massacre of Glencoe—the darkest episode in the history of the reign of William III.—is familiar to almost every reader. Beside other massacres of more modern date, it looks insignificant in size; but its cold-blooded, deliberately-planned wickedness, and the treachery, the falsehood, the unspeakable villainy of the man who planned it, have given a lurid horror to the deed, and damned its perpetrator to everlasting infamy. In the valley of Glencoe, on the borders of Argyll and Inverness, were some fifty cottages, inhabited by about 200 persons. A party of more than a hundred soldiers were quartered on these people, by whom they were treated with all possible kindness, and with whom they lived some twelve days. Before dawn on the morning of the thirteenth day, the soldiers rose up at the word of command, and commenced an indiscriminate slaughter. Over thirty persons, men, women, and children, were butchered; the rest fled to the mountains, where most of them perished of cold and hunger in that terrible February. The few who returned came back to find their homes a heap of blackened ruins, and their cattle driven off by the inhuman murderers.

The chief guilt of this savage deed rests with the younger Dalrymple. The proofs are indisputable. We have the evidence of his own letters to the commanding officer of the party. "Your troops," he wrote, "will destroy entirely the country of Lochaber, Lochiel's lands, Keppoch's, Glengarry's, and Glencoe's. Your powers shall be large enough. I hope the soldiers will not trouble the Government with prisoners." I think, by the way, that I recollect the use of a somewhat similar phrase not very long ago in connection with a certain campaign in Asia—and it was not used by Asiatics either.

But this is not all. It was not Dalrymple's fault that the massacre did not assume gigantic proportions. As Mr. Green remarks, " He had hoped that a refusal of the oath of allegiance (to William) would give ground for a war of extermination." In this he was disappointed. By the appointed day Lochiel, Glengarry, Keppoch, and the other Highland Chiefs had taken the oath. Macdonald of Glencoe came in, the very last day, to Fort William; but, as there was no person there to administer the oath, he had to travel to Inverary, which he reached six days after the appointed time. The evidence of Macdonald's submission was suppressed by the Dalrymples, the father having a hand in the business as well as the son. An order, conveniently vague in its language, was laid before the King, which the monarch, according to

The Dalrymples.

Burnet, signed without reading. The rest we know. The truth only came to light but slowly, and then the sole punishment the younger Dalrymple received was dismissal from office. That was his sole punishment then; but he will ever remain gibbeted in history with Guise and Alva, with Kirk and Claverhouse, with Soojah Dowlah and Shefket Pasha, as a pitiless man of blood, who spared neither age nor sex, slaying not as a soldier, but as an assassin. One feels some little satisfaction in recording that the posterity of the author of the Glencoe Massacre has died out, and that the title and estates are now held by the descendants of one of his younger brothers.

LXXII.

The Somersets.

THE *Spectator*, in noticing the reprint of the first series of " Our Old Nobility," expressed a doubt whether this kind of writing could be productive of useful results. The editor of the *Spectator*, at the time of the first Reform agitation, was of exactly the opposite opinion, for he devoted special supplements to information of a somewhat kindred character, from which, however, I have derived hardly any assistance. I venture to hope that, as the work of the *Spectator* proved useful in regard to electoral reform, my own will not be altogether ineffective when the subject of Land Tenure Reform comes to the front. I believe, too, that more recently the *Spectator* published a series of articles on " The Great Governing Families of England," which have furnished me with several useful hints, although the great houses were therein treated far too tenderly. This very phrase, " Great Governing Families," used as recently as 1865, and equally applicable now, expresses a most disagreeable truth. Believing, as I do, in government by the people and not by a few great houses, I humbly venture to hope that I may assist in tearing off the mask of a gigantic imposture, and lead some tenants of the great houses to understand that they are under no obligation to those who receive their rents, and especially that they are under no obligation to sacrifice their political convictions to please the owners of the soil they till or the houses which they inhabit.

Let us take, for instance, his Grace the Duke of Beaufort, who owns in—

Gloucestershire	16,610 acres
Monmouth	27,299 ,,
Brecon	4,019 ,,
Wilts	1,939 ,,
Glamorgan	1,215 ,,
Total	51,082 ,

With a rental of £56,209.

The Somersets. 91

The Gloucestershire estates were partly acquired by purchase. The far-famed seat at Badminton, which has a park ten miles in circumference, was purchased of the Botelers in 1608 by a younger son of the head of the house of Somerset, and was bequeathed by his only daughter to the Somerset who was afterwards created the first Duke of Beaufort, by whom the mansion was erected in 1682. Other manors in Gloucestershire appear to have been acquired by purchase still more recently. But it is in the counties on the Welsh border that I am more particularly interested. Monmouthshire returns two Conservatives, one of whom is a son of the Duke. That the overwhelming majority of county electors in South Wales are Liberals I presume that no one who knows anything of the district would doubt for a moment. Nowhere is Nonconformity more staunchly Liberal than in South Wales, and nowhere does Nonconformity appear in such strength. It is the territorial tradition alone that makes the return of a Conservative in either of these counties possible. That evil tradition has been recently broken in Brecon, for which the Liberal candidate, who in 1874 was defeated by a majority of 558, now sits as member. That which is possible in Brecon is possible in Monmouth; but the tenantry of the Duke of Beaufort and other territorial magnates have yet to learn that when they have paid their rents they have discharged their obligations in full. The Somersets are Plantagenets; and the Herberts, from whom they derived most of their Welsh property, were Normans. They represent the power of the sword, the forcible dispossession of the weak by the strong. Time has consecrated the conquest, and I have no desire to disturb it, though my fathers dwelt in Wales long before the first of their ancestors set foot upon its soil. But so long as Welshmen who cultivate their lands sacrifice their convictions at the polling-booth, and vote as their landlord or his agents order them, so long they wear the shameful badge of conquest. The ballot was brought into use to protect their liberties; those who do not make use of the advantage are slaves. The Duke of Beaufort may lord it over the soil, but when he tries to lord it over our consciences every true-hearted Welshman should cry—Hands off!

"Old John of Gaunt, time-honoured Lancaster," third son of Edward III., had a family by his first wife, his eldest son being Henry IV.; by his mistress, Catherine Swinford, whom he afterwards married, he had three sons and a daughter who took the name of Beaufort from a castle in France, where they were born. The second of these sons was the Cardinal Beaufort of Shakespeare, the eldest was created Marquis of Somerset and Dorset. The son of the latter was created Duke of Somerset, and had an only daughter, who was married to Edmond Tudor, Earl of Richmond, and became mother of Henry VII. He also left an illegitimate son, Charles, who took his father's title as a patronymic. Charles Somerset was therefore the half-brother of the mother of Henry VII., and, as was to be expected, he shared in the spoils of the final victory of the House of Lancaster. He obtained a number of employments from Henry, but, what was of far greater importance to the fortunes of his descendants, he became a great lord of the soil by his marriage with the daughter and heiress of William Herbert, Earl of Pembroke and Huntingdon, through whom he acquired the larger part of that nobleman's estates. He was Lord Chamberlain to Henry VII. and Henry VIII.; in the reign of the former monarch he was known in right of his wife's possessions as Baron Herbert; by the latter monarch he was created Earl of Worcester.

We must now turn to the Herberts, whose early history is somewhat obscure. It is not quite clear who the original Herbert was. According to one account he was the bastard son of Henry I.—the bar-sinister frequently appears when dealing with the Somersets. According to another account, he was Lord Chamberlain to that King, whose mistress he married. We need not go into the troubled history of South Wales in those times, but pass on to William Herbert, first Earl of Pembroke. As a simple Knight he distinguished himself in the French campaigns of Henry V., but his fortune was made by espousing the Yorkist cause. The strength of the Lancastrian cause had lain chiefly in the North and West; the bloody fight at Towton was followed by enormous confiscations, and one of the chief gainers thereby was Herbert, who obtained immense grants of lands in South Wales. For instance, I find, in Jones's "History of Brecknockshire," that Edward IV.,'very early in his reign, granted the castle, town, manor, and lordship of Crickhowel, Ystradyw-isaf, and Tretower, with other large possessions in Wales, to Sir William Herbert. Pembroke, Haverfordwest, Tenby, and several other places in Pembrokeshire were acquired in like manner, as also several estates in Glamorgan and elsewhere. The right of the Tory Duke of Beaufort to compel Liberal Welshmen to vote as he pleases rests upon a grant of estates confiscated by Edward IV., because their former owners supported the King whose father Herbert had served as a soldier.

We may trace the Monmouthshire estates most easily by means of the ancient buildings; the possession of a castle usually indicates the ownership of much of the surrounding property. Monmouth Castle—the birthplace of Henry V., who was hence called Henry of Monmouth—was granted by Henry III. to one of his younger sons, whose descendant, Blanch, married John of Gaunt. Raglan Castle, one of the principal seats of the Somersets till it was deposited in the time of the Civil War, was held by several Norman families in succession, and was probably derived by the Herberts from one of them by marriage. Chepstow Castle, where Henry Marten, the Regicide, was immured for several years, appears to have been purchased by the Earl of Pembroke. Tintern Abbey was granted to the Earl of Worcester in the reign of Edward VI. I presume, but am not able to state with certainty, that the Glamorganshire property of the Somersets, at Oystermouth, near Swansea, and elsewhere, was formerly part of the Herbert estates, and obtained in like manner with the rest.

Of the subsequent history of the Somersets there is little of interest to record. The fourth Earl of Worcester, who had been Master of the Horse to Elizabeth, was made Lord Privy Seal to James I., with an annual salary of £1,500 for life. The fifth Earl is said to have expended £300,000 in the cause of kingly despotism, and he and his son used their great influence to waste the lives of Welshmen in the battles of Charles I., as their ancestors had done during the Wars of the Roses. Clarendon speaks of the Earl of Worcester as the richest man in the kingdom, and in the time of the Commonwealth the estates were worth no less than £20,000 per annum. Early in the Civil War Charles I. created the Earl of Worcester a Marquis. The second Marquis was a dabbler in Science, and published " A Century of Inventions," from one of which the idea of the steam-engine is said to have been derived. The third Marquis was created Duke of Beaufort by Charles II.; he made an ineffectual effort against the

Prince of Orange, but subsequently took the oath of allegiance. For the next generation or two the Somersets were regarded as timid Jacobites, without the courage of their opinions.

During the present century I count no less than five Somersets in the Church (the Duke has twenty-four livings in his gift), and twelve in the Army. Most of the latter, of course, rose to a high position. The most distinguished of them was Lord Fitzroy Somerset, who served through the Peninsular War, lost an arm at Waterloo, subsequently held several lucrative military offices, and was created Lord Raglan. At the outbreak of the Crimean War he was appointed Commander-in-Chief of the British Army, which post he held when the victories of Alma and Inkerman were won. He died in the Crimea during the siege of Sebastopol.

Before the constituencies of South Wales, whether borough or county, allow themselves to be overawed by the territorial influence of the Duke of Beaufort, I would entreat them to consider whether they owe anything to him or his. The very lands he holds are his by right of conquest. The Somersets have always been on the side of tyranny, and when they have not been Catholics they have always been High Churchmen. If they had had their way, Charles I. would have trampled under foot the liberties of his country; James II. would have ruled England through the Jesuits; Nonconformists would still be excluded from holding any public office, and would yet have to pay Church-rates. Is there a Welsh Nonconformist who is degraded enough to sell his soul and dishonour his conscience for such a race?

LXXIII

The Wyndhams.

THE patent of nobility held by Lord Leconfield dates only from 1859, and yet, if we take into account the fact that his estates have been acquired not by purchase, but by matrimonial alliances, he is fully entitled to rank among "Our Old Nobility," especially as his Irish estates have descended by bequest for more than a thousand years, and the greater part of his English estates for considerably more than half that period. It is a case of "New Men and Old Acres," so far, at least, as the connection between the two is concerned; for the Wyndhams can only in that sense be regarded as new men. They are a Saxon family, anciently seated at Wymondham, in Norfolk, from which place they are supposed to derive their name. Mr. H. W. Wyndham still holds 6,483 acres in that county, and is, I believe, the son of the hero of an extraordinary case which those of my readers who have arrived at middle life can hardly fail to remember. We must not, however, look in Norfolk for the estates of Lord Leconfield. A Wyndham in the reign of Henry VIII. obtained a good share of the spoil of the monastic houses; and his son and grandson both married Somersetshire heiresses. Later on, the Norfolk property fell to a younger son; and the Somersetshire property, at Orchard and elsewhere, to an elder son, one of whose descendants was created a Baronet. From this latter line Lord Leconfield is descended, but we must not look for his estates in Somersetshire. The second Baronet was Sir William Wyndham, a statesman of the reigns of Anne and George I., who, according to Lord Stanhope, held the threads of the whole Jacobite conspiracy in 1715, and narrowly escaped condign punishment through the influence of his father-in-law, the Duke of Somerset. The son of Sir William Wyndham became afterwards Earl of Egremont; and the father of the present Lord Leconfield was the eldest illegitimate son and adopted heir of the third Earl.

Succeeding as he did to vast estates, it was only natural that he should be created a Peer. The Egremont title only takes us back to 1749, but it takes us to a period when the Wyndhams succeeded to estates which had been in the possession of great Norman houses for centuries. Lord Leconfield (Leconfield is in Yorkshire) holds estates in six different counties as follows:—

Sussex	30,221 acres.
Yorkshire	24,733 ,,
Cumberland	11,147 ,,
Clare	39,048 ,,
Limerick	5,298 ,,
Tipperary	273 ,,
Total	110,720 ,,

With a rental of £88,484.

He also has no less than twenty-four Church livings, one of which is worth £1,538 and a house; another, £1,371 and a house: the total annual value of them all, exclusive of residences, being £10,393.

The Yorkshire, Sussex, and Cumberland estates are part of the ancient inheritance of the Percies. When speaking of the Percies, I said that for a hundred years they were a powerful family before they set foot in Northumberland. For their ancient home, where they settled soon after the Conquest, we must go to Yorkshire, in the neighbourhood of Spofforth, where they once had a magnificent mansion, the ruins of which are, I believe, still in existence. These estates are now the property of Lord Leconfield. By marriage the great houses of Percy and Louvaine became united. The Louvaines acquired their possessions by an enormous Royal grant. Adeliza, Queen of Henry I., had a brother, Joceline de Louvaine, to whom were granted vast estates in Sussex, at Petworth and other places in that county. Petworth Park, which is twelve miles in circumference, and the rest of the Percy estates in Sussex, are now the property of Lord Leconfield. William the Conqueror granted a large part of Cumberland to Ranulph de Meschines, one of his followers, who, in turn, granted great estates at Egremont and elsewhere, in the same county, to his brother William. From him the Egremont property passed by marriage to one family after another, till at length an heiress brought the domain to the Percies. The

Egremont estates are now the property of Lord Leconfield. There have been a few small modern acquisitions by purchase in Sussex, and possibly in Yorkshire and Cumberland; but by far the greater part of the English estates of Lord Leconfield have passed constantly either by descent or bequest, ever since the Norman period. He certainly could not complain if Parliament should ever see fit to re-impose upon the land the ancient burdens which his forefathers undertook as the condition upon which their lands should be held.

I must now proceed to show how these great ancestral estates of the Percies passed to the Wyndhams. Charles, sixth Duke of Somerset—known to history as the "Proud Duke"—married the daughter and heiress of the Duke of Northumberland. Ultimately the Percy estates were divided between the Duchess's son's daughter and her daughter's son. Her son's daughter married Sir Hugh Smithson, who became the first of a new line of Percies, and who was the occasion of the only witty saying ever uttered by George III. Not satisfied with being created Duke of Northumberland, Smithson vainly applied for a Garter. "I am the first Duke of Northumberland to whom it has been refused," said he. "Yes," said King George, "and he is the first Smithson that ever asked for it." The daughter's son of the Duchess was Charles Wyndham; Sir William Wyndham, his father, having married the daughter of the sixth Duke of Somerset. On the death of the seventh Duke of Somerset without issue, the Seymour title and estates passed to a distant kinsman, and the Earldom of Egremont (a brand-new title), with that portion of the Percy estates which did not pass to Smithson, was inherited by Charles Wyndham.

We must now pass to Ireland, and here we tread upon ground which has passed in unbroken succession, either by inheritance or bequest, from a time beyond which the memory of man or the records of history run not to the contrary. The estates in Clare and elsewhere were formerly in the possession of the O'Briens, Earls of Thomond, descended from the ancient Royal line of Brien Boroihme, who fell at the Battle of Clontarf in 1014. In the wilds of the West of Ireland the O'Briens were acknowledged as Kings of Thomond till, in the reign of Henry VIII., that title was relinquished for two Irish peerages, the Earldom of Thomond and the Barony of Inchiquin. The Barony of Inchiquin is still held by the O'Briens, with 21,884 acres in Clare and Limerick. The Earldom of Thomond exists no longer, but the estates formerly appertaining thereto are now the property of Lord Leconfield. The Wyndhams, however, do not possess O'Brien blood as well as the O'Brien estates. The eighth Earl of Thomond married the sister of Sir William Wyndham's wife, and left his estates to a kinsman, with remainder to Sir William's youngest son, who subsequently succeeded to them, but died without issue. Thus these estates passed into the Wyndham family.

The history of the Wyndhams is certainly a very curious one. At the Reformation they were simple Norfolk squires; in the reign of Charles II. the head of the elder branch had become a Somersetshire baronet, but, by a series of matrimonial accidents, about one hundred and thirty years ago, the family had achieved a complete change of base. Prior to that time the Wyndhams do not appear to have held a single acre of the vast estates now owned by Lord Leconfield. The marriage of the Jacobite statesman, Sir William Wyndham, has resulted in the acquisition by his descendants of the lands held for so many centuries by the Percies and O'Briens.

The Wyndhams, as a rule, have not been distinguished as tax-eaters; their good fortune has placed them above necessity. Yet there was one of them, the brother of one of the Earls of Egremont, who was a most exemplary sinecurist. This was the Hon. P. C. Wyndham, who, about half a century ago, was Secretary of the Council, Remembrancer of the Court of Exchequer, and Clerk of Common Pleas in Barbadoes, also Registrar in Chancery, and Clerk of the Patents in Jamaica, all which duties were of course discharged by deputy, and brought their fortunate holder an annual income of £5,500.

A relative of the present Lord Leconfield, the Hon. P. S. Wyndham, has sat for nineteen years for West Cumberland, or, rather, for the 11,000 acres owned by the family. Two other Wyndhams figure as considerable landowners—Mr. William Wyndham, who owns 2,866 acres in Somerset and 5,734 in Wilts; and Captain A. W. Wyndham, who has 62,25 acres in Mayo.

LXXIV.

The Dundases.

THERE are several branches of this fortunate family, two of which possess peerages. The Earl of Zetland owns in Yorkshire 9,623 acres; in Fife, Stirling, Clackmannan, and Dumbarton, 13,110 acres; in Orkney and Shetland, or Zetland, 43,446 acres. With regard to the latter, Sir Walter Scott, in a note on Magnus Troil, one of the characters in "The Pirate," says:— "The Udallers are the allodial possessors of Zetland, who hold their possessions under the old Norwegian law, instead of the feudal tenures introduced among them from Scotland." The introduction of feudal tenures was nothing more or less than a permanent robbery of the landowners and their descendants. The land was theirs absolutely till the abominable feudal tenures were introduced. In 1643 the islands were granted to the Earl of Morton, and this grant was confirmed in 1707, and made absolute in 1742. Twenty-five years after the Earl of Morton sold his rights (?) to Sir Lawrence Dundas, ancestor of the Earl of Zetland, who had made a great fortune as an army contractor. Army contractors in those days made immense fortunes with astonishing rapidity. Apparently the Dundases of this branch have still further advanced their fortunes by marriages into the Fitzwilliam and other landed families. But I must not dwell upon the House of Zetland, my purpose rather being to show of what stuff peers were made at the beginning of the present century.

The first Lord Melville obtained a peerage in 1802. For many years he had been the confidant and coadjutor of Pitt. He was a son of a Lord President of the Court of Session, and, as Fox said, "ever showed an eagerness to heap up emoluments and to systematise corruption." In 1775 he was appointed Lord-Advocate of Scotland, and for a period of thirty years he held a succession of rich offices, sometimes three or four together. When he held one of the chief offices in the Cabinet he was appointed Privy Seal of Scotland, and at the same time his wife obtained a pension of £1,500 a-year. He also had a grant of the Stewardship of Fife, with arrears of pay amounting to £3,000, arrears which the very persons who signed the warrant declared they were unacquainted with.

Sir Erskine May rightly says, in regard to that period, that, "with free institutions, the people were governed according to the principles of despotism." One of the Bills passed at that time empowered the Crown to secure and detain persons suspected of conspiring against the King's person and government; another provided that a prisoner, on the evidence of a single witness, and undefended by counsel, might be sentenced to capital punishment; another provided that if a meeting of twelve or more persons remained together for one hour after being ordered to disperse, the offenders should suffer death. Well might Fox declare that "every man who talked freely might be, and would be, in the hands and at the mercy of Ministers." Such was Toryism in its palmiest days. For all these things, next to Pitt, Dundas was responsible. I think of the true and brave men whom he hunted down, caused to rot in gaol, or to be transported beyond the seas; and then it is with a stern satisfaction that I proceed to describe the disgrace and downfall of their persecutor.

Lord Melville, who had held various lucrative offices for thirty years, was a pluralist who was at the same time Minister of War, President of the Board of Control, and Treasurer of the Navy. The latter office was practically a sinecure, the work being done by a deputy. Former Treasurers had made much gain by keeping large balances in their hands—dirty profits which the elder Pitt proudly refused to touch—but on Melville's appointment, at his own suggestion, this evil custom was made illegal, and his salary was raised from £2,000 to £4,000; and yet in 1803 it was discovered by a Committee of Inquiry that Alexander Trotter, the deputy of Lord Melville, contrived for several years to have balances in his hands deposited with Coutts, the banker—one of Trotter's relatives—ranging from £40,000 to nearly half a million. For some years these balances constantly exceeded £100,000, and with this money Trotter habitually discounted bills and speculated in stocks.

Trotter entered the Navy Office as a junior clerk at £50 a year, with a slowly rising increment. After a time he was

The Dundases.

appointed deputy by Melville, at a salary of £500, which was afterwards increased to £800. In 1791 this man's dividends from stock in his possession were only £80; in 1802 they were £11,308, and he had purchased considerable landed property. Even according to his own statement, Trotter's property derived by marriage and inheritance did not exceed £10,000; and yet he estimated that he was worth £65,000 when he was examined before the House of Lords. If this latter statement was correct, somebody else must have made considerable gains beside Trotter himself, and the question at once arises whether Lord Melville was a partner in his fraud. This it is impossible to determine with certainty, because the precious pair burnt the documents that might have incriminated them. I quote the statement made by the Cort Committee and signed by its chairman, the late Rev. Dr. Booth, a statement which is fully borne out by the proceedings leading up to Lord Melville's trial. "When in 1803 Parliament had appointed a Commission of Naval Inquiry to examine the irregularities of the Treasurer, Lord Melville, and his paymaster, Alexander Trotter, they mutually agreed, a few weeks before the sitting of the Commission, by a joint release exhibited on the subsequent impeachment of Lord Melville, to burn, and accordingly did burn, their accounts for £134,000,000 of public money, which had passed through their hands." The very last thing which an honest man, with an inquiry pending over his head, would have done, would have been to burn the documents which he knew would be called for. In the face of such conduct Lord Melville's personal denials go for nothing.

Lord Melville, however, admitted that he had a general knowledge of Trotter's practices. But that was not all. Trotter, when examined before the Commission of Inquiry, refused to answer whether his chief had shared in his unlawful gains. But that was not all. It was shown that when Lord Melville left office for a short time that he was a defaulter to the extent of £13,000, and that when he came into office again £7,600 of the deficiency was still unpaid. It was shown, further, that when he had promoted this junior clerk with a paltry salary to the office of paymaster that he had borrowed £10,000 and £20,000 of him at a time; and that, in all, so far as could be ascertained, Trotter had advanced to his chief £46,000, partly with interest, but much of it without any interest. Further, it was shown that with some of these sums Trotter had purchased stock on Lord Melville's account. It would be easy to quote a multitude of damning facts which came out at the trial, but my space forbids. I have, however, quoted quite enough to justify the declaration of William Wilberforce that he could not find words sufficiently strong to express his utter detestation of Lord Melville's conduct; and I must add that, after his lordship had been heard in his own defence at the bar of the House of Commons, the same eminent man protested that "he considered his defence an aggravation of his guilt." Lord Melville had, of course, to resign the places that he held, and his name was struck off the Privy Council. Ultimately, he was tried by the House of Lords on ten counts, and acquitted by majorities ranging from 27 to 135; but, as Miss Martineau says, "it was felt at the time, and has been felt since, impossible that many, if any, should believe him actually innocent of the charges brought against him."

I cannot forbear contrasting the treatment of Lord Melville and Henry Cort. Cort was an inventor who had made most important discoveries in the manufacture of iron, on which he spent £20,000. In 1789 Mr. Adam Jellicoe, Deputy-Paymaster of the Navy, with the consent of his superiors, advanced Cort £27,000, and entered into partnership with him. When Jellicoe died a few years after, it was discovered that he had stolen this money and other sums from the office. The ironworks were seized, but, instead of being retained or sold by the Government, they were actually handed over to Jellicoe's son—Cort, who was probably innocent, being turned out. Now let us turn to Lord Melville. Cort died in 1800, and a few days after Lord Melville presented a memorial to the Lords of the Treasury, setting forth the value of Cort's inventions and asking on that account a release of £25,000, the amount for which he was responsible owing to Jellicoe's defalcations, his own deficiency at the time being £190,000. He obtained the release. And what did Cort get? A few years after, Lord Melville's own son was First Lord of the Admiralty, and reported that Cort's merits had been sufficiently recognised by the pensions conferred on Cort, his widow, and children, viz.:—£160 a year to Cort, received for six years; £100 to his widow, received for sixteen years; and £20 to her children after her death.

The Dundases.

The Dundas family have proved themselves to be the most voracious set of tax-eaters in modern times. It is impossible to trace them all; and, if I did, it would be wearisome. As it is, my list is a tolerably long one. The first Viscount Melville died in 1811, and in the same year I find an annual pension of £1,000 granted to the Viscountess. The second Viscount had nearly a score of relatives in receipt of places or pensions. He himself was Lord Privy-Seal of Scotland (£2675), which, I believe, was a life office, and which he obtained in 1811. He died in 1851. If he held the office till his death, he must have netted over £100,000 therefrom. Then there was a Lady Elizabeth, who, I presume, was his sister, and who was granted in 1801 a pension of £300, and lived on till 1852. The second Viscount's eldest son was a General in the Army, Governor of Edinburgh Castle, and Colonel of the 60th Foot. His second son was a Vice-Admiral, and was for some years a Lord of the Admiralty, with a salary of £10,000. His third son, the present Lord, was Storekeeper-General of the Navy. His fourth son went into the Church, and obtained the Crown living of Epworth, value £988 and a house. The family motto is, *Quod potui perfeci*—" I have done what I could"; and it must be allowed that they have done a great deal in putting public money into their own pockets.

Now let us pass to the Zetland branch, the chief of which formerly held the title of Baron Dundas. The second son of the first Lord Dundas was a Colonel in the Army. Another son, by favour of the Fitzwilliams, into whose family his father had married, for many years held two rectories, with two houses and £829 per annum. Afterwards his son was appointed to one of them (Harpole), £529 and a house. Another son was a Vice-Admiral, and for some time a Lord of the Admiralty (£1,000); and another was a Lieutenant-General. There was also a William Dundas, M.P., a cousin, I believe, of Lord Melville, who held three or four Scotch sinecures for many years, whose united annual value was between three and four thousand pounds. I find also a Dundas as Commander-in-Chief and Governor of Landguard Fort; another as Joint-Keeper of the Signet; another as Governor of the Cape of Good Hope; another as Governor of the Prince of Wales's Island; another as Commissioner of Excise; another as Commissioner of the Navy at Bombay;

another with a pension of £300 for himself and £300 for his children; and another, a female, with a pension of £780. It is quite possible that one man held more than one office, and it is very likely that I have omitted to mention some offices altogether; if so, my excuse must be the number of the tribe. I must not omit to mention that it was a Dundas who suggested in the House of Commons, during the disturbances over Lord Robert Grosvenor's Sunday Closing Bill, that the mob should be dispersed by cannon. Of late years this fortunate family have not had such opportunities of living upon the public purse; yet I find one—the Hon. Robert Dundas—who had been in the Admiralty forty-two years, and who on his retirement in 1869, had a salary of £1,300, receiving an annual allowance of £1,072. Another was a Colonial Governor for twenty-two years; and yet another has been in turn Solicitor-General and Judge Advocate-General twice.

The Boyles.

"TREASON, sacrilege and proscription," says Gibbon, "are often the best titles of ancient nobility." The Boyles are not very ancient, but to them the third item in this statement is most appropriate. In the present paper I am speaking exclusively of the Irish Boyles; the Boyles Earls of Glasgow are quite a distinct house. Until the time of Elizabeth the ancestors of the Earl of Cork and Orrery and of the Earl of Shannon were an obscure Herefordshire family. In that reign the founder of the house, a younger son of a younger son, was a law student in London, so impecunious that he was unable to continue his studies, and therefore resolved to become an adventurer in Ireland. One of his descendants, the present Earl of Cork and Orrery, has in

Cork	19,689 acres
Kerry	11,552 ,,
Limerick	2,762 ,,
Wexford	231 ,,
Somerset	3,398 ,,
Total	37,632 ,,

With a rentroll of £19,166.

Another descendant, the Earl of Shannon, has 12,743 acres in Cork, with a rentroll of £9,322. The first Earl of Cork, who arrived in Ireland in 1588—less than three hundred years ago—tells us in his autobiography, "All my wealth was £27 3s. in money, a diamond ring, a bracelet of gold, a taffety doublet, a pair of black-velvet breeches laced and cut upon taffety, two cloaks, competent linen and necessaries, with my rapier and dagger." A modest inventory this; he was very much like the typical country boy, who reaches London with the traditional half-crown in his pocket. However, like the "undertakers"—most appropriate name—who went over to Ireland in Elizabeth's reign, in order to enrich themselves, he did not very long remain in this impecunious condition, and before his death he could compute his income at £50 a day, exclusive of houses and parks.

Boyle had not been long in Ireland when he laid the foundation of his fortunes by a marriage with a Limerick heiress, who brought him an estate of £500 per annum. His rise was so rapid that his purchases of lands excited the unfounded suspicion that he was in the pay of Spain, and he came over to England to justify himself. After a short imprisonment he was released by Elizabeth, and appointed Clerk of the Council in Munster. The rebellion of Fitzgerald, Earl of Desmond, though a misfortune to Boyle at the outset, proved in the end to be greatly to his advantage, as he obtained a large part of the confiscated Desmond property. Sir Walter Raleigh, too, who had acquired considerable lands in Munster, in 1602 sold them to Boyle for the small sum of £1,500. This property, the greater part of which is now in the possession of the Duke of Devonshire, is worth considerably more than £30,000 per annum. Later on he appears to have obtained grants of land as assignee of Carew and others. He also obtained by purchase the estate of Marston, in Somerset, which is still the seat of the family. Boyle, who had been created Earl of Cork, in his old age assisted Charles I. in preparing for his expedition against the Scots at a cost of £20,000, a very large sum in those days. I am not surprised at his rapid acquisition of confiscated lands, but looking at his purchases, the lavish scale of his expenditure, and his pecuniary assistance to Charles I., and to the poverty of Ireland, I cannot understand whence he obtained so much money. From an English point of view, it was no wonder that he became known as "the Great Earl of Cork;" but the Irish must have regarded him very much as a Zulu dispossessed of his lands regards a Dutch Boer. An inquiry having been made into the condition of Munster in 1611, it was reported that all Lord Cork's lands were inhabited by English. We are also told that "he encouraged the settlement of Protestants, the suppression of Popery, and the transportation of many septs and barbarous clans from the fruitful province of Leinster into the wilds of Kerry"—very agreeably, no doubt, to the new colonists of the fruitful province, but very much to the disadvantage of those who were driven away to the wilds.

The Earl of Cork appears to have taken particular care of

his relatives. His brother obtained two Irish Bishoprics—Cork and Cloyne, and Ross. Another relative became Archbishop of Tuam, and yet another Bishop of Waterford. Somewhat later one of the descendants of the priestly Boyles became Archbishop of Armagh, and obtained a considerable grant of lands in Wicklow. Subsequently he became Lord Chancellor of Ireland, and his son, who inherited his estates, was created Viscount Blesinton, a title now extinct.

The sons of the first Earl of Cork inherited the abilities or the good luck of their father. Three of them were created Irish peers in his lifetime, and the fifth, Robert Boyle, distinguished for his reputation as a philosopher, more than once refused a peerage. The second son, Viscount Boyle, was killed in the Irish Rebellion of 1642. The eldest son (afterwards second Earl) further advanced his fortunes by a marriage with the daughter and heiress of Clifford, Earl of Cumberland, who possessed large property in the North of England. He took the Royalist side in the Civil War, but contrived to escape the sequestration of his estates, and after the Restoration was appointed Lord High Treasurer of Ireland, and was created Earl of Burlington. His great-grandson, the fourth Earl, claimed and obtained the ancient barony of Clifford, and at his death his daughter and only child, who married a Duke of Devonshire, carried the Clifford property and part of the Irish estates to the Cavendishes. He was distinguished for his architectural taste, and was the builder of Old Burlington House in Piccadilly; Cork Street is still to be found at the end of the Burlington Arcade. Burlington House, as well as Chiswick House which had been acquired by purchase, passed to the Cavendish family.

At the death of this Earl the Cork title and estates passed to the Earl of Orrery, whose descendants still possess both titles. We must now go back to the third son of the first Earl who in his father's lifetime had been created Lord Broghill, and who was a conspicuous figure in the time of the Commonwealth. Frequent allusions are made to him in Cromwell's letters, he having been one of the Protector's principal lieutenants in the subjugation of Ireland. He was a prominent member of Cromwell's first Parliament, and sat upon the Committee on Kingship. to which scheme he was strongly favourable; if we may trust a family chaplain, with the base design of making Cromwell unpopular. From the

Cromwell Parliament he obtained two grants of confiscated lands, one to the value of £1,000 per annum, and the other of 2,000 acres of cultivated soil. After the Protector's death, Lord Broghill sent his younger brother to invite Charles II. over to Ireland, for which service the said brother was created Viscount Shannon at the Restoration, a title which expired with his grandson. Broghill himself was created Earl of Orrery, and appointed to a number of lucrative offices in Ireland. Like the aristocratic Protestants of the time of the Tudors, the aristocratic Puritans of the time of the Stuarts were quite ready to make their convictions subordinate to their interests. Broghill had much more substantial rewards than an earldom. Besides his numerous offices, he had five grants under the Irish Act of Settlement, which, by the way, was drawn up by his own hand. He also farmed the excise of beer and spirits in Ireland, and on the suppression of his office as President of Munster he obtained a pension of £800 per annum. Later on I find him obtaining a grant of £5,000, and of £500 per annum from Crown Lands.

The fourth Earl of Orrery was a distinguished scholar, who bequeathed his library and philosophical instruments to Christ Chureh College, Oxford, where he was educated, and after whom Mr. George Graham, the inventor of "The Orrery," bestowed the name on that astronomical instrument. His son, the fifth Earl, as I have already indicated, became also fifth Earl of Cork. A younger grandson of Lord Broghill, first Earl of Orrery, after filling the offices of Speaker of the Irish House of Commons, Chancellor of the Exchequer, and Lord Justice, was elevated to the Irish Peerage under the title of Earl of Shannon. His descendant sits in the House of Lords under the English title of Baron Carleton, and possesses 12,743 acres in Cork, with a rentroll of £9,322.

Apart from the unquestionable wrongs which the Irish have had to endure at the hands of successive generations of confiscators, the world has not had much reason to regret the rise of the Boyles to affluence and power. Literature, art, and science have found in them earnest patrons, and even ardent votaries. One of them obtained an elaborate eulogy from Burnet; another was complimented as "the generous Burlington" by Gay; another was the friend of Swift; and yet another the friend of Pope, to whom the poet dedicated his essay on "Taste," and wrote a number of letters. Lord Beaconsfield has told us, in one of his earlier works, that "greatness no longer depends on rentals, the world is too rich; nor on pedigrees, the world is too knowing;" and this truth the Boyles have generally appeared to recognise. In more recent times the Boyles have hardly retained the prominent position they formerly occupied; but the present Earl of Cork is known as one of the most consistent and active members of the Liberal party.

LXXVI.
The Herberts.
(POWIS BRANCH.)

HAT which Ireland was to English adventurers in the sixteenth and seventeenth centuries, India was in the eighteenth. Between the two classes, however, there was a wide difference. The Irish, unlike the natives of India, saw the soil of their country appropriated by landlords of another race; but many of the English adventurers, at great cost, effected vast improvements in the country. The natives of India were fleeced unmercifully by Englishmen, whose chief object was to get as much wealth out of the country in the shortest possible time, and then take it away with them. I have not yet dealt with any landlords of the Nabob class, and I therefore now propose to take the house whose founder was immeasurably superior to most Anglo-Indian nabobs.

Three earls bear the name of Herbert—Pembroke, Carnarvon, and Powis. Of the first I have already spoken; of the last I now propose to speak. Strictly speaking, the Earl of Powis is not a Herbert, but a Clive; but in the female line he is descended from the Herberts, and inherits a considerable portion of the estates once held by a branch of this great Norman-Welsh house. He owns in

Shropshire	26,986 acres.
Montgomery	33,545 ,,
Total	60,531 ,,

With a rent-roll of £62,925.

The union of the two houses of Herbert and Clive can hardly be described as an alliance of new men and old acres, for the Clives are certainly as old a family as the Herberts, and held lands in the Marches of Wales long before the Herberts were known in the district. But to the Clives, at the beginning of the last century, there must have appeared an immense distance between themselves and the owners of that stately pile in Montgomeryshire known to the Welsh as Castell Coch, or the Red Castle, and to the English as Powis Castle. For though some of the Clives had sat in Parliament as county members, the father of Robert Clive had but an estate of £500 a-year, followed the profession of a solicitor, was in embarrassed circumstances, and was glad to accept an Indian writership for his eldest son at a time when the East India Company was nothing more than a society of traders.

I have no space to describe, even in the most cursory manner, the brilliant and rapid career of Robert Clive in India. In 1744 he obtained a writership, in 1747 he temporarily exchanged the pen for the sword, and achieved his first successes. Soon after he was appointed to the lucrative office of Commissary-General. In 1751 he again distinguished himself as a military leader, and at the age of 27 he returned to England with such large gains in the shape of prize-money that he was able to extricate his father from pecuniary embarrassment, and to excite the wonder of the Metropolis by his extravagant mode of living. In two years he returned to India. I am more concerned with his gains than with his career as a soldier and administrator. Having set up in the room of Sujah Dowlah, a wretched tyrant, one of that Prince's officers, Meer Jaffier, as Nabob of Calcutta, he received enormous gifts from the man whom he had placed in power. At one time Meer Jaffier presented him with £210,000, and afterwards with the quit-rent for life of the lands held by the East India Company near Calcutta, amounting to not far short of £30,000 per annum. By the time Clive had reached the age of 34 he had an annual income of upwards of £40,000, and there is every reason to believe that he might have made yet larger gains if he had so chosen. Meer Jaffier, at his death, bequeathed to Clive a legacy of £70,000, which the legatee generously devoted to the relief of Indian soldiers.

While it is impossible to acquit Clive of the charge of beating villians by their own weapons, among which forgery was included, it must be remembered that his enormous gains were not wrung, like the gains of many of his successors, directly from the sufferings of the wretched natives. He played for high stakes with high players. The wealth he obtained was from princes, not from ryots, and it was not the fruit of personal extortion. In his later years, too, the efforts of Clive were strained to the utmost to restrain the rapacity of those who had been dazzled and demoralised by his own astonishing career. Fiercely assailed as Clive was after his final return to England, it is now generally recognised that the worst charges against him were unjust, and that the final judgment of Parliament will also be the final judgment of history.

It was but natural that Clive, in the midst of his successes, should determine to become a great landowner. In his native county, Shropshire, the Walcots, of Walcot Hall, had been settled for many generations. Clive availed himself of an opportunity to purchase the Walcot estates, which have since remained in the possession of his descendants, Walcot Hall being one of the seats of the Earl of Powis. But he wanted a residence nearer London. Sir John Vanbrugh, the architect for whom was composed the well-known epitaph—

"Lie heavy on him, Earth, for he
Has laid full many a load on thee,"

purchased some land at Esher, in Surrey, whereon he built himself a house. In 1715 it was sold to Pelham, Duke of Newcastle and Earl of Clare, by whom the house was greatly enlarged and beautified. The Duke added to the property partly by purchase and partly by enclosing a heath, and after his second title the place was called Claremont. Kent, a celebrated landscape gardener, was employed in laying out the grounds of—

"Esher's peaceful grove,
Where Kent and Nature strive for Pelham's love."

At the death of the Duke, Clive purchased the property and rebuilt the house at a cost of £100,000. The neighbouring peasantry used to say that the great, wicked lord had built the walls so thick in order to keep out the Devil, who would one day carry him away. At Clive's death the place was sold; and, after passing through several hands, it was purchased by the Government as a residence for the amiable Princess Charlotte, who there died in childbed. Of late the mansion has been the residence of the Orleans family. To return to the Clives, Robert Clive received a peerage, and at his death was succeeded by his eldest son. who married the sister and heiress of the last Earl of Powis of the Herbert creation.

I find it more difficult to obtain information in regard to

The Herberts.

Welsh property than in regard to English, but I have little doubt that the Herberts owed their property in Montgomeryshire to the favour of the Crown. During the reigns of the Norman and Plantaganet kings the Marches or borders of Wales were the scene of constant struggles between the Welsh and the Barons. At length Mortimer, Earl of March, the favourite of the Queen of Edward II., became the most powerful baron in that district, seating himself at Wigmore, in Herefordshire. He came to an ignominious end, but his descendants obtained the restoration of their lands. A Mortimer heiress at last brought them by marriage to the Royal Family, and for some time they were in the possession of the Crown. The great stronghold on the English side was Montgomery Castle, which appears to have been given into the custody of Sir Richard Herbert by Edward IV. By what process this castle, and the great estates in Montgomeryshire, ultimately came into the absolute possession of the Herberts I am unable to say, but it is not at all probable that they acquired either by purchase. Powis Castle itself, by the way, was purchased by the Herberts of the Greys in the reign of Elizabeth. The Richard Herbert just mentioned was brother of William Herbert, Earl of Pembroke, and, like him, was a staunch adherent of the Yorkist cause during the Wars of the Roses. Richard Herbert, during a Welsh war, laid siege to Harlech Castle, which made a stout defence. It is said that the popular Welsh tune, "The March of the Men of Harlech," was composed in commemoration of the event; if so, the English words now wedded to the tune are sadly out of place. There is another story in reference to this siege which I would fain believe to be true. Dafydd ap Ivan ap Einion only surrendered the castle on condition that his life should be spared; nevertheless Edward IV. would have executed his vanquished foe had not Sir Richard Herbert demanded of the King that either he should restore the brave Welshman to the castle, and send some one else to take it, or else take his own life instead of his prisoner's. Sir Richard, like his brother, was afterwards beheaded by the victorious Lancastrians. One of his younger sons re-obtained possession of Montgomery Castle, and in the reign of Henry VIII. was Steward of the Marches of North Wales and East Wales. His son, as already noted, increased his estates by purchase. Of the grandsons of the latter the fifth was George Herbert, the poet;

the eldest became Lord Herbert of Cherbury. Cherbury, by the way, is a little town on the Shropshire side of the border, two or three miles from Montgomery, and has given its name to one of the Hundreds of the County of Salop. Lord Herbert of Cherbury, chiefly known for his Deistical writings, after acting as Ambassador to France, was elevated to an Irish peerage by James I., and to an English peerage by Charles I.

Of the succeeding Lords Herbert of Cherbury there is little noteworthy to record. Twice the peerage expired, and twice it was revived in favour of the nearest kinsman, who inherited the estate. One of the Herberts of Cherbury married a niece and heiress of the Marquis of Powis—also a Herbert—by which means the family estates were considerably augmented. The Herberts of the Powis line, by the way, narrowly escaped forfeiture through adherence to James II. and his son; but the son obtained the reversal of the outlawry which the father had incurred. The second Lord Clive, who, as lord of the manor of Llanyblodwell, was the landlord of my own great grandfather, after his marriage with the heiress of the Herberts, was created Earl of Powis.

LXXVII.

The Trenches.

"GODLINESS is profitable to all things, having the promise of the life that now is"—especially if there be a National Church gorged with wealth upon which younger sons can be quartered. The Tories have fought repeated and obstinate battles for the maintenance of the Irish Protestant Establishment. It is well, therefore, that the people should remember how that institution worked, and to whose advantage. As I have already glanced at the history of the Beresfords, I do not think that I could find a better illustration than the Trenches. There are two branches of the house. The Earl of Clancarty owns in

Galway	24,010 acres
Roscommon	1,454 ,,
Total	25,464 ,,

with a rent-roll of £11,142. Lord Ashtown has in

Yorkshire	6,386 acres
Eight Irish Counties	44,175 ,,
Total	50,543 ,,

With a rent-roll of £28,202,

We shall see presently by what sinister means the peerages were obtained. Mr. Henry Trench has also 10,760 acres in six Irish counties, with a rent-roll of £4,714. The Trenches therefore hold between them more than 80,000 acres of land in Ireland, every inch of which has been acquired during the last three hundred years. It is hardly necessary to remark that the Trenches are not an Irish family, but belong to that numerous class of adventurers who, in the sixteenth and seventeenth centuries, "undertook" the exploitation of the sister island. They profess to be of French extraction, being descended from a Protestant refugee who settled in Northumberland about 1575. According to one account, Frederick Trench settled in Galway in 1605; according to another, in 1631. Not long before, the whole of Connaught had been the scene of most frightful cruelties, which were perpetrated by the English upon the unhappy inhabitants. Writing of the year 1577, Mr. Froude says:—"When the people were quiet there was the rope for malefactors, and death by natural law for those whom the written law would not touch. When they broke out there was the blazing homestead and death by the sword for all, not for the armed kerne only, but for the aged and infirm, the nursing mother, and the baby at the breast." Writing of the year 1582 the Four Masters say, " Neither the sanctuary of the saint nor of the poet, neither the wood nor the forest valley, the town nor the bawn, was a shelter from the Captain (Brabazon) and his people, till the whole territory was destroyed by him." Such was the condition of Connaught a few years before the first Trench made his appearance there. Frederick Trench is said to have purchased the extensive estate of Garbally, in County Galway. Irish estates were certainly cheap in those days; but Northumberland was not then a money-making county, and I am at a loss to conceive whence these Huguenot refugees could have obtained the purchase-money. However, whether they obtained a direct grant, or bought cheaply from those who had so lately received a grant of confiscated lands, matters very little.

The great-grandson of this Frederick Trench, Richard by name, married the heiress of David Power, of County Galway. As the Clancarty branch of the Trench family now call themselves Le Poer Trench, I presume that the Powers were descendants of the Roger Le Poer who accompanied Strongbow to Ireland, and was a large gainer by the earliest of the many confiscations that have taken place in the island. By this marriage Richard Trench's estate was considerably increased. His son was created Baron Kilconnel, in 1797, and his eldest son sat in the last Irish Parliament, voted for the Act of Union on condition of receiving certain promised rewards. Almost immediately after the Act had passed the father was made a viscount, and the year following he was advanced another step in the Peerage as Earl of Clancarty. That name has been recently made familiar by a popular play, and therefore I may as well explain in passing that the Earldom of Clancarty held by Donough McCarty, the hero of Mr. Tom Taylor's drama, had become extinct. The new Earl, however, was descended, through the Powers, from a sister of Donough McCarty. The sons of the first Earl of Clancarty of the new creation were all born with a silver spoon in their mouths. The eldest, who voted for the Act of Union as Member for County Galway, obtained his own reward, apart from the reversion of his father's new title, in the shape of an appointment as one of the Commissioners on the affairs of India, and subsequently of the sinecure of Irish Postmaster-General. He was afterwards appointed Ambassador to Holland, and, on his retirement from that easy post, obtained a modest pension of £2,000 per annum. For a man who never displayed any remarkable abilities, he certainly was successful at the trade of politics.

The second son of the first Earl was brought up to the Church, and became first Bishop of Elphin, and afterwards Archbishop of Tuam and Bishop of Clonfert. Though he had in the two latter dioceses only 3,000 Protestant families to look after, he received the enormous annual income of £17,326. His eldest son went into Holy Orders, and was, of course, well provided for, his father having numerous good livings in his gift. The next son of the first Earl became an Admiral; two out of his three sons were also quartered upon the Irish Church. The next son was in Holy Orders, and became Archdeacon of Ardagh, with three fat livings, whose united annual value was £2,206; his eldest son became a pluralist in that diocese of Tuam which proved such a mine of wealth to the fortunate Trenches.

Let us now turn to the other branch of the family, of which Lord Ashtown is the head. The younger son of the first Trench who settled in Ireland went into Holy Orders, and became Dean of Raphoe. He, or one of his immediate descendants, appears to have acquired lands in the County of Galway. A little later, Frederick Trench acquired lands in Tipperary by his marriage with the heiress of Francis Sadleir. Of his sons, the third became Dean of Kildare; *his* eldest son, in turn, being quartered on the Irish Church. Frederick Trench's eldest son was M.P. for Portarlington, and afterwards the first Lord Ashtown.

The Act of Union, it will be remembered, was passed by

one vote in the Irish House of Commons. That vote was the vote of the Member for Portarlington. How was it gained? There had been previous rumours that the Ministers had entered into negotiations with him, but that his conditions were too exacting. As a certain class of voters hang back till near the close of the poll, so with Mr. Trench. He even went so far as to rise in his place and declare that he should vote against the Ministry. Cooke and Castlereagh conferred a short time together, and then Cooke went and sat down by the side of Trench and had a short conversation with him. A few minutes afterwards Trench had the unblushing audacity to rise, and, amid the disgust of the House, declare that he had thought better of the subject since he had unguardedly expressed himself, and was now prepared to vote with the Ministry. As Sir Jonah Barrington says, "scarcely was there a member of any party who was not disgusted. . . . Mr. Trench's venality excited the indignation of every friend of Ireland." A few months after Mr. Trench became Lord Ashtown. With regard to the Ashtown estates in Yorkshire, I need only remark that they have been acquired by marriage with the Olivers, who derived them in the same way from the Gascoignes, a family to whom the famous Chief-Justice Gascoigne belonged.

Lest the *Spectator* should again ask *Cui bono?* I will ask the question myself, and endeavour to answer it. Here is a family which, as late as the reign of Elizabeth, was unknown in Ireland; it now owns more than 80,000 acres of Irish soil. It has had no other means of acquiring this large property than by the exploitation of the Irish people or by marriage with other houses of the same class. Its gains by the Irish Protestant Establishment may be reckoned by hundreds of thousands, I might almost say millions. And, like other great Irish landlords, the Trenches have the right to evict from their holdings the descendants of those who by their labour and energy have given to the soil of Ireland the value which it now possesses. The demand of the Irish tenant farmer is for fixity of tenure, that so long as he pays his rent no one shall be able to dispossess him of his holding. If the greater portion of the soil of England was held by men of another race and another creed, who had fastened upon the country within the last three hundred years, is it not very likely that Englishmen would make a similar demand? The Norman merged into the Englishman centuries before most of the families that now rank as great Irish landlords set foot in Ireland. The English people can never thoroughly understand the Irish Land Question until they look at it from the Irish standpoint.

LXXVIII.

The Howards.

(CARLISLE BRANCH.)

THE lamented death of the late Mr. C. Howard, M.P., brother to the Earl of Carlisle, reminds me that I have as yet only glanced at the ducal line of that great family. Beside the Duke of Norfolk, the Earls of Suffolk, Carlisle, and Effingham, Lords Howard de Walden and Howard of Glossop, and the Earl of Wicklow, all bear the same famous name, and all except the last are undoubtedly descended from the same stock—an honour which the Earl of Wicklow also claims. Taking the estates of all these, and of three Commoner Howards, I find that this fortunate family owns more than 211,000 acres of land in the United Kingdom. The Earl of Carlisle, though not the wealthiest of the Howards, has more extensive estates than the Duke of Norfolk himself. He owns in—

Cumberland	47,730 acres.
Northumberland	17,780 ,,
Yorkshire	13,030 ,,
Total	78,540 ,,

With a rentroll of £49,602.

Those who are familiar with "The Lay of the Last Minstrel" will recollect "Belted Will Howard," one of the prominent characters in the poem, but who, as Scott tells us in his notes, by a poetical anachronism was introduced into the romance a few years earlier than he actually flourished. It was "Belted Will Howard" who was the founder of the Cumberland branch of the family. He was a younger son of the fourth Duke of Norfolk, who was beheaded in the reign of Elizabeth, having been drawn into treason through Mary Queen of Scots. In the following reign, Lord William Howard was restored in blood. It was a marriage with a Dacre heiress that made him a great landholder.

The Dacres settled in Cumberland very soon after the Conquest. They are said to have been kinsmen of De Meschines, a Norman, whom William created Earl of Cumberland, and to whom he granted the whole county. De Meschines granted the barony of Gillesland to the ancestor of the Dacres. There is a place called Dacre, in Cumberland, but it is doubtful whether the family derived their name from the place, or the place derived its name from the family. Scott says that the family took the name to commemorate the part played by one of them at the Siege of Acre; but Mr. Howard, the author of "Memorials of the Howard Family," regards this as a groundless fiction. Be that is it may, for some centuries the Dacres were one of the most powerful families in Cumberland, taking an active part in the incessant border wars. By marriage with an heiress one of them acquired the barony of Greystoke, which also had been granted by De Meschines to another of his Norman associates. In time there appeared two branches of the Dacre family—the Lords Dacre of the North, and the Lords Dacre of the South. The title held by the latter branch still exists, the heir presumptive to it being the present Speaker of the House of Commons. Lord William Howard married one of the three sisters and co-heirs of the last Lord Dacre of Gillesland. Each of these sisters, by the way, married a Howard. By this marriage Lord William became possessed of Naworth Castle, the ancient seat of the Dacres of the North, and of the barony of Hinderskelle, near Malton, in Yorkshire, on which estate Castle Howard, a mansion built by Sir John Vanbrugh, was subsequently erected. Greystoke barony came into the possession of the Dukes of Norfolk, and is now owned by one of the younger branches of the ducal house.

The Barony of Dacre of Gillesland was revived at the Restoration in favour of Lord William Howard's descendant, and in addition he obtained the higher titles of Viscount Morpeth and Earl of Carlisle, and was at one time Ambassador to the Czar of Muscovy, and at another Governor of Jamaica. The third Earl was for a time First Lord of the Treasury. The fourth married the heiress of one of the co-heirs of Cavendish, Duke of Newcastle; but, as he left only daughters by that lady, I presume his share of the Newcastle property passed to them. He married, secondly, a daughter of the fourth Lord Byron—hence the connection of his son, the fifth Earl, with the Byron family.

Men are sometimes kept in remembrance by the strangest accidents. The fifth Earl of Carlisle was Lord Lieutenant of Ireland. He published some poems, which ran through three or four editions; and some tragedies, which gave rise to Dr. Johnson's somewhat toadyish remark, "that when a man of rank appeared in the character of an author, he deserved to have his merit handsomely allowed." But these things, and the Earl himself, would have been long since entirely forgotten, had not the Earl been the guardian of Lord Byron. To the Earl of Carlisle the "Hours of Idleness" were dedicated "by his obliged ward and affectionate kinsman, the author." But the guardian treated the ward with studied coolness, or, at any rate, the ward fancied that he did so; and in "English Bards and Scotch Reviewers" the "affectionate kinsman" attacked the noble author of the forgotten tragedies of "The Stepmother" and "The Father's Revenge," in lines which the author himself afterwards pronounced as "much too savage":—

> "What heterogeneous honours deck the peer!
> Lord, rhymester, petit-maître, pamphleteer!
> So dull in youth, so drivelling in his age,
> His scenes alone had damned our sinking stage;
> But managers for once had cried, 'Hold, enough!'
> Nor drugged their audience with the tragic stuff.
> Yet at their judgment let his lordship laugh,
> And case his volumes in congenial calf;
> Yes! doff that covering where morocco shines,
> And hang a calf-skin on those recreant lines."

Byron afterwards scribbled on his copy of the book, opposite this passage, "Miserable record of misplaced anger and indiscriminate acrimony;" and, in a well-known passage in "Childe Harold," he alludes to a younger son of the Earl who fell at Waterloo:—

> "Yet one I would select from that proud throng,
> Partly because they blend me with his line,
> And partly that I did his sire some wrong,
> And partly that bright names will hallow song!
> And his was of the bravest, and when shower'd
> The death-bolts deadliest the thin files along,
> E'en where the thickest of war's tempest lower'd,
> They reached no nobler breast than thine, young, gallant Howard."

The seventh Earl, known for the greater part of his life as

Lord Morpeth, was one of the most deservedly popular noblemen of the present century. His father was a member of Lord Grey's Cabinet, without portfolio. Lord Morpeth, like his father before him, entered Parliament for Morpeth, which was then a pocket borough of the family. In 1827 he was the seconder of Sir Francis Burdett's motion in favour of Catholic Emancipation; a little later, in an eloquent speech, he seconded Sir Fowell Buxton's resolution in favour of the abolition of Slavery in the Colonies. As early as 1832 he declared himself in favour of the remission of the Advertisement Duty and the Stamp Duty on Newspapers. Throughout the prolonged debate on the first Reform Bill he steadily supported the popular cause, having by that time become one of the members for the great county of York. He held office in several Liberal Administrations as Secretary for Ireland, as Commissioner of Woods and Forests, as Chancellor of the Duchy of Lancaster, and twice as Lord-Lieutenant of Ireland. It is rarely that an Irish Viceroy can be denominated popular, but the Earl of Carlisle was one of the most popular Viceroys that have ever held office. In the Conservative reaction of 1841 he lost his seat for the West Riding of Yorkshire; but a few years after he was re-elected to Parliament, and voted in the majority with Sir Robert Peel for the Abolition of the Corn Laws. Sanitary Reform, Factory Legislation, the Education of the People, and Mechanics' Institutes found in the Earl of Carlisle a warm and earnest supporter. He won for himself an honourable position in literature. Besides his poems, he published volumes of travels in America, Turkey, and Greece; lectures on the writings of Pope and Gray, and on the importance of Literature to Men of Business; and in his elder years he evinced the same interest which he had manifested in his youth as to the Slavery Question by writing a preface to "Uncle Tom's Cabin."

The seventh Earl of Carlisle, who was never married, was succeeded in 1864 by his next surviving brother, a clergyman, who in 1832 obtained the living of Londesborough, in Yorkshire, a little parish of 324 inhabitants, value £798 and a house, which, strange to say, he still holds. He is over seventy years of age, and has never married. Mr. Charles Howard, the late Member for East Cumberland, had an only son, Mr. George Howard, who was recently elected Member for East Cumberland. Mr. George Howard is married to a daughter of the second Lord Stanley of Alderley, and has given promise, by his consistent Liberalism, of faithful adherence to the principles which have made the Carlisle branch of the Howard family one of the most popular of the great houses.

LXXIX.

The Pratts.

LET the Churchills and the Nelsons, and even the Wellesleys, hide their diminished heads while I speak of the Pratts. The Duke of Marlborough, Lord Nelson, and the Duke of Wellington, splendidly as they were rewarded, at any rate left an indelible record on the history of their country. One fell in the moment of victory, and the others proved their prowess on many a hard-fought field. I have to tell of a man without any record that anyone cares to remember, who yet received in the course of his lifetime a million of public money. It is safe to say that if he had never lived he never would have been missed. Though several times an office-holder, he cannot claim a place in the ranks of English statesmen. He is as utterly forgotten as the great-grandfathers of the vast majority of those who read this page. And yet from first to last he must have received a million of money from the taxpayers of this country. We pay our Prime Ministers during their short and uncertain tenure of office a paltry £5,000 per annum, and usually, if they choose to accept it, they are in a position to claim a pension of £2,000 when they retire; but I have to speak of a man who never did anything for his country worth mentioning, and who received a million as his reward. Beside him even the Anglo-Indian Nabob of the last century sinks into insignificance. I was warned long ago that my materials would soon be exhausted; that after twenty or thirty families had been glanced at little would remain to be told; and yet I have dealt with no less than seventy-eight families and have not yet noticed the Pratts.

But, withal, the Pratts can boast of a singularly unique distinction, of which they may well be proud. I doubt if there is any other noble family which can fairly make a like claim. We have seen that there have been many roads to the Peerage. The Court, the field, the deck, the Bar, the Exchange, illicit love, and unlawful gain have all largely contributed to swell the ranks of the Peerage; but where shall we find a Barony like that of Camden, which was directly obtained through the services which the first Lord Camden rendered to the cause of popular liberty? There is not a particle of exaggeration in the eulogism which Lord Campbell has pronounced upon him :—" Englishmen to the latest generation will honour his name for having secured personal freedom by putting an end to arbitrary arrests under general warrants, for having established the Constitutional rights of juries, and for having placed on on imperishable basis the liberty of the Press."

The very name of Camden has an aroma of antiquity about it, derived doubtless from the author of " Britannia " ; but the Camden peerage is of quite modern date. A little over a hundred years ago the first Lord Camden received his title from Camden Place, Kent. The Camden estates consist of :—

Kent	7,214 acres
Sussex	3,755 ,,
Brecon	6,430 ,,
Total	17,399 ,,

With a rent-roll of £16,380.

We need not trouble ourselves with the early history of the Pratts; suffice it to say they were impoverished by the Civil War, and that John Pratt, an eminent lawyer, who flourished at the beginning of the last century, restored the fortunes of the house. In the year 1714 he was elevated to the position of Lord Chief Justice. He appears to have purchased the Wilderness Estate, in Kent, near Sevenoaks, and Bayham Abbey, in Sussex; though, strange to say, Lord Campbell asserts that he left his family in almost abject poverty. His son, Lord Chancellor Camden, purchased the seat at Camden Place Chislehurst, now the residence of the ex-Empress Eugénie, and at one time the abode of Camden, the antiquary. From this place he derived his title. Lord Chancellor Camden married the heiress of Nicholas Jeffreys, of the Priory, Brecon, through whom the Welsh estates were derived. The Brecon property is chiefly spoil of the monastic houses, but had been obtained by purchase by the Jeffreys family.

Lord Chancellor Camden was a younger son, for whom little provision was made save an excellent education. From Eton, where he made the acquaintance of the elder Pitt, he proceeded to Cambridge, and thence to the Bar. For some time he made no progress, and, in despair, he was about to take Holy Orders, when Henley, the leader of his circuit—afterwards Lord Northington—befriended him, and, having obtained a brief for him as his junior, stayed away on the plea of illness, and allowed Pratt to win the cause alone. Henceforward Pratt's rise was rapid, and he was appointed Attorney-General in the Ministry of the elder Pitt. Thence he was elevated to the seat of Lord Chief Justice of the Common Pleas. John Wilkes having been arrested on a general warwarrant, *i.e.*, a warrant not specifying the name of the person, Pratt issued his *habeas corpus* to the Lieutenant of the Tower, and discharged Wilkes from custody. In subsequent actions for damages brought by persons who had been arrested on general warrants, Pratt used the strongest language of denunciation against the proceedings of those in power, and he pronounced a warrant to search for and seize the papers of persons prosecuted for libel as utterly illegal and void. His independent conduct gave him well-merited popularity, and he became one of the idols of the people, as witness the portrait of him, with its inscription, that still hangs in Guildhall as a memento of the gratitude of the citizens of London. The City was, even then, the staunch and loyal supporter of popular rights, and those who served the people might always reckon on the aid and sympathy of the Corporation. When the first Rockingham Ministry assumed office, a forgotten Law-lord stood in the way of Pratt's elevation to the Woolsack; but he had become the idol of the people, and it was necessary, in obedience to the popular demand, that something should be done for him. Therefore it was that he was elevated to the Peerage under the title of Lord Camden. The Rockingham Ministry was succeeded by that of Chatham, and Camden's old schoolfellow and lifelong friend appointed him Lord Chancellor. At that time there was no regular provision of £5,000 per annum for ex-Lord Chancellors, and, in exchanging the permanent position of Lord Chief Justice for an uncertain position on the Woolsack, Lord Camden was quite justified in stipulating for a retiring pension of £1,500 per annum, and the reversion of an Exchequer Tellership for his eldest son. When Chatham ceased to take an active part in public business the Ministry reverted to unpopular courses. Though Camden approved of the expulsion of Wilkes from the House of Commons, he disagreed with his colleagues as to the advisability of his expulsion after the freeholders of Middlesex had re-elected him, as also in the foolish and suicidal course which was taken in the dispute with the American Colonies. At last, on Mansfield's insinuation that he was a consenting party to the measures for coercing America, Camden openly broke away from the Ministry. Henceforth he staunchly supported Chatham in his vain endeavours to restrain the English Government from the folly and crime of war with the revolted colonies. The closing years of Lord Camden's life were marked by a steady and consistent support of the popular cause. He pleaded eloquently for justice to Ireland; he denounced the abuses of the Pension List, declaring that, if necessary, he was ready to give up his own, though no pension in existence had been better earned; he shared the younger Pitt's youthful views on the necessity of Parliamentary Reform, and strongly supported them; and, above all, he was the main cause of the passage through the House of Lords of Mr. Fox's Libel Bill, which for ever settled the question that juries and not judges should decide what was and what was not a libel. Lord Camden who had been some years previously advanced to an earldom, died in 1794, at the ripe old age of 81, leaving behind him a name that will ever be precious to the hearts of free Englishmen.

I pass now to the second Earl, who was subsequently created a Marquis. At the age of 21 he received the sinecure appointment of a Tellership in the Exchequer. Two years after, he was appointed a Lord of the Admiralty, and, a little later, one of the Commissioners of the Treasury. In 1795 he was Lord-Lieutenant of Ireland; in 1804, Secretary of State for the Colonies; in 1805, Lord President of the Council, an office which he held, with a short interruption, till 1812. But all the while he was a Teller of the Exchequer. In that year a stout old Radical, Mr. Creevy, brought before Parliament the scandalous amount of emoluments which Lord Camden received from his office. At the time of his appointment to the post, which it must not be forgotten was a sinecure, he did not receive from it more than £2,500 a-year. During the American War the profits rose to £7,000, and in 1807 to no less than £23,000. In 1812 we were in the thick of the struggle with Napoleon Bonaparte, and the nation was much distressed by the cost of the prolonged war; nevertheless, when Mr. Creevy, after proving his case, proposed that the profits of Lord Camden should be limited to some fixed and settled sum of money, more suited to the present means and resources of the nation, his demand was rejected. The scandal, however, had become so great, and was so constantly denounced, that Lord Camden resigned his claim on the extra emoluments of his sinecure, which was worth at that time, according to the "Georgian Era," between thirty and forty thousand pounds per annum. It appears, however, that it was not until five years afterwards that he resigned his full claims. Then, having received for doing nothing the enormous sum of £740,000, he agreed to take £3,683 annually for his arduous labours. As he lived till 1840 he must have received about £85,000 more.

The second Marquis died a year or two ago, and was succeeded by his son, an infant only a few months old.

LXXX.
The Ryders.

AM beginning to feel at home at last. So far as one can judge of race by location, I apprehend that my ancestors—British, Saxon, and Danish—were in England long before the Norman. Still, as these were all conquered races—mere Afghans and Zulus, who, by the divine right of triumphant scoundrelism, calling itself superior civilisation, had to put their necks beneath the yoke—I ought to feel the vast superiority of those whose fathers came over with the Conqueror, But when I reach the Ryders I begin to feel at home. The British aristocracy is not altogether an exclusive caste. The great-great-grandfather of the Earl of Harrowby kept a shop in Smithfield; I had a great-grandfather who kept a shop in Fetter-lane, not five minutes distant. Among our Lares and Penates we still keep a pair of broken images which once figured in the shop window of our ancestor; I wonder whether Lord Harrowby still keeps among his household gods the identical yard-stick with which his ancestor measured silks and calico, Lord Harrowby is too good a man to be offended at being reminded that his forefathers rose from the ranks. I might also remind Lord Sandon when, like a consistent Conservative, he votes against the Burials Bill, he votes to perpetuate one of the odious badges of inferiority under which those from whom he sprang once suffered.

The term "Liberal-Conservative" is not so often heard now as it was five-and-twenty years ago, but it still represents a mental temperament which must exist as long as the Conservative party itself. However loyal Conservatives may be to their party, there are divers shades of Conservative feeling. Culture, travel, religion, philanthropy, each in their own several way, temper the Conservative instinct. Take, for example, the Conservatism of the Earl of Beaconsfield, the Marquis of Salisbury, and Mr. Cross. Every thoughtful Liberal, as soon as he gets away from specific questions, will at once recognise that they are of a different species. The first we despise, the second we hate, the third we reason with. In the adventurer we know that success is the only morality, in the landlord that class-privilege is the criterion of politics, in the Liberal-Conservative that reason and sentiment have considerable weight. Family traditions are frequently an important element in the political life of great houses, and it would be easy to point out several aristocratic families of an essentially Liberal-Conservative type. Of these the Ryders will form a very fair example.

There has always been a strong dash of Puritanism in the Ryders, which may perhaps be attributed to the fact that their earliest ancestor, of whom anything positive is known, was a Nonconformist minister. The Rev. Dudley Rider (they spell the name with a "y" now) was Rector of Bedworth, in Warwickshire, then a good living worth £200, and now of the value of £562 annually. This he renounced for conscience sake when the Act of Uniformity was passed in 1662. It is stated, too, that he also sacrificed a good estate, for his uncle, who had made him his heir, refused afterwards to have anything to do with a man who had incurred the odium of Nonconformity. After his ejection from Bedworth, Mr. Rider removed to Weddington, from whence he was driven by the iniquitous Five Mile Act, passed by the Tories of those days. After preaching at King's Lynn and elsewhere, he retired into private life, and died in 1683.

The eldest son of the Rev. Dudley Rider became a tradesman at Nuneaton; his son went into the Church, and became Archbishop of Armagh. The second son came to London, and opened a mercer's shop in Smithfield. He appears to have been faithful to the Nonconformity of his father, for his children were sent to a Dissenting academy at Hackney. His second son, who appears to have been originally intended for a Dissenting minister, studied at Edinburgh and at Leyden, and, having entered himself as a student in the Temple, threw off the Nonconformity which was then an insuperable bar to his professional advancement. While at the University he seems to have suffered from straitened means, but he had a happy faculty of pushing his way in the world, and was fortunate enough to be the friend and fellow student of Lord King, by whom he was recommended to Walpole. In 1733 he was appointed Solicitor-General, and four years after

Attorney-General. His time of office was unmarked by any exciting event save the Jacobite Rebellion of 1745, Sir Dudley Ryder appearing for the prosecution at the trial of the chiefs of the Rebellion. Once he had the misfortune, by order of the House of Commons, to prosecute an audacious printer for a libel on that august assembly; but, though he tried to bully the Jury into a verdict of guilty, they acquitted the prisoner; and Sir Dudley had the additional mortification, on returning home, to be compelled to treat a mob to drink the health of the Jury. In 1754 hé was made Lord Chief Justice; but Lord Hardwicke obstinately objected to his elevation to the peerage. Two years afterwards, the Duke of Newcastle needing votes in the House of Lords, it was intimated to him that he would be created a peer, but before the patent of peerage was made out he suddenly expired, and the Government was shabby enough to withhold the title from his son. The son, however, having sat for Tiverton nearly twenty years, zealously supporting Lord North's Ministry, was at length raised to the Peerage by the title of Lord Harrowby. Harrowby, by the way, is a small place in Lincolnshire, not far from Grantham. He adopted as his family motto, *Servata fides cineri*—" The promise made to my ancestor's ashes is now kept"—very appropriate under the circumstances.

The first Lord Harrowby had three sons. The first sat in his father's lifetime for Tiverton, as did also the second, who held at different times several lucrative offices. The third went into the Church, and became Bishop of Lichfield; one of his sons had a canonry in Lichfield Cathedral. The second Lord Harrowby, a staunch supporter of Pitt, and that statesman's second in the Tierney duel, filled a number of offices in his lifetime. He was successively Under-Secretary of State, Comptroller of the Household, Treasurer of the Navy, Paymaster of the Forces, Ambassador to Berlin, President of the Board of Control, and President of the Council. In 1809 he was advanced to an Earldom. He appears to have been a moderate Conservative, for whom the stiff Toryism of the Wellington Administration was too strong. Although a staunch supporter of Catholic emancipation, he was a prominent member of the Evangelical party, and took a warm interest in their religious and philanthropic societies.

His eldest son, the present Earl, who is now over 80 years of age, originally sat for what was once the family borough of Tiverton. Before the passing of the first Reform Bill the election of members was vested in the Corporation of that borough, and it deserves to be recorded in Lord Harrowby's honour that, having declared himself in favour of Reform, the Corporation of Tiverton in 1830 refused to re-elect him. In the following year, however, he was elected for Liverpool, and his name appears in the Division List as voting in favour of the second reading of the Reform Bill of 1832. Faithful to the Liberal-Conservative tradition, he also voted for the Abolition of the Corn Laws. He continued to sit for Liverpool till 1847, when his father's death removed him to the Upper House. Faithful also to the Puritan traditions of the family, Lord Harrowby has always been a warm supporter of the institutions of the Evangelical party. He has been Secretary to the Board of Control, Chancellor of the Duchy of Lancaster, and Lord Privy Seal. As he was first elected for Tiverton in 1819, his legislatorial career has extended over 60 years. Probably no living legislator can boast of so long a period of active service.

The Earl of Harrowby owns in

Staffordshire	4,940	acres
Lincoln	4,253	,,
Gloucester	3,207	,,
Warwick	225	,,
Total	12,625	,,

With a rent-roll of £22,696.

All of this has doubtless been acquired in a perfectly legitimate manner. Sandon Hall, near Stone, in Staffordshire, was purchased by the first Lord Harrowby, in 1776, of Lord Archibald Hamilton, the Dukes of Hamilton having previously acquired the estate by marriage.

Lord Sandon, the eldest son of the present Earl, is better known to the world now than his father. I once had to transact a little business with him, and his urbanity contrasted very favourably with the manner of some men with whom I had previously been brought into contact on the front Opposition bench. He seems to have inherited the family traditions. According to Dod, he formerly ranked as a Liberal, and even now his Conservatism has not the flippancy of Mr. Cavendish Bentinck or the pugnacity of Lord Cranbrook. Of all the members of the present Government, not even excepting the ever suave and courteous Chancellor of the Exchequer, he seems the last man to create political enemies. He sat for Lichfield for three years, but since 1868 he has sat, as his father did before him, for Liverpool. It will be remembered that he was one of the members of the first London School Board.

The Ryders have certainly had their share of good things in both Church and State, but not to such an extent as to give them a reputation for greediness, or occasion anything like scandal.

LXXXI.
The Edens.

IT has sometimes been urged against the direct representation of labour and the payment of members that thereby a door would be opened to professional politicians. Using the term in no opprobrious sense, it is obvious we have not a few professional politicians. Journalists are professional politicians, so are not a few lawyers who enter upon a Parliamentary career, so are others who belong to neither of these classes. I think I have already furnished proofs that the profession of politics has been eminently advantageous to not a few of our great families; but there are some noble houses whose members have uniformly followed the profession of politics, except those who were provided for in the Church, the Army, or the Navy. Let us take the Edens for example.

The Edens cannot be ranked among the great territorial houses. Neither Lord Auckland nor Lord Henley appear in the list of landowners holding 5,000 acres and upwards. Sir William Eden owns 6,096 acres in Durham, and 1,832 in Yorkshire, and Mr. John Eden owns 5480 acres in Durham. Small as are their landed possessions, and modern as are their titles, the Edens have a remarkable, if not a very eventful, history. They have been certainly liberally rewarded by the nation for their services, and of one of them, at least, it may be safely said, that, so far from his services being valuable, it would have been a good bargain for the country if it had paid him ten times the amount received simply to do nothing at all.

The Edens are an old Durham family, who held lands of the Bishop of Durham as far back as the fifteenth century, By what exact process they rose from tenants to landlords I am unable to say; but in the reign of Charles II. one of them, who greatly advanced the fortunes of the House by a marriage with a Lambton heiress, was created a Baronet. The third Baronet had five sons. The eldest succeeded him; the second was appointed Governor of Maryland, and his descendants subsequently inherited the title and estates of the family. The fourth son obtained the appointment of Deputy-Auditor of Greenwich Hospital; and of his sons, one became a Lieutenant-General in the Army, with the colonelcy of a regiment; another became an Admiral, and has been Secretary to the First Lord of the Admiralty, Commodore Superintendent at Woolwich, Aide-de-Camp to the Queen, and a Lord of the Admiralty; another was Assistant-Comptroller of the Exchequer, and another was in the East India Company's service. The third and fifth sons of the third Baronet were both advanced to the peerage, the one as Lord Auckland, the other as Lord Henley. I proceed to glance at both branches of the house. If the lengthy catalogue of places and pensions becomes wearisome to the reader, I shall have all the more claim upon his sympathy in the patient endeavour to trace them all out.

William Eden, afterwards the first Lord Auckland, at the age of twenty-nine was appointed Director and Auditor of that ancient sink of corruption, Greenwich Hospital. The next year he was made an Under-Secretary of State. A seat was soon provided for him in the Duke of Marlborough's pocket borough of Woodstock. Next he became a Commissioner of the Board of Trade, and then Chief Secretary for Ireland, in which latter capacity he was not remarkably successful; Mr. Massey speaks of him as escaping with difficulty from Dublin amid the execrations of the populace. He also acted as Vice-Treasurer for Ireland. In the early part of his career he had had some experience in diplomacy, as one of the Commissioners for negotiating Peace with America, and during Pitt's administration he acted at different times as Ambassador to France, Spain and Holland. He was at first created an Irish Peer, but afterwards obtained an English Peerage. Somewhat later he was Postmaster-General, and he finally retired in 1801 on a pension of £2,300 and £700 for his wife. He died in 1814 and his wife in 1818. The pay of Ambassadors ranged from five to eleven thousand pounds. Altogether, Lord Auckland must have found the profession of politics extremely profitable. He had two daughters, who had a pension of £204 each.

He obtained for his eldest son one of those lucrative sinecures, an Exchequer Tellership; but he died in his father's

The Edens.

lifetime. The next son, the second Lord Auckland, had a pension of £300, dating from 1814, and another of £400, dating from 1820, and he lived on till 1849. In Earl Grey's Ministry he held both the offices of Master of the Mint, salary £3,000, and the President of the Board of Trade, salary £2,000. In 1835 he was appointed Governor-General of India (salary £25,000), and remained there till 1842. He is distinguished as being the author of the first Afghan War. The history of that shameful and criminal folly is too well known to need repetition here. Suffice it to say that it resulted in the total destruction of a British Army in Afghanistan, and in the Indian authorities being compelled to set again upon the throne of that country the very man whom they had displaced. The war began successfully, and when the British troops were in possession of Cabul, Lord Auckland ordered that "Afghanistan" should be inscribed upon the colours, and the English Government hastened to elevate him to an Earldom. The disgrace and disaster followed a little later on. Remembering this, it may be as well to defer Lord Lytton's advance in the Peerage till we can see the end of the second war, because history, which has repeated itself more than once before now, may yet do so again.* Of this wretched war, Miss Martineau well says that "it does not become those at home, who were misled, to forget this great folly and crime, or to attempt to cover it with cant about the glory of our arms." As to Lord Auckland's responsibility, I again quote the same historian:—"It has often been said that the way to have peace in India is to send out soldiers rather than civilians as Governors-General, and certainly this declaration of war goes far to confirm the saying. It is scarcely conceivable that a great military ruler could have done an act so rash as Lord Auckland did." The second Lord Auckland, who, besides the above-named offices, was at one time Auditor of the Exchequer and First Lord of the Admiralty, died in 1849, without issue, when the Earldom expired, but the Barony was inherited by his next brother.

The third Lord Auckland had gone into the Church, and, after holding minor appointments, was elevated to the Bishopric of Sodor and Man in 1847. Less than two years

---

* This chapter was printed long before the recent Cabul Massacre occurred.

after he succeeded to the barony, but he still continued to hold his Bishopric. In 1854 he was translated to the richer See of Bath and Wells, which he continued to hold till 1869, when, being seventy years of age, he retired. He died the following year, and was succeeded by his eldest son. Of his other sons, one went into the Navy, and another into the Indian Civil Service.

The first Lord Auckland's youngest brother, Clerk to the Auditor of Greenwich Hospital, went into the Diplomatic Service, and acted as British Ambassador at various Courts. He married the sister and co-heir of Henley, Earl of Northington, and ultimately was created an Irish Peer, with the title of Baron Henley. The second Lord Henley (who dropped the family name of Eden for that of Henley) married a sister of the late Sir Robert Peel, and obtained a Mastership in Chancery, value about £4,600 per annum, which he continued to hold after succeeding to the title. His brother, who went into the Church, obtained the living of Beaksbourne (£247) and Harbledown (£385 and a house), and subsequently of Bishopsbourne (£527 and a house).

It is worth while to glance at the Edens who are now in the Church; they will serve to show what "a feast of fat things" the Church of the Poor provides for the cadets of aristocratic houses who go into her service. There is one who is Vicar of Ticehurst (£820 and a house); another is Prebendary of York, also Vicar of Aberford (£364 and a house); another is Vicar of Sedgefield (£1,800 and a house); another is Vicar of Wymondham (£761 and a house).

Even at the present day we have not done with the Edens as pensioners. A Mr. Frederick Eden, who was in the Civil Service, retired in 1867, his salary then being £866 per annum, and his retiring pension is £317. The late Sir William Eden, Bart., was also Custos Brevium of the Court of Common Pleas, and received for forty years in that capacity the sum of £786 18s. 8d. annually—in all £31,457. He died in 1873, but the annual £786 18s. 8d. is still paid to his son. Have we not already paid the Edens enough, and more than enough, for their brilliant services? So long as the Eden Baronetcy does not want an heir is the British nation compelled to keep on paying them nearly £800 per annum for doing nothing?

My almost interminable list of Eden places and pensions is

not quite exhaustive. I have come across two or three other Edens who, I am sure, held offices at some time or other, of whom I could not obtain particulars. I have, however, stated quite enough to show that they have uniformly acted up to the family motto, *Si sit prudentia*—"If there be but prudence." Thank Heaven we live in an enlightened country, where the members of aristocratic houses serve the State purely from patriotism and public spirit. We have not among us placemen, adventurers, and office-seekers, even as those Americans! We make our Parliament the close preserve of wealthy men, and carefully keep out those whose moderate means might tempt them to turn politics into a trade. What need of more Burts, so long as we have plenty of Edens?

LXXXII.

The Thynnes.

THE history of the Thynnes is singularly uneventful; except the murder of one member of the house it presents hardly any feature of interest, save in the acquirement of the property which the Thynnes possess. The Marquis of Bath, however, is fully entitled to a place in "Our Old Nobility," though his superior title is not a hundred years old, and his second title a little less than two hundred. He is the owner of Longleat, one of the most magnificent mansions in the country, which is surrounded by a park of 4,500 acres, and his landed possessions amount to 55,425 acres, with a rent-roll of £67,002, situated as follows:—

Wilts	19,977 acres
Somerset	8,214 ,,
Salop	3,508 ,,
Hereford	699 ,,
Monaghan	23,027 ,,

Lord John Thynne has also 14,981 acres in Cornwall, Bedford, and Devon, with a rent-roll of £13,461.

The Thynnes were Poitevins, who came over to England in the reign of John, to assist that tyrant in fighting his rebellious barons. For some time they were known by the name of De Boteville. Geoffry de Boteville, one of the Poitevin adventurers who came over to assist John, subsequently held certain lands at Stretton and Boteville in Shropshire, under the great Earl of Arundel. Twice they lost a part of these lands, but some portion of them was held by William Thynne, Master of the Household to Henry VII. Either William Thynne or his brother was Chief Clerk of the Kitchen to Henry VIII. Sir John Thynne, the son or nephew of Henry VIII.'s Clerk of the Kitchen, died, in the reign of Elizabeth, one of the richest landowners in the South of England. At the time of the Reformation the Thynnes certainly held no lands at all, save a small estate in Shropshire; in the reign of

Elizabeth they were in possession of most of the great estates in Wilts and Somerset now held by the Marquis of Bath. Their rise as a great territorial house was prodigiously rapid; and yet, save as regards Hornsingham, a manor of 2,000 acres, held by Lord Hungerford, who was attainted, and whose property in this place was granted to John Thynne, they do not appear to have acquired much by any direct grants from the Crown. How are we to account for their great landed acquisitions in such a short space of time?

Sir John Thynne (who was knighted at the Battle of Musselburgh) was the favourite and secretary of the Protector Somerset. I have already alluded to the frightful rapacity of the statesmen of the days of Edward VI., and need not dwell upon it further now. It is stated in the records of the Thynne family that Sir John was twice imprisoned in the Tower along with his master, and that the second time he only escaped with a fine of £6,000 and the loss of several great offices and good leases. He seems to have played a very safe and clever game. He did not obtain direct grants from the spoil of the monastic houses, but he made extensive and advantageous purchases from those who did. When such vast estates were being flung away right and left by those whose duty it was to conserve the property of the Crown, there must have been plenty of good bargains in land, and Thynne, as the Secretary of the Protector Somerset, must have had choice opportunities of making them. But whence had he the means? He seems to have had some connection with the City of London, for in the Thynne records there is an agreement between himself and the Corporation, that he should hold the office of Packer of the City of London, on payment of a sum of £66 13s. 4d. annually to the Corporation. But, beyond this, he had the good fortune to marry the daughter of Sir Richard, and the sister and eventually co-heir of Sir Thomas Gresham, the great London merchants. With this lady he had as a dowry the manors of Buckland and Laverton, in Wilts, the manor of Foston, in Leicestershire, and lands in half-a-dozen parishes in Yorkshire. In the course of his life he was purchaser of lands in about 40 different parishes, the vendors being Somerset himself, the Earl of Oxford, Lord Stourton, Lord Seymour of Sudeley, and a number of others. The site of the mansion of Longleat, where was formerly a small monastic house, was purchased of

Sir John Horsey. Most of the extensive park and surrounding lands were purchased of the Court of Augmentations, and before the Reformation had been parcel of the extensive possessions of the rich Abbey of Glastonbury, which had been given as a dowry to Queen Katharine Parr. I note that in the time of the Commonwealth another Wiltshire manor was purchased by Sir James Thynne; but, for the most part, the extensive estates of the Marquis of Bath in Wilts and Somerset are the same as were acquired by his prudent ancestor, whose lucky marriage provided the ready cash, and whose Court connections provided the ready opportunity. Sir John Thynne was Comptroller of the Household to the Princess Elizabeth, but he appears to have been too timid to attend upon her in the hour of danger, and to have been deservedly neglected by her in the time of her prosperity. Her accession to the Throne brought him no honours nor rewards, and he appears to have occupied himself with the building of Longleat, which it took him twelve years to erect in its original form.

Sir John Thynne, eldest son of Sir John, followed his father's example in going to the City for a wealthy bride. He married the daughter and heir of Sir Rowland Hayward, twice Lord Mayor of London, who brought him on her marriage a considerable estate in Shropshire. His great-grandson, Thomas Thynne (popularly known as "Tom of Ten Thousand," because of his great wealth) was murdered by some ruffians hired by Count Königsmark, the disappointed lover of Lady Elizabeth Ogle, a great heiress, of whom Thynne was the accepted suitor. The story, illustrated in stone upon the tomb of Thomas Thynne in Westminster Abbey, is too well known to need detailed recapitulation here. On the death of Thomas Thynne the estates passed to a younger descendant of Sir John Thynne, who was almost immediately afterwards created Viscount Weymouth, with remainder to his younger brother. He died without male heirs, and was succeeded by his nephew, with whom the title nearly expired; but he left a posthumous son, who subsequently married Lady Louisa Carteret, granddaughter of Granville, Earl of Bath, and daughter of John Carteret, Earl Granville. The possessions of the Carterets and Granvilles subsequently passed, through this marriage and the marriage of one of the Leveson-Gowers, to the Thynnes and the Leveson-Gowers. The title

The Thynnes. 143

of Earl Granville has recently been revived in an offshoot of the latter house. Younger sons of the first Marquis of Bath held the title of Baron Carteret, which is now extinct; but I presume that the estates are those now held by Lord John Thynne, a younger son of the second Marquis.

The first Marquis of Bath, the title being evidently selected from the connection of the family with the Granvilles, who had held the Earldom of that place, was created Marquis in 1789. For a period of about thirty years he held various offices, being successively Lord of the Bedchamber, Groom of the Stole, Master of the Horse, and Secretary of State. Of the succeeding holders of the title there is nothing noteworthy to record. They were consistent Conservatives in the time of the signing of Magna Charta—they have been consistent Conservatives almost ever since. Before the passing of the first Reform Bill, the Thynnes had possession of the rotten borough of Weobly, and of one of the close Corporation seats for Bath itself.

As a rule, the Thynnes seem to have been moderate in their demands upon the national purse; but then it must be remembered that their wealth is great, and that they are not so numerous a clan as the Edens or the Beresfords. There is one exception, the Rev. Lord John Thynne, who, as a landowner with a rental of £13,461, might be reasonably expected to leave to less favoured men the rewards of the Church, even if he were anxious to take part in its sacred work. Yet I find that this nobleman has been Canon of Westminster for the last forty-eight years, with £2,500 a year and a residence; and, further, that he had a sinecure rectory in Somerset, given to him by his father or brother, value £168 and a house, from 1832 to 1872. What with incomes and residences, he must have had from the Church in the course of his life over £130,000. Lord John had a brother, Charles, who was formerly a Prebend of Canterbury, and Rector of Longbridge (another family living), but he went over to Rome. There is another Thynne in the Church, a son of the Rev. Lord John Thynne, who is Rector of Kilkhampton (£712 and a house), one of his father's livings, and also Prebendary of Exeter.

The present Marquis of Bath, though nominally a Conservative, has manifested an independence which entitles him to considerable respect. Throughout the discussions arising out of the Eastern Question he has been a warm supporter of the enlightened policy which would fain have combined Europe in an endeavour for the peaceful and gradual deliverance of South-Eastern Europe from the Ottoman yoke. The Marquis repeatedly contributed to the funds of the Eastern Question Association; and he has still more recently shown his warm interest in the cause of the Bulgarians by proceeding on a visit to Eastern Roumelia.

LXXXIII.

The Vanes.

A S the present Duke of Cleveland calls himself Powlett, I suppose I ought to use that name ; but, seeing that the family patronymic has been changed from Vane to Powlett, and from Powlett back to Vane, and from Vane back to Powlett again, perhaps some succeeding Duke may choose to resort once more to the illustrious name which his ancestors bore, and by which the family is best known. I may also explain at once that the present Dukedom of Cleveland is not the bastard Dukedom that owed its origin to the adulterous connection of Charles II. with Barbara Villiers, wife of the Earl of Castlemaine, who was created Duchess of Cleveland by her Royal paramour. That title descended to her eldest son by Charles II., but subsequently expired. One of the Vanes, however, married a female descendant of Barbara Duchess of Cleveland.

The Duke of Cleveland owns land in nine counties, as follows :—

Durham	55,837 acres.
Salop	25,604 ,,
Sussex	6,025 ,,
Somerset	4,784 ,,
Northampton	3,482 ,,
Kent	2,440 ,,
Cornwall	1,997 ,,
Wilts	1,511 ,,
Devon	1,085 ,,
Total	102,774 ,,

With a rent-roll of £91,784.

To him belongs Raby Castle, Durham, one of the most stately ancient mansions in the North of England, and the hoary ruin of Barnard Castle, that frowns from its precipitous cliff over Teesdale ; and yet it is only from the days of the Stuarts that the Vanes could be reckoned among our great houses. They have accumulated about 100,000 acres in less than 300 years.

The pedigree of the Vanes claims that they originally came from the borders of Wales; but at the earliest time of which anything definite is known of them (Henry VI.), Henry Vane held the Manor of Hilden, in Kent. How it was acquired I know not, and it does not much matter, as it was sold not long after. At the beginning of the Reformation, then, the Vanes were plain Kentish squires, and they appear to have been zealous supporters of the Reformed Faith. Sir Ralph, the son of Henry Vane, obtained a considerable grant of lands at Shipbourne, in Kent, formerly belonging to the monasteries of Tunbridge and Dartford, which are, or at any rate were till recently, in the possession of his descendants. Sir Ralph was one of the *entourage* of the Protector Somerset. Sharing in his prosperity, he shared likewise in his fall, and was finally hanged upon Tower Hill. If Burnet is to be believed, he was a man who merited a better fate. Though Sir Ralph died an ignominious death, his lands passed to a kinsman who narrowly escaped a similar fate for his share in Wyatt's rebellion.

The next heir of the property was the real builder of the fortunes, if not of the greatness, of the house. Throughout the history of James I. and Charles I. the name of Sir Henry Vane often occurs, though his fame has been altogether obscured by that of his illustrious son. Clarendon speaks disparagingly of him; and, indeed, he does not appear to have been anything more than a successful courtier. It was as a courtier that he rose to be a great landowner. Clarendon says that "his fortune was not great, but he found many ways to improve it," which is quite true, as we shall see. In the reign of James I. Vane was appointed Cofferer to the Prince of Wales; after the accession of Charles he was Comptroller of the Household, and subsequently Secretary of State.

We must now go back a little. In the reign of Elizabeth, Charles Neville, Earl of Westmoreland, was engaged in an abortive rebellion to release Mary Queen of Scots and restore the old Catholic faith. Mr. Froude represents him as rather driven into rebellion by fear than any other cause. He escaped, and took refuge in the Low Countries; but all his vast possessions were confiscated. After the accession of James, he pleaded hard to be restored to his lands, inasmuch

The Vanes. 147

as he had espoused the cause of James's own mother; but the King, who had plenty of favourites to provide for, turned a deaf ear to the unfortunate Earl. I believe some of the Neville estates were in Shropshire—at Wem, for instance, where the Duke of Cleveland now holds property; but the greater part of the property was in Durham. Raby Castle had been in their possession for centuries; so also had Barnard Castle, which, on the confiscation of John Balliol's English estates, had been granted by the King to the Beauchamps, from whom it passed by marriage to the Nevilles. The Bishop of Durham, who was almost a King in the county, had a legal right to such forfeitures; but, in spite of adverse legal decisions, the Nevilles held fast to their grant.

After the flight of the last Neville, Earl of Westmoreland, the estates remained for a time in the possession of the Crown, but in 1613 they were granted to Carr, the King's favourite. A year or two after, on Carr's disgrace and forfeiture, Raby, Barnard Castle, and Brancepeth, were granted to trustees for the augmentation and support of Prince Charles for ninety-nine years. Almost immediately the trustees granted the remainder of the term to Vane, the Prince's Cofferer, and in 1626 he obtained the reversion in fee for £1,500 fine, to be held in socage under £51 10s. rent, the woods to be surveyed and valued separately, and the fees of the several officers, £52 6s. per annum, to be discharged. Just the kind of bargain which we might have expected to be driven by a courtier of that period. Sir Henry appears to have done an extensive business in land-jobbing. I find that he sold Hadlow, in Kent, which he had inherited, and bought Fairlawn and Wrotham in that county. Doubtless he had other good bargains which have escaped my notice. Considering the advantages he had derived from his position at Court, his conduct in supporting the Parliamentary party in the later years of his life certainly savours of ingratitude. But as he grew old he came under the influence of his son, the Vane—

"Young in years, but in sage counsel old,"

of Milton's sonnet.

Of the younger Vane it is needless for me to speak at length here. There is hardly one of the heroes of the Commonwealth that has so stainless a record. The man whom Milton praised, whom Cromwell feared, whom Charles· II. dared not allow to live, needs no poor eulogy of mine. He had been appointed Treasurer of the Navy, and is said to have relinquished profits of £30,000 per annum for the benefit of the Commonwealth. Of all the leading Republicans of that age Vane was the most consistent, the most philosophic, the most statesmanlike. Cromwell takes beyond question the first place among the historic Independents, but the second place among that noble band must be accorded to Sir Harry Vane. His death was the best testimony of his greatness. He was the only man who died upon the scaffold for his share in the Great Rebellion who was not actually a regicide; and he was executed because, as Charles II. wrote, he was "too dangerous a man to let live if we can honestly put him out of the way." He died on Tower Hill "like a prince," as a Cavalier who was present testified—a patriot and a statesman well worthy to be associated with Sydney and Russell.

Sir Christopher Vane, son of the great Sir Harry, was knighted by Charles II., and created a peer by William III., with the title of Baron Barnard. He married the sister and co-heir of John Holles, Duke of Newcastle. He appears to have taken no active part in public life, but, like Mrs. Craik's well-known hero of fiction, John Halifax, he aided in supporting public credit at a critical moment by paying large sums of money into the Bank. The third Lord Barnard, who married the daughter of the Duke of Cleveland, son of Charles II., held the lucrative office of Paymaster of the Forces, and gained two steps in the peerage by his elevation to the Earldom of Darlington in 1754.

The third Earl of Darlington, who was created Marquis of Cleveland in 1827, was one of those wise and statesmanlike nobles who so largely aided in saving the country from a revolution half a century ago. We are accustomed to indulge in sneers at "the Whigs" in these days, and the debt of gratitude which the country owes the Whigs of 1832 is too often forgotten. For my part I would rather prefer to remember their virtues than their failings. Let us take the Marquis of Cleveland, for instance. He seems to have considerably increased his landed property by purchase. I have stated above that the Vanes have property in Somerset, Cornwall, and Sussex. A portion of this seems to have been acquired for political purposes, though, under the circumstances, with a most laudable object. The Marquis commanded no less than six borough seats, before the passing of the first Reform Bill, viz., two each for Ilchester, Camelford, and Winchilsea. Of that Bill he was an ardent supporter. Taunted with being a borough-monger, the Marquis frankly declared that he had purposely, at great expense, obtained the control of his boroughs because such property was so often used for improper purposes, and there was no other mode of counteracting those who thus used it. A nomination borough he declared to be "a species of property, if such in any sense it could be called, that could be desired only for the sake of two objects—either for the sake of Parliamentary influence, or for the pecuniary advantages to be derived from a sale of seats in the House of Commons; and if such property was bad in one sense, it was bad in the other, and therefore it ought to be put an end to both ways." It is said that the purchase of the property that gave the Marquis of Cleveland the command of these seats cost him something like a quarter of a million, and, as the seats gave the property an artificial value, the Marquis deserves as much credit for his patriotic conduct as if he had directly subscribed a large sum to the Reform agitation. The year after the Reform Bill passed his conduct was appropriately recognised by the Reform Ministry by his elevation to the Dukedom of Cleveland. He married the daughter and co-heir of Powlett, the last Duke of Bolton. The Powletts, of whom I have before spoken, were a family who grew rich out of the spoils of the monastic houses. That portion of the Bolton estates which came to the family was inherited by a younger son, who ultimately succeeded to the Dukedom of Cleveland, but he died shortly after, and the dukedom and estates came into the possession of his younger brother, who is the present duke.

LXXXIV.

The Wemyss-Charteris-Douglases.

WHAT a graceful and dignified speech was that which Lord Elcho delivered in the British House of Commons on the Zulu War. The modern fashion is to scream at our enemies like fish-fags, and blackguard them like costermongers. Poor Shere Ali was the object of our abuse so long as he lived; now it is Cetewayo's turn. We have it on the word of Lord Elcho that he is a gorilla; we have it also from Lord Elcho, on the eminent authority of a German newspaper, that he caught his brother alive and tortured him to death. True, that a better authority, Bishop Colenso, declares that there is no foundation for the story. No matter; Cetewayo is our enemy; and if the stories about him are not true, they ought to be.

Impelled, I suppose by the " gorilla " speech, a correspondent asks me—Who is Lord Elcho, and how comes it that he represents a Scottish constituency? He is the eldest son of the Earl of Wemyss and March, and has been for many years member for Haddingtonshire—formerly as a Liberal, and latterly as a Conservative; and he showed his appreciation of his constituents by flinging the contents of his cigar-case among them on the hustings, when the seat was contested by that renowned Scottish farmer, the late Mr. Hope, of Fenton Barns. He sits for the county, not because the Haddingtonshire farmers are less Liberal than those of most other Scotch constituencies, but because his father owns 10,136 acres of land in that county. For a similar reason, doubtless, Sir G. Montgomery sits for the counties of Selkirk and Peebles, in the latter of which the Earl of Wemyss and March owns 41,247 acres. Besides these estates, the Earl has 4,789 acres at Stanway, in Gloucestershire, obtained either by purchase or marriage. A century and a half ago Stanway was held by the Tracy family, who had a grant of the same at the dissolution of the monasteries. The Earl also has 3,010 acres in the neighbourhood of Elcho, Perthshire, where the family once had a castle; 1,261 acres in Berwick, and 1,504 in Midlothian—61,947 acres in all; with a gross rent-roll of £56,742.

The Wemyss family claim to be descended from that Macduff, Thane of Fife, who slew the murderer and usurper, Macbeth. It must be remembered, however, that it is only in tragedy that Macbeth was a murderer and usurper. Duncan was killed at Bothgowan, near Elgin, which, as Mr. Burton, remarks, was near, if not actually within the territory ruled by Macbeda; Duncan being there with aggressive designs. How the Wemyss family first obtained lands in Fife I know not, but in the fourteenth century they had two additional grants from the King, and another in the sixteenth. Their connection with Fife appears now to be merely titular, as they have sloughed off the old skin; and, while the name of Wemyss represents their ancient origin, those of Charteris and Douglas indicate the manner in which they have acquired most of their present possessions.

Until the reign of Charles I. they were commoners; but that monarch created the head of the house Lord Elcho, and subsequently Earl of Wemyss. These favours did not hinder him from manifesting his Covenanting sympathies during the Civil War, and his son, Lord Elcho, who married a daughter of Balfour of Burleigh, followed his example, and was defeated at a battle in Perthshire by Montrose. By a subsequent marriage, this last had an only daughter, in whose favour a new patent of peerage was obtained. Her son, who was Lord High Admiral of Scotland, and a Commissioner of the Treaty of Union, married the daughter of the first Duke of Queensberry. It is through this alliance that the Wemyss family derive a very large portion of their property.

The first Douglas, Duke of Queensberry, who died at the age of forty-eight, according to Burnet, who describes him as " very covetous," came into a much impaired fortune, but he greatly increased it. For a long time he was Lord High Treasurer of Scotland, and rendered himself odious by exacting ruinous fines from the Presbyterian gentry, who obeyed the law by going to church, but left their wives at home. He increased his fortune so much that he purchased for his second son, who was created Earl of March, the lands and lordship of Neidpath, in Peebles, from the Hays, ancestors of the

Marquis of Tweeddale. It was not all of the Earl of March's lands that were obtained by purchase. The Duke of Queensberry in 1688 obtained a grant of the principal part of the revenue of the Cross Church, Peebles, consisting of sundry houses in the West Port, Edinburgh, of lands in the parish of Cramond, and fifty acres of rich glebe lands—only four acres being left for the minister. This property he gave to the Earl of March. In 1707 there was an additional grant. "Among other favours," says the "Statistical Account of Scotland," he obtained the grant of Forton, and that donative had been deemed of so much value that it was named in the deed of entail of the March estates." The issue of the Earl of March subsequently succeeded to the Queensberry title and estates, but at the death of the fourth Duke without issue the Dukedom passed to the Duke of Buccleuch, the Marquisate to another kinsman, and the Earldom of March, with the estates held by the first Earl, to the seventh Earl of Wemyss.

But in the mean time the fourth Earl had contracted a splendid marriage with the daughter and heiress of Colonel Francis Charteris, of Amisfield, Haddingtonshire. Of this personage I have had some difficulty in gaining information, except that in his own day he is described as "notorious," and a "gambler," and that he was tried and condemned for a heinous crime, with difficulty obtaining a pardon. Looking over the works of Swift, edited by Sir Walter Scott, I came across the following remarkable epitaph, with the following foot-note by the editor:—" This epitaph on a man infamous for all manner of vices was written by Dr. Arbuthnot." It runs as follows:—" Here continueth to rot the body of Francis Chartres, who, with an inflexible constancy and inimitable uniformity of life, persisted, in spite of age and infirmities, in the practice of every human vice excepting prodigality and hypocrisy; his insatiable avarice exempted him from the first, his matchless impudence from the second. Nor was he more singular in the undeviating suavity of his manners than successful in accumulating wealth; for, without trade or profession, without trust of public money, and without bribe-worthy service, he acquired—or, more properly, created—a ministerial estate. He was the only person of his time who could cheat without the mask of honesty; retain his primeval manners when possessed of £10,000 a year; and, having daily deserved the gibbet for what he did, was at last condemned for what he could not do. O, indignant reader, think not his life useless to mankind! Providence connived at his execrable designs to give to after ages conspicuous proof and example of how small estimation is exorbitant wealth in the sight of God, by his bestowing it on the most unworthy of all mortals." I think that this will do as a companion picture to Lord Elcho's gorilla. If Dr. Arbuthnot had lived till now, he might have found another respect in which the life of Colonel Charteris was not useless to mankind, inasmuch as we owe it to his acquisition of property that Lord Elcho sits for Haddingtonshire.

The eldest son of the fourth Earl of Wemyss was engaged in the Jacobite Rebellion of 1745, and was attainted in consequence. The father died in 1756, but the son lived on an exile till 1787. At that time the Wemyss family had a narrow escape of being snuffed out, but as the next brother had not been implicated in the rebellion he was mercifully allowed to succeed to the family title and estates.

It only remains to be said that the Wemyss family, unlike most of the great Scotch houses, have never shown voracious tax-eating propensities. They have furnished at various times not a few gallant soldiers to the British Army and officers in the Navy. If they are too belligerent in their propensities, at any rate, unlike the Jingo mob who howl for war without the least intention of fighting themselves, the family of Wemyss are always ready to take a fair share of the risks. A younger brother of Lord Elcho was killed at Balaclava, and more recently his lordship's second and eldest surviving son died at sea of fever and dysentery, brought on by the hardships of the campaign in Ashantee. Charteris-Douglas-Wemyss; it seems a strange combination—the successful gambler, the oppressor of the Presbyterians, and the soldier of the Covenant. Were I a Scotchman, I should regard the worldly successes of the first and second as far less glorious than the defeat of the third.

LXXXV.

The Walpoles.

THE County of Norfolk has furnished to the country an unusually large proportion of able and successful public men—the Townshends, Nelsons, Cokes, De Greys, and many others. Among them the name of Walpole will take no mean place. The Earl of Orford, the present head of the house, owns 12,341 acres of land in Norfolk, with a rent-roll of £15,313. The Walpoles claim to have been settled in the county prior to the Norman Conquest; and it is certain that, not long after that event, they held lands of the Bishopric of Ely, at the place from whence they derive their surname. Somewhat later they acquired the manor of Houghton, which was for a lengthened period the seat of the family, and at which place Sir Robert Walpole erected a magnificent mansion. In the reign of Elizabeth the heir of the Walpoles was indicted for treason; but his forfeited lands were granted to his next brother, to whom his father also bequeathed his own lands at his death. The grandfather of Sir Robert sat in the Restoration Parliament, and his father was also at one time a member of the House of Commons.

It is not my province here to deal at length with Sir Robert Walpole's conduct of public affairs. Suffice it to say that, with all his faults, he was a wise and able statesman, who rendered inestimable services to his country. It cannot be denied that, if he used his opportunities to enrich himself and his family, his personal gains were but small when compared with the great increment of national prosperity which resulted from the policy which he steadfastly pursued. His memory need shrink from no comparison with his immediate predecessors or successors. I have only to do with him as an example of the fact that several of our great families have been built up by pursuing the profession of politics.

Sir Robert's father was a simple country squire of moderate

fortune—between £2,000 and £3,000 a year. Robert, who was a younger son, was originally intended for the Church; but, on the death of his elder brother, he was called home to assist his father in the management of the estate, and at that time not unfrequently sold beasts at market. Early in life he entered Parliament as a member of the Whig Party. In 1708 he was appointed Secretary at War, and in the following year Treasurer of the Navy. Two years after he was accused of corruption in regard to a Forage Contract in Scotland, was expelled the House of Commons, and imprisoned in the Tower—punishments which were more the result of party malignity than of the gravity of his offence. At the accession of George I. Walpole obtained the lucrative posts of Paymaster of the Forces and Treasurer of Chelsea Hospital; and shortly after he became First Lord of the Treasury and Chancellor of the Exchequer. In 1717 he went into opposition, but two years after he was conciliated by the offer of the Paymastership, and in 1721 he again became First Lord of the Treasury. Declining a peerage at the time (which, however, he accepted for his son), he continued to hold office till 1742, when he retired, and was created Earl of Orford, with a pension of £4,000 a year. George I. gave to Sir Robert Walpole the patent place of Collector of Customs for his own life and that of his two elder sons; but afterwards, Sir Robert having obtained for his eldest son the great place of Auditor of the Exchequer, and for his second son that of Clerk of the Pells, bequeathed £1,400 a year out of the first-named place to his third son, Horace, and £400 to his second son, Edward. In regard to the personal and family gains of Sir Robert Walpole I may quote Mr. Abraham Hayward, who says in his Essays:— "When Sir Robert Walpole became Prime Minister, his paternal estate was computed at less than £3,000 a year. During his tenure of office, he lived magnificently; he laid out enormous sums (popularly computed at £150,000) on buildings and pictures; and he more than quadrupled his private income, besides providing for his sons by patent places to the tune of £14,000 a year between them. We shall not much mend the matter by accepting Archdeacon Coxe's palliation that 'Sir Robert had been a large gainer by the South Sea Bubble.'" At the first Earl of Orford's death, he was succeeded by his eldest son, who, in addition to the rich sinecure above mentioned, was a Lord of the Bedchamber and Ranger of St. James's and Hyde Parks.

A younger son of the first Earl was Horace Walpole, whose letters are almost worth all the money he ever obtained from the public revenue. Horace, who was born in 1717, writing in 1782, gives the following account of his patent places:— " My father," he says, " in my youth gave me the two little patent places I still hold—Clerk of the Estreats and Comptroller of the Pipe—which together produce about £300 per annum. When I was about eighteen or nineteen he gave me the place of Inspector of the Imports and Exports in the Custom House, which I resigned in about a year on his giving me the patent place of Usher of the Exchequer, then reckoned worth £900 a-year. . . . I was content with what he had given me, and, from the age of twenty, I was no charge to my family." I presume that most men, under similar circumstances, would be quite contented with what their fathers had given, and would be satisfied to be at no charge to their families so long as they could draw £1,200 a-year from the nation for doing nothing. In these cases we must always bear in mind that the duties of the offices were always discharged by a deputy. The best of it for the office-holder was that the emoluments of these places usually tended to increase rather than to diminish. Horace Walpole's was a case in point. In 1744 he estimates his sinecures at a value of £2,000 a-year, and in 1780 he declares the net value of the chief of them to be worth £1,800, taking an average of the previous twelve years. The Commissioners of Accounts, who had taken the emoluments for that year alone, had put down the value of the place at £4,200 per annum, but as Horace Walpole furnished a plausible explanation, showing that the profits greatly fluctuated, we must be content to take his own estimate of the average value on a series of years. At the death of the third Earl without issue, who sold the celebrated Walpole collection of pictures to the Emperor of Russia for the comparatively small sum of £45,000, Horace Walpole came into the title. With him the male issue of Sir Robert died out. The great statesman, however, had a daughter, who was married to the Earl of Cholmondeley, and the splendid mansion which he built at Houghton is now the property of the Marquis of Cholmondeley, her descendant.

Sir Robert, however, had a younger brother, whom he promoted in the diplomatic service, and who, having purchased the Manor of Wolterton, near Aylsham, in Norfolk, was elevated to the peerage, with the title of Baron Walpole of Wolterton. The eldest of his sons, at the death of Horace Walpole, inherited the Walpole barony, which had been conferred upon Sir Robert's heir in his father's lifetime, but the other honours expired. A few years afterwards the title of the Earl of Orford was revived in his person, and is still held by his great-grandson.

The Walpoles have since continued to dip into the Exchequer now and then. In 1830 there was an Edward Walpole, who was a clerk in the Treasury and private secretary to the Chancellor of the Exchequer, with a salary of £900 a year; also an F. Walpole in the Home Office, with salary and allowances of £682. A little later I find the Earl of Orford in the enjoyment of a pension of £706, and his brother, a colonel in the Army, with an appointment in the Foreign Office. There was also a Rev. R. Walpole in the possession of the family livings of Itteringham, £378, and Tivetshall, £1,026, with a house to each. The latter is held by a Walpole now.

There is yet another branch of the family of whom I must say a word. The first Lord Walpole of Wolterton had a younger son, whose son for many years had a lucrative diplomatic post at one of the minor German Courts. All this gentleman's sons have been well provided for. The eldest, the Rev. Thomas Walpole, has for thirty-four years been Rector of Alverstoke, Hants, with £1,345 and a residence. Sir Robert is a Lieutenant-General in the Army, and since 1869 has had the colonelcy of the 65th Foot. John, who for thirty-three years was in the Civil Service, and was Assistant-Secretary to the Emigration Board (salary £660), retired in 1864 on a pension of £330. Charles, after forty years in the Inland Revenue Department, retired when he was receiving £1,000 per year, with a pension of £663. The most fortunate of all is the Right Hon. Spencer Walpole, M.P. for Cambridge University, who, beside being for six years a Commissioner of Church Estates, was Home Secretary in three short-lived Conservative Ministries—four or five years in all—and who for his eminent services has received for seventeen or eighteen years a pension of £2,000 per annum.

LXXXVI.

The Erskines.

THE family of Erskine is poor in possessions, but rich in titles, and richer still in honours—in honours chiefly won by one of its cadets, who rose by sheer force of ability from penury to the Woolsack, and who wrote upon his escutcheon the proud motto, "Trial by Jury." The name of Erskine is born by the Earl of Buchan, the Earl of Kellie, and Lord Erskine. Besides these, there is Goodeve-Erskine, Earl of Mar, and St. Clair Erskine, Earl of Rosslyn. Not one of these appears to possess an estate of 10,000 acres. This relieves me for once from the tedious task of tracing out the sinister and tortuous ways by which wealth has been derived, and affords me an ample opportunity of dwelling upon the brilliant career of one whose eloquence was only equalled by his lofty patriotism, and whose services to his country deserve to be held in imperishable remembrance. To me this is a congenial task. I am jealous of the historic continuity of English Liberalism. I can understand and pity a Russian Nihilist to whom yesterday is as great a blank as to-morrow; for an English Nihilist I cannot but feel contempt.

The Earldom of Mar was in existence at the period of the Norman Conquest, and its origin is lost in antiquity. At various times its possessors have played an important part in Scottish history. In the fourteenth century a grand-daughter of one of the Earls of Mar married Sir Thomas Erskine, and one of their descendants was elevated to the peerage with the title of Lord Erskine. The direct male line of the old Earls of Mar having died out, Queen Mary, in 1565, restored the title to the fifth Lord Erskine. In the Civil War the family suffered greatly, and, although the estates were restored on the accession of Charles II., a great part of them had to be sold. The Earl of Mar took an active part in the Jacobite Rebellion of 1715, and was attainted in consequence. In 1824 the title was revived in favour of one of his descendants, who

The Erskines. 159

was succeeded by his son; but, he dying without issue, the Earldom passed to the son of his eldest sister who had married Mr. William James Goodeve. The Earldom of Kellie was obtained through the marriage of one of the Erskines into the family which held that ancient Earldom. The Earldom of Rosslyn is a modern creation, obtained by Alexander Wedderburn, Lord Loughborough, who was Lord Chancellor in 1793. At his death the title passed to his nephew, an Erskine, who was descended from the seventh Earl of Mar.

This seventh Earl of Mar was the favourite of James I., from whom he received large grants of confiscated Church lands, formerly belonging to Dryburgh and other monastic houses, which were erected into the Barony of Cardross, and passed to the issue of his second son, who married the Countess of Buchan. By the middle of last century the Buchan branch of the family was almost in as unfortunate a condition as the heirs of the attainted Earl of Mar. Possibly they had suffered in political troubles, for some of them were staunch Covenanters; certainly, one of them had squandered a large portion of his inheritance. The fifth Earl was reduced to a miserable income of £200 a year, lived in a flat at Edinburgh, and was compelled to move to cheaper lodgings at St. Andrews. He had three sons; the eldest, his heir, succeeded him, and contrived in half a century to increase his income from £200 to £2,000. The second became an able and successful practitioner at the Scotch Bar. Of the third, who afterwards became Lord Erskine, I am about to speak more particularly.

Thomas Erskine, as a lad, was anxious to be educated for a learned profession; but what could a poor lord, with but £200 a-year, do for a third son, save provide him with porridge and kail, which seems to have been the lad's ordinary fare? He could not even buy him a commission in the Army, so the boy was sent to sea as a midshipman. Four years passed, and young Erskine returned home, soon after, attending the funeral of his father, which was conducted at Bath by Whitfield, of whom the Earl was an adherent. With the small legacy bequeathed him, Erskine purchased an ensigncy, and, with only his pay to support him, he was rash enough at the age of twenty to rush into matrimony with an amiable young lady of no fortune. After enduring two or three years of poverty as a subaltern in a marching regiment, Erskine's casual attendance at the Assizes fired him with the resolve to make a determined effort to forsake the Army for the Law. He entered himself as a student at Lincoln's Inn, and also as a student at Cambridge—he, as the son of a nobleman, having the right to take a degree without examination, which degree, once obtained, shortened his legal probation by two years. It was a hard struggle. He took lodgings for his young wife in Kentish Town, and had to be content with mean fare and shabby clothes. He had no legal connections to push him forward; and, as he himself said, when he obtained his first brief he had barely a shilling in his pocket. But he had only been at the Bar a few months when a happy accident brought him fame and fortune at a single bound. Some men equally worthy of success have to fight their way inch by inch for half a lifetime. Fortunately for Erskine and for England it was otherwise with him.

An action for libel had been brought against Captain Baillie, lieutenant-governor of Greenwich Hospital, because, after vainly appealing to the Government to redress the flagrant abuses in that institution, he had published the facts of the case. Shortly before the trial, Erskine, who was quite unknown to Baillie, was present at a dinner at which Baillie attended, and happened to express himself strongly in conversation on the case. Baillie asked his attorney to retain Erskine as junior counsel for his defence. The fee was but one poor guinea, and four senior counsel had to appear before him. After the others had spoken the case was adjourned till the next morning, and then Erskine rose and electrified the Court with a speech which was a masterpiece of invective, in which he attacked the prime author of the abuses, Lord Sandwich, with withering scorn. Captain Baillie won his case, with costs, and Erskine's fame at the Bar was at once secured.

A few months after, Erskine acted as legal adviser to Admiral Keppel, who was tried by court-martial on a groundless charge of incapacity, and the Admiral, on his acquittal, presented him with £1,000. In four years and a half Erskine was computed to have not only paid his debts, but to have made £9,000, and to have acquired a practice of £3,000 per annum. From 1783 to 1806 he is said to have had, on the average, a dozen special retainers a-year, with a minimum fee of 300 guineas each. In all he is said to have made £200,000;

he appears to have invested his money unwisely, and to have died comparatively poor.

For many years Erskine was the chief legal advocate of English liberty against the infamous attacks of tyrannical Tory Governments. In defending Lord George Gordon he made a successful stand against the attempt to bring a man to the scaffold on a charge of constructive treason. In the case of Stockdale, the publisher, he made an equally successful stand against libel prosecutions by vote of the House of Commons. In the case of Thomas Paine, for publishing "The Rights of Man," he vindicated the independence of the Bar by accepting a retainer for Paine, though warned that if he did so he would lose his office as Attorney-General of the Prince of Wales. But his crowning triumph was his successful defence of Hardy, Horne Tooke, and Thelwall, who, as members of the London Corresponding Society, were tried for high treason. Hardy, the brave shoemaker, whose tombstone any one may see against the railing of Bunhill Fields when passing up the City Road, was tried first. Scott, afterwards Lord Eldon, spoke for nine hours for the prosecution, and a whole week passed before the prosecution closed. For seven hours Erskine spoke in Hardy's defence, till his voice failed, and hardly rose above a whisper amid the hushed stillness of the court. At the close of the trial his exertions were rewarded with a verdict of Not Guilty. The trials of Horne Tooke and Thelwall followed, and in each case Erskine was equally triumphant. In another trial Erskine earnestly contended that in libel cases juries should be judges, not merely as regards the publication of the libel, but as to the libel itself—a principle afterwards embodied in Fox's Libel Bill. Once he appeared to prosecute in a case affecting the liberty of the Press, at the instance of the Society for the Suppression of Vice, who proceeded against the publisher of Paine's "Age of Reason;" but on it appearing that the Society pressed for a vindictive punishment he repudiated its action, and refused to appear in its behalf again.

As a debater in Parliament, and as Lord Chancellor, Lord Erskine did not achieve remarkable success, and he was severely blamed for appointing his son-in-law a Master in Chancery just before his retirement. That solitary act of nepotism, however, is venial indeed when we compare him with those who came before and those who followed after.

Almost the last public act of his life was to write a pamphlet in which he earnestly pleaded the cause of the oppressed Greeks. Well might Lord Brougham write of this true nobleman—"He resisted the combination of statesmen, and princes, and lawyers—the league of craft and cruelty formed to destroy our liberties—and triumphantly scattered to the winds the half-accomplished scheme of an unsparing proscription. Before such a precious service as this, well may the lustre of statesmen and of orators grow pale; and yet this was the achievement of one not only the first orator of his age, and not among its foremost statesmen, because he was beyond all comparison the most accomplished advocate, and the most eloquent that modern times have produced."

LXXXVII.

The Vernons.

AT the time of the marriage of the Princess Louise Sir William Vernon Harcourt excited some ridicule by alluding to his distant connection with royalty. I do not know why he should have been laughed at; he might, had he chosen, have claimed some connection more or less remote with almost half the great families of England, and with a few in France beside. The very names are indicative of Norman descent. Both Harcourt and Vernon are in Normandy, the latter on the direct line from Dieppe to Paris.

We will take the Vernons first, Harcourt being but a name assumed by a younger son of the house on coming into possession of the Harcourt estates, which descended through his mother, a Harcourt heiress. The Vernons came into England with the Conqueror, and acquired great estates in Derbyshire. Sir George Vernon of Haddon Hall died leaving two daughters, one married to a Stanley, the other to a Manners, by whom the extensive Vernon property was in-inherited. But the house had already thrown off several branches. One of the Vernons married a Staffordshire heiress; later on another Vernon married the heiress of that property; later still another Vernon married another Vernon heiress of Haslington, in Cheshire. Yet another married the sister of Sir Peter Venables, also a Cheshire heiress; and he, in 1762, was created Lord Vernon. The second wife of this nobleman was the sister of the first Earl Harcourt; by her he had a numerous family, of whom more hereafter. More recently a Lord Vernon married into the Warren family, an ancient Cheshire house which had, since the days of the Plantagenets, been seated in that county, on lands which are rich in coal. Thus by successive marriages the Vernons have been able to acquire a moderate estate of 9,801 acres in all, in Derbyshire, Cheshire, and Staffordshire; I am only surprised that it is not larger. There is little notable in their

11—2

history beyond mere marrying and giving in marriage. I turn now to the Harcourts, whose story is of far greater interest.

The Harcourts are said to have been descended from a Saxon Prince, who lived in Denmark, and accompanied Rollo on his piratical expedition to Normandy. There were two branches of the family who came over with the Conqueror to England. In the reign of Henry I. the representative of the elder line was Earl of Leicester, but his posterity died out. The head of the younger branch commanded the Norman archers at Hastings. From him, according to one antiquary, the Scotch Hamiltons and the French Montmorencies are descended. His grandson had considerable grants of English land from the Crown. In the reign of Richard I. a Harcourt became possessed, in right of his wife, a Norman heiress, of Stanton Harcourt, in Oxfordshire, which for centuries was the seat of the family. Henceforth the Harcourts played a not inglorious part in English history. One of them fought with Simon, the patriot Earl of Leicester, at Evesham; another, a Yorkist, was slain in the Wars of the Roses; another, a Lancastrian, bore the standard of Henry VII. at Bosworth; another fought at the Battle of the Spurs; another was associated with Raleigh in his efforts to colonise America; another was in Sir Horace Vere's campaigns in the Low Countries, and was killed in the Irish War in 1643. The son of this last suffered much in estate by his steady Royalism during the Civil War, for which he obtained no compensation from Charles II. beyond the barren honour of a knighthood. His son was destined to play a prominent, but yet a somewhat timid and inglorious part in the reigns of William III., Anne, and George I.

Simon Harcourt was by education and conviction not only a Tory but a Jacobite. Onslow describes him as "a man very able, but without shame." He conducted the impeachment of the illustrious Lord Somers, and defended the worthless Sacheverel, but his greatest dishonour was his conduct of the prosecution of Defoe for writing "The Shortest Way with Dissenters," in which he displayed a savage vindictiveness, and, in Defoe's belief, a bad faith, which will be remembered as long as the name of the man whom he persecuted. In the reign of Anne, Harcourt became successively Solicitor and Attoney-General, Lord Keeper and Lord Chancellor. He was leagued with Bolingbroke in the plot to procure the restoration of James at the Queen's death; but the prompt and decisive action of the Whig nobles disconcerted the conspirators, and, finding himself overmatched, Lord Harcourt not only took the oath to George I., but himself administered them to the Council. He was, however, dismissed from office; but, though his Jacobite opinions were well known, he had been too prudent to compromise himself as Bolingbroke had done, and so escaped a prosecution. During the Jacobite Rebellion of 1715 he cautiously sat on the fence, waiting to jump till it was quite safe, and so escaped once more. In his later years he contracted a friendship with Sir Robert Walpole, who induced him at length to accept the Hanoverian Succession as a *fait accompli*. Out of his official emoluments he saved sufficient to purchase considerable additions to his ancestral estates, particularly Nuneham Courtenay where his grandson and successor, who was created Earl Harcourt, built a mansion, and laid out an extensive park. This Harcourt line died out in 1830. The last Lord Harcourt having left his property to his wife's family on condition that they should assume his name. The present head of the Harcourt family is Mr. J. S. Chandos Harcourt, of Ankerwycke Priory.

We must return now to the first Lord Vernon, who, as I said, married as his second wife the sister of the first Earl Harcourt. His eldest son by this marriage ultimately inherited the Vernon title and estates. The next son, Edward, who married a daughter of the first Marquis of Stafford in 1830, inherited the Harcourt estates, consisting of 5,720 acres in Oxfordshire. He went into Holy Orders, and when quite a young man was made a Canon of Christchurch; at the age of thirty-four he obtained the Bishopric of Carlisle; not long after he was translated to the richer see of Salisbury; and a few years after he became Archbishop of York. This was in 1807, and he lived on till 1847. In the course of his lifetime Archbishop Harcourt must have received from the Church considerably over half a million of money—three-quarters, I think, would be nearer the mark—and taking residences and offices into account, he and his reverend sons must have had altogether about a million from that source. The Archbishop had quite a patriarchal family, no less than ten sons and four daughters. The family motto is *Ver non semper viret*—The spring does not always flourish—which he inferentially translated into "Make hay while the sun shines." With a princely revenue, to say nothing of the Harcourt estates, he might have provided for his family himself; but what need was there to do so when the rich milch cows of Church and State were ready to hand? Of his ten sons no less than eight were provided for in the Church, the Army, and the Navy. The eldest son, being heir to the Harcourt estates, of course had no need to choose a profession. The second son was Rector of Rothbury (£1,106 and a house), and Rector of Kirkby-in-Cleveland (£600 and a house), a sinecure; likewise Chancellor and Commissary; also Prebendary of York. He afterwards became Canon of Carlisle (£1,000 and house). The third son was Vicar of Bishopsthorp (£300 and a house) and Rector of Etton (£700 and a house); also Canon of York. By the way, nearly all the preferments of the clerical Vernon-Harcourts were given them by their father, or obtained through his influence. The eldest son of Canon Vernon-Harcourt has succeeded to the Harcourt estates, and is a member for Oxfordshire; his brother is Sir William, the Liberal member for Oxford, who not long ago reminded his Sheffield audience that he was a Yorkshireman. The fourth son of the Archbishop was an Admiral in the Navy. The fifth was a Colonel in the Army. The sixth became Chancellor of the Diocese of York, and married an heiress who brought him the mansion of Grove Hall, in Nottinghamshire. The seventh, an Admiral in the Navy, married the widow of Mr. W. Danby, of Swinton Park, who had bequeathed her for life 11,441 acres in Yorkshire. The eighth went into Holy Orders, and became a Prebendary of Carlisle. The ninth became a Colonel in the Army, and Equerry to the late Duchess of Kent.

If we put aside the Sparkes and Norths and Pretymans, it would perhaps be difficult to find a more striking instance of the abuse of Church patronage than this. Yet by some no doubt I shall be accused of holding up the Church itself to contempt, even as Milton was when he denounced "the hireling wolves whose gospel is their maw." But it was only a few days ago that I read in the columns of a leading Conservative journal a pitiful complaint from one who gave the clerical history of several fellow students of high attainments for whom the richest Church in Christendom had barely provided a piece of bread. It is true that the worst scandals of

Pluralism belong to a past generation, but it is equally true that the Church of England is still largely degraded into a system of outdoor relief for the younger sons of the territorial aristocracy. It is commonly reported that there is a strong disposition on the part of some members of the Royal Commission to palter with the great evils of patronage; it is all the more necessary, therefore, that they should be constantly kept before public notice.

LXXXVIII.

The Greys.

(STAMFORD AND WARRINGTON BRANCH).

THERE are so many of this fortunate family in the English Peerage that I cannot glance at them all, but the Stamford and Warrington branch is of so much importance, both in a territorial and historical point of view, that I cannot pass them by unnoticed. Twice at least has this house played an important part in our history, and, owing in great part to fortunate marriages, its estates are both large and valuable. The Earl of Stamford and Warrington owns in—

Cheshire	8,612 acres.
Lancashire	5,231 ,,
Leicestershire	9,012 ,,
Stafford	7,339 ,,
Salop	606 ,,
York and Worcester	161 ,,
Total	30,961 ,,

With a rent-roll of £58,395.

The late Mr. Joseph Kay, in his excellent work on the Land Question, says:—" It would be a most interesting subject of inquiry, had we only the means of following it out, to ascertain how each of the great estates came to be formed. How many were created by the industry and personal efforts of some ancestor; how many were the grants of Sovereigns to their favourites; how many were gradually amassed by successive marriages of convenience; how many were obtained by ambitious statesmen, in the troublous times of our rough island story, by the attainder and death of rivals; how many were either created or immensely increased by grants of the vast possessions of the religious houses and of the

Roman Church ; how many were the results of our fierce and bloody civil wars and struggles. It would, indeed, be a curious and instructive study." At the time when these words were written I had already commenced my task, and, indeed, they had not fallen under my notice till very recently; but no words could have more accurately laid down the plan which I have endeavoured to follow. The space and time at my disposal have necessarily left these sketches far from complete; but had I not imposed upon myself the most severe condensation, my work would have been obviously unfitted for the columns of a newspaper, and I trust that as it is I have placed in the hands of the general reader the most important facts in regard to the agrarian history of each of the houses with which I have dealt. If a more detailed inquiry is desirable, I have made the way easier for those who shall come after me. After this brief digression, I return to the family whose name stands at the head of this article.

The Greys of Stamford and Warrington owe their estates to several of the circumstances mentioned by Mr. Kay, but chiefly to successive marriages of convenience. The Greys were a Norman family, who rose into prominence in the times of the early Plantagenet Kings. The founder of this branch of the house was a younger son of Lord Grey de Ruthin, who, in the reign of Henry VI., married the granddaughter and heiress of the last Lord Ferrers of Groby. Bradgate and Groby, in Leicestershire, had been acquired by a Norman house at the Conquest, and had passed by successive marriages to the Ferrers family. Since the marriage of Edward de Grey into the Ferrers family these Leicestershire estates have been in the possession of his descendants. The eldest son of this marriage fell in the Lancastrian cause at St. Albans, and Edward IV. married his widow, through whose influence her son, Sir Thomas Grey, was created Marquis of Dorset. His grandson, the third Marquis of Dorset, married the daughter and heiress of Charles Brandon, Duke of Suffolk, whose Duchess was the sister of Henry VIII. The Marquis was elevated to the dukedom of Suffolk in the reign of Edward VI. His three daughters. the eldest of whom was the unfortunate Lady Jane Grey, died without issue. The Duke himself was beheaded for his share in Wyatt's rebellion. Thus the sudden greatness of the house for a time was eclipsed, but in the reign of James I. it partially regained its prosperity.

Lord John Grey, a younger brother of the unhappy Duke of Suffolk, obtained a grant of Pergoe, in Essex, which was part of the Royal manor of Havering-atte-Bower. His son Henry sold the Essex property, but acquired a considerable estate in Staffordshire. Enville had been acquired by the marriage of another offshoot of the Greys with a Staffordshire heiress, and the last heir of that branch, who was childless, sold the property to Henry Grey, who was created Lord Grey of Groby by James I. His grandson married the daughter and co-heiress of William Cecil, Earl of Exeter, through whom he became possessed of the castle, manor, and borough of Stamford. I have already shown in a previous article that the Cecils derived their property almost exclusively from royal grants. Early in the reign of Charles I. Lord Grey of Groby was created Earl of Stamford; from the same monarch he received a grant of lands in Charnwood Forest. The Earl and his eldest son, Lord Grey of Groby, were ardent supporters of the Parliament during the Civil War, and both of them had military commands. Lord Grey of Groby was especially active, and after the relief of Gloucester and the Battle of Newbury he received the special thanks of the House of Commons. He is said to have had more to do with Pride's Purge of the Long Parliament than Colonel Pride himself; and his signature appears second, between those of Bradshaw and Cromwell, on the death-warrant of the King. During the Civil War he made great sacrifices in the cause, but he subsequently received large grants from the Parliament, both in land and money. It was voted that lands in Leicestershire, to the value of £1,000 per annum, should be settled upon him, and with his pecuniary rewards he made extensive purchases. Somewhat later he quarrelled with Cromwell, and engaged himself in plots, for which he was imprisoned. Fortunately, perhaps, for his family, he died just before the Restoration, but his father lived on till 1673. The elder grandson of the first Earl, dying without issue, was succeeded by his son, and he by his son, who contracted another advantageous marriage with the daughter and heiress of Booth, the last Earl of Warrington.

The Booths had acquired fortune very much in the same way as the Greys. They were an old Lancashire family, one

The Greys.

of whose younger sons had married a Cheshire heiress named Venables. Dunham Massey and other lands in Cheshire, spoils of the Norman Conquest, had passed by successive marriages to the family of Venables, and thence in the same manner to the Booths. In the reign of Henry VIII. Sir William Booth married the heiress of the Asshetons, the ancient possessors of the valuable manor of Ashton-under-Lyne, which is still held by his descendants. During the Civil War Sir George Booth was a leading member of the Presbyterian party, and gave his support to the Parliament. Towards the close of the Commonwealth period he appeared in arms for Charles II., but was defeated after a sharp encounter by Lambert, and made his escape disguised as a woman. The following year he acted as one of the deputation to invite Charles back, and received as his reward from the King the title of Lord Delamere, and from the Parliament £10,000. Lord Delamere was accused in the reign of James II. of treasonable correspondence with Monmouth, but was acquitted. At the coming of the Prince of Orange he raised Cheshire for William, and gained two steps in the peerage, being created Earl of Warrington. He was also awarded a pension of £2,000 a-year, which, strange to say, was not paid. At the death of George Booth, second Earl of Warrington, the estates passed to the Earl of Stamford, who had married his daughter, and their son and his descendants have since held both titles.

It will be seen that though the Greys are an old family, the greater part of their estates are still older, that is, that they have descended by inheritance in unbroken succession from Norman times. The Asshetons, of Ashton-under-Lyne, the Venables and Fittons of Dunham Massey, the Ferrers o Groby, the Lowes of Enville, all of whom were ancient houses, have one by one been merged into the house of Grey. What has not been acquired in this manner has been acquired almost entirely by Royal or Parliamentary grants. Necessarily the wealth of this house has been immensely increased by the industry and enterprise of the people of Cheshire and Lancashire. I have given the gross rental of the estates of the Earl of Stamford and Warrington, but I have little doubt that it conveys but an inadequate idea of his wealth. Certainly it gives us no information as to his prospective wealth, seeing that our system of leases in the manufacturing towns secures not only to the landlord a considerable share of the present profits of industry, but in the future an exaction of yet larger sums from those whose capital and labour have, without exertion on his part, given to his lands a value of which his ancestors never dreamed.

LXXXIX.

The Bruces.

THE Bruces are a Norman family, who came over with the Conqueror, and obtained large grants of land in the North of England. In the reign of Henry I. one of them, having ingratiated himself with the King of Scotland, obtained from that Monarch large grants of land in Annandale; and, not long after, the Bruces became allied by marriage with the Scottish Royal House. For some time the Bruces were half English, half Scotch. Robert Bruce's father had a house near London, at Tottenham, Middlesex, the name of which is still preserved in Bruce Castle School, which was opened as a branch of the Birmingham establishment kept by the Messrs. Hill more than a generation ago. The English estates of the Bruces were confiscated in the time of the Plantagenets; and England knew them not again as landowners till the beginning of the seventeenth century.

From one of the younger branches of the Bruce family was descended Sir Edward Bruce, of Kinloss, who was employed by King James in several embassies to the Court of Elizabeth, and who became the intermediary of that Monarch's confidential correspondence with the younger Cecil before his accession to the English Crown. Like the rest of the needy Scottish courtiers, Bruce accompanied his master to England; and, in the very first year of James's reign, obtained for life the great place of Master of the Rolls. The following year he was created Earl of Elgin. His son, early in the reign of Charles I., was created Baron Bruce of Whorlton, in the English Peerage. Whorlton, in the North Riding, and the dissolved Cistercian Abbey of Jerveaux (Urevale), had been granted by Henry VIII. to the Earl of Lennox, but subsequently reverted to the Crown, and is said to have been regranted by James I. to Edward Bruce of

Kinloss. The second wife of the second Earl of Elgin was the widow of the Earl of Oxford, and the daughter of the elder Cecil. According to one account, the Bruces had large grants from King James of lands at Tanfield and elsewhere in Yorkshire, at one time in the possession of the Marmions; but there is evidence to show that the elder Cecil had previously received a grant of these lands from Elizabeth; consequently, they must have been brought into the family by the marriage with Cecil's daughter. Whichever account be true, they were derived by the direct favour of the Crown, whether of Elizabeth or James matters little. The eldest son of this marriage was created Earl of Ailesbury. The next heir made a most fortunate matrimonial alliance, his wife being the sister and sole heiress of William Seymour, Duke of Somerset, one of the wealthiest nobles in the kingdom.

It is unnecessary here to recapitulate the history of the Seymours. Suffice it to say that one of them had married the daughter and co-heiress of Sir William Sturmy, of Chadham and Wolf Hall, in Wiltshire. The Sturmys, from the days of Henry II., had been hereditary Bailiffs of the Royal Forest of Savernake, where is now situated Tottenham Park, the chief seat of the Marquis of Ailesbury. This is only another instance of the tendency of hereditary guardianship to develop into ownership. The Protector Somerset in the reign of Edward VI. obtained—or, rather, appropriated to himself—immense grants of land belonging to the Crown, which, however, he was ultimately compelled to disgorge. Marlborough Castle, Bradon, and Savernake Forests, and other lands derived from his ancestors, were restored to him. The present Marquis of Ailesbury owns in

Wiltshire	37,993 acres.
Yorkshire	15,502 ,,
Bucks	1,566 ,,
Total	55,061 ,,

With a rent-roll of £59,716.

It will be seen from the foregoing account that nearly all this has been derived at various times by grants from the Crown.

The Earl of Ailesbury whose marriage resulted in the acquisition of the Seymour estates played a half-hearted part at the Revolution of 1688. He was one of the first to invite the Prince of Orange over, but he resolutely refused to swear allegiance to him as King. His son married Lady Anne Saville, daughter and co-heiress of the Marquis of Halifax; but the Saville property passed to her daughter, and, as there were no male children, the Earl of Ailesbury obtained a new patent of peerage as Baron Bruce of Tottenham, with remainder to a nephew, to whom he bequeathed his estates. The Earldom of Ailesbury then expired, and the Scottish Earldom of Elgin passed to the Earl of Kincardine, who was descended from a brother of Edward Bruce of Kinloss, the courtier of James I. The two earldoms have been since held by his descendants, some of whom have achieved distinction in the public service. The seventh Earl, who was Ambassador at Constantinople, brought home the "Elgin Marbles" from Greece, and the eighth Earl was not many years ago Governor-General of India.

The nephew, Thomas Brudenell, was a younger son of the Earl of Cardigan. The Brudenells were small landowners in Oxon and Northampton in the time of the Plantagenets. One of them, who was Lord Chief Justice in the reigns of Henry VII. and Henry VIII., made considerable purchases of land at Staunton Wyvill in Leicestershire, and Deene in Northamptonshire, the latter place being the chief seat of the family. One of his descendants received a baronetcy from James I., and had a peerage from Charles I. Lord Brudenell was a staunch Royalist, and suffered a long imprisonment in the Tower, for which he was compensated at the Restoration by being created Earl of Cardigan. The eldest son of the second Earl of Cardigan, who died in the lifetime of his father, married Lady Frances Saville, daughter of the Earl of Sussex, who subsequently became heiress to her brother's estates. These Savilles, according to Allen's History of Yorkshire, were an illegitimate branch of the family, who, by address and Court favour, had outstripped the legitimate line. Their lands are situated in Yorkshire. The grandson of the Saville marriage rose to a dukedom, for, having married the co-heiress of the Duke of Montagu, he was, after the death of his father-in-law, created Duke of Montagu. He died without issue, and his next brother succeeded to the Earldom of Cardigan, which continued to be held by the Brudenells till 1868, when the last Earl—he who led the Light Brigade at the charge of Balaclava—died without issue, and the Earldom of Cardigan passed to the Marquis of Ailesbury. The late Earl of Cardigan held in—

Northamptonshire	6,343 acres
York	4,361 ,,
Leicester	2,280 ,,
Total	12,984 ,,

With a rent-roll of £16,130.

What will be the ultimate disposition of these lands I am unable to say. In the new Domesday Book they are set down as held by the trustees of the late Earl, whose widow resides at Deene, the old seat of the Brudenell family.

In 1821 the then Earl of Ailesbury, who had steadily used the family electoral influence for the Government, was raised a step in the Peerage, being created a Marquis. The first Reform Bill swept away most of the Parliamentary influence of the Brudenell Bruces, but they still have one representative in the House of Commons, who nominally sits for the little borough of Marlborough. The present Marquis, as Lord Ernest Bruce, sat for that place from 1832 till his accession to the peerage in 1878. Marlborough has barely 600 electors, while several boroughs which also return only one member have more than ten times that number. Among these are Swansea, Bury, Burnley, Dewsbury, Dudley, Walsall, Gateshead, South Shields, Stockton, Huddersfield, and Wednesbury. The last-named has more than thirty times the number of electors possessed by Marlborough; the contrast is a beautiful example of our electoral anomalies.

The present Lord Aberdare, Henry Austin Bruce, belongs to a Welsh family, he being the second son of Mr. J. Bruce-Pryce, of Glamorganshire.

XC.

The Agar-Ellises.

THE rapid rise of prosperous houses in comparatively modern times is sometimes a perplexing enigma. Take, for instance, the Agar-Ellises, or the Ellis-Agars. About a century ago, in the short space of twenty years, three of them obtained peerages; and they own between them at the present time more than 87,000 acres. The family motto is, *Non hæc sine numine*—"These things are not without the Deity;" and I am almost inclined to add that He alone knows how they obtained them. Viscount Clifden has an Irish seat, Gowran Castle, anciently one of the strongholds of the Butlers; he has an English seat at Holdenby, in Northamptonshire—a name for ever associated with that renowned Elizabethan courtier, Sir Christopher Hatton. Evidently this is a case of New Men and Old Acres. Viscount Clifden owns in

Northampton	4,774 acres.
Bucks	2,976 ,,
Somerset	2,537 ,,
Oxon	1,107 ,,
Middlesex	36 ,,
Ireland	38,464 ,,
Total	49,894 ,,

Almost all the Irish estates are in Kilkenny. The rent-roll is £36,583. Certainly this is a considerable accumulation in two hundred years.

Gowran Castle, Kilkenny, was an ancient seat of the Butlers, which was besieged in the Irish Wars of the Commonwealth, and, with the surrounding lands, was granted to Ireton, then Lord Deputy. It did not revert to Ormonde at the Restoration, but was granted, with other forfeited estates of the regicides, to James, Duke of York, from whose trustees it was purchased by a certain Charles Agar. The Agars are said to have been a Huguenot family, who escaped from

France in time of persecution, and settled in Yorkshire. How Charles Agar was able to buy this extensive estate I know not, but it must be remembered that Irish lands were very cheap in those days. Not very long after another Yorkshire adventurer, a certain Sir William Ellis, went over to Ireland, and became secretary to Tyrconnel. Sir William had a brother, Welbore Ellis by name, who also went over to Ireland, and, being in Holy Orders, obtained the Bishopric of Meath. The Bishop ultimately became the heir of his brother, the Secretary, and the grandson of Charles Agar married the only daughter of the Bishop. The eldest son of this marriage, after having held lucrative offices in Ireland, was created Viscount Clifden in 1781. The second son was a Commissioner of Customs; the third was created Earl of Normanton, of whom I shall have more to say hereafter.

The Bishop of Meath had a son, also named Welbore Ellis. The father, being only a poor Bishop, had his son educated free of expense, first of all as a King's scholar at Westminster, and afterwards at Christ Church, Oxford. Welbore soon entered Parliament, and for many years held highly-paid offices, as a Lord of the Admiralty, Vice-Treasurer of Ireland, Secretary at War, Treasurer of the Navy, and Colonial Secretary. The only distinguished services which I can discover that he rendered to his country were that he strenuously opposed any concessions to the American colonists, and that he moved the committal of Lord Mayor Crosby to the Tower for daring to maintain the freedom of the Press against a tyrannical House of Commons. He was the "Grildrig" of Junius, who describes him as a little mannikin and the most contemptible creature in the world, who, whether he made or suppressed a motion, was equally sure of disgrace. Even Lord Stanhope speaks of him as "a man who was ridiculed for his diminutive stature, not in him redeemed by any loftiness of mind." Nevertheless, he appears during the many years in which he held office to have amassed a large fortune. Having gone over to Pitt in 1793, he was rewarded the following year with an English peerage, under the title of Baron Mendip. As he left no issue, his title and fortune passed to his great-nephew, the second Viscount Clifden.

This nobleman, by the way, was one of those Irish borough-mongers who received bribes at the passing of the Act of Union in the shape of compensation for the loss of their patronage. Almost ever since the Agars obtained possession of Gowran they had possessed two seats for the borough of that name in the Irish Parliament. One of them usually occupied one of the seats, and, judging by the number of offices they obtained, it must have been quite a mine of wealth to them. When the Act of Union passed Viscount Clifden received £15,000 for the extinction of his pocket borough. With this comfortable sum in hand, coupled with his placeman great-uncle's fortune, it need not surprise us that soon after he appears as a considerable purchaser of land in England. About 1830 Viscount Clifden purchased the manor and estate of Lenborough, in Buckinghamshire, and the still larger estate of Holdenby, in Northamptonshire, came into his hands in the same manner. Holdenby, the ancient seat of the Hattons, was purchased by James I., who gave it to his son Charles, with whose later history its name will always be associated. It was confiscated and sold during the Commonwealth, but at the Restoration Charles II. resumed possession of it. He appears to have granted it to his brother James Duke of York, who in turn gave it to a French officer, whom he created Earl of Feversham. Feversham's representative sold it to the Duke of Marlborough, in whose family it remained till the third Duke sold it to Viscount Clifden, who had married his eldest daughter. This nobleman held the office of Clerk of the Privy Council in Ireland, a sinecure with £1,450 a-year. At this period the Agar-Ellises were steady and consistent Whigs, being staunch advocates of Catholic Emancipation and Parliamentary Reform. The eldest son of the second Viscount Clifden was created a peer of the United Kingdom, with the title of Baron Dover, in the lifetime of his father, whom he predeceased. His grandson, the present holder of the title, is a minor.

I have previously mentioned that a younger brother of the first Viscount Clifden was created Earl of Normanton. Many of my readers have unconsciously trodden upon his tombstone on entering the door at the north transept of Westminster Abbey, and in the fourth bay of the north aisle of that Abbey they may see his monument. It is a somewhat curious production. There is a representation in bas-relief of the new Protestant Cathedral at Cashel, which his lordship was instrumental in building. There is a figure, too, of the Earl, in full canonicals, handing to another clergyman an

open book, on which are the words, "Be not weary in well-
doing"—a maxim which he certainly did not lose sight of,
especially when we remember the Apostolic dictum that "He
that desires the office of a Bishop desireth a good thing."
The sculptor has also introduced two or three forlorn Irish
beggars to indicate the prelate's kindly disposition. But the
most remarkable feature of the monument is a little cherub
putting a mitre upon his lordship's head. As the Yankee
editor said, when he received a poem describing how the
angels laid a new-born baby on the young mother's lap,
"That may be very good poetry; but it's not the road such
things usually come in this world." Leaving the realms of
imagination, and coming down to plain facts, Charles Agar,
having taken Holy Orders, was so fortunate as to be appointed
Chaplain to the Lord-Lieutenant; and soon after the first
piece of preferment fell to him, in the shape of the Deanery
of Kilmore. When about thirty years of age, he was elevated
to the Bishopric of Cloyne; and, about ten years after, to
the Archbishopric of Cashel. In 1801 he was translated to
the Archbishopric of Dublin, and he lived on till 1809. He
had an eye to temporal as well as spiritual dignities, for he
was successively created a Baron, a Viscount, and an Earl.
I cannot discover that either he, or his son, or his grandson,
married rich heiresses; so I must conclude that the greater
part of the landed possessions of the Earl of Normanton
were derived from the savings of the Archbishop and his
heir. As the first Lord Normanton was a Prelate of the Irish
Church for nearly forty years, he had ample opportunities of
saving a considerable sum; and I believe his son achieved
yet greater things by studious frugality. However that may
be, the present Earl of Normanton, whose grandfather was
only the younger son of an Irish commoner, now owns no
less than 37,336 acres of land in half-a-dozen English and
Irish counties, with a rent-roll of £41,011.

XCI.
The Hamiltons.

THE Hamiltons, like the Bruces, are of Norman extraction, and, like many great Scotch families, they owe almost everything to the direct favour of the Crown. The present Duke of Hamilton figures in the new Domesday Book as the owner in

Bute	102,210 acres
Lanark	45,731 ,,
Suffolk	4,939 ,,
Linlithgow	3,694 ,,
Stirling	810 ,,
Total	157,384 ,,

The gross rental is £140,526. Heaven and Mr. Padwick alone know what it is net. The estates are in the hands of trustees, and the Duke has an allowance. As the Duke is richer in titles than a Royal baby in Christian names, I will not recount them all. Suffice it to say that he is not only the Premier Peer of Scotland, but also Duke of Brandon in the Peerage of England, and that his peerages are sixteen in number.

Almost every acre of his vast domains in Scotland are derived directly by grants from the Crown. His proprietary rights are of course no more affected by this fact than by his unwise use of his enormous income. But we may well echo Oxenstiern's exclamation as to the little wisdom with which the world is governed, when we reflect that our ancestors placed it within the power of their monarchs to grant to their favoured followers the power for themselves and their descendants through all time to take tithe and toll of the produce of the soil of great tracts of land which have constantly grown in value owing to the industry of the whole population. The grantors, of course, could not foresee that the posterity of the grantees would ultimately derive such immense revenues for doing nothing at all; but when I hear people lamenting that rents over a large part of Scotland have gone down about 25 per cent., I cannot greatly pity the people whose ancestors obtained everything for nothing.

The chief seats of the Duke of Hamilton in Scotland are Hamilton Palace, Lanarkshire ; Kinnell House, Linlithgow ; Brodrick Castle, Isle of Arran, Buteshire. They form convenient landmarks in tracing the history of the family. The Lanark and Linlithgow estates have been, with short interruptions, in the possession of the Hamiltons ever since the days of King Robert Bruce. A certain Sir Walter Hamilton having attached himself to that monarch, although he had previously sworn fealty to Edward I., was rewarded with extensive grants of lands, particularly of the barony of Cadzow and the estate of Kinnell. On the former estate is now erected Hamilton Palace (called a palace because Mary, Queen of Scots, once resided there), one of the most magnificent mansions in the kingdom. The Kinnell estate has in modern times acquired greatly increased value from its collieries. Kinnell House was for a time the residence of Dugald Stewart, at which place he died.

The greater part of the Hamilton estates are situated in Arran, the larger of the two islands which form the county of Bute. Arran was anciently a domain of the Scottish Crown, but in the fifteenth century it was given as a dowry to the Princess Mary on her marriage with Boyd, who was created Earl of Arran. During one of the frequent domestic convulsions of the time Boyd had to flee for his life, and his estates, as well as those of his brother, were confiscated about 1468. Of the lands in question Mr. Burton says:—" These domains were all forfeited to the Crown, but were not, in the usual manner, put at the disposal of the Crown to give away at pleasure. The Act of Forfeiture rendered it incompetent for the Crown to alienate any of them without the consent of Parliament, and assigned the greater portion of them as a principality for the heir of the Crown." This Act, however, did not long prevent the Hamiltons from obtaining possession of Arran. Boyd soon died in exile, and the head of the house of Hamilton married his widow, the Princess Mary. In 1503— less than forty years after the Act had been passed—the eldest son of this marriage obtained a grant of the island from King James IV., and since that time it has been held by his descendants.

As if the Scottish Monarchs had not already done enough for the Hamiltons, I find that James VI. of Scotland, in the year 1606, granted to the head of the family the lands of the rich Abbey of Aberbrothock, in Forfarshire, a proceeding which moved Archbishop Abbot to an humble remonstrance, in which, after expressing his disappointment that the property had not been devoted to ecclesiastical uses, he ventured to hope " that two out of the poor clergy would receive small holdings out of this great domain." The lands in question, I believe, are not now in the possession of the Duke of Hamilton.

The Suffolk estates are a modern acquisition. Easton in Suffolk was purchased by a Dutch officer, who was illegitimately descended from one of the Princes of Orange. He appears to have been a great favourite with William III., by whom he was created Earl of Rochford. The last Earl of of Rochford bequeathed these estates to a Duke of Hamilton, who was his half-brother.

The history of the house of Hamilton is so constantly interwoven with the history of Scotland that it would be impossible for me to give even a brief epitome thereof. My business, however, is with the lands rather than with the men. The second Earl of Arran was created Duke of Chatelherault in France, with a French pension, in order to induce him to consent to the marriage of Queen Mary with the Dauphin. At one time they seemed likely to lose possession altogether in favour of a certain Captain Stewart, but the fourth Earl, uniting with other nobles in a military demonstration, obtained possession of the King, regained his lands, and was created Marquis of Hamilton. The third Marquis, an ardent Royalist, was created a Duke after the outbreak of the Civil War between Charles I. and his Parliament, and was beheaded in Old Palace Yard in 1749. His son, the second Duke, was mortally wounded at the Battle of Worcester, and, leaving only daughters, the estates fell to his sister, Lady Anne Hamilton, who married Lord William Douglas. From that time the Dukes of Hamilton have been Douglas-Hamiltons. On the failure of the elder male line of the great house of Douglas, the Douglas-Hamiltons laid claim to the great Douglas estates, but after prolonged litigation they were finally defeated. Since the death of the fourth Duke, who was a leading statesman at the time of the Hanoverian settlement, the Hamiltons have not been distinguished except as house builders, art collectors, and patrons of the turf.

The male line of the Hamilton family is represented by the Duke of Abercorn, who was a few years ago created a Duke by the grace of our Sovereign Lord, Benjamin I. This branch of the Hamiltons, like the other, owes everything it possesses to the direct favour of the Crown, or to what it has saved out of its extensive grants. The Duke of Abercorn owns in—

Tyrone	51,919 acres
Donegal	15,860 ,,
Edinburgh	1,500 ,,
Renfrew	662 ,,
Sussex	8 ,,
Total	69,949 ,,

With a rent-roll of £45,954.

All this has been acquired within the last three hundred years.

Claud, fourth son of the Hamilton who was created Duke of Chatelherault, obtained from James VI. a grant of the barony of Paisley. The Hamiltons, by the way, also obtained possession of the rich Abbey of Paisley, which they subsequently sold. I presume that the lands they still hold in Renfrew are a remnant of these grants. The eldest son of Lord Paisley was created Earl of Abercorn—a place with which, I believe, the Hamiltons have now no local connection—by the same monarch. But James had now come into possession of the Crown of England and Ireland, and he made to the Earl of Abercorn extensive grants of land in the barony of Strabane. A younger brother of this Earl was made Constable of Toome Castle, Antrim, for life, and had a grant of 400 acres in Longford and 2,000 acres in the barony of Strabane. Another younger son also had grants of lands in Tyrone and Tipperary, and, after the Restoration, of other lands in Cork, besides several lucrative offices. The eldest son of this last, who was one of the favourite courtiers of Charles II., obtained a grant of an estate in Meath, and £900 per annum out of the firstfruits and tenths of the dioceses of St. David's, Hereford, Oxford and Worcester. His eldest son, who was one of the Privy Councillors of James II., went over to the side of the Prince of Orange, and assisted in the relief of Londonderry. By this time the eldest line had died out, and the Earldom of Abercorn was held by a descendant of the third son of the Duke of Chatelherault. He held fast to James II., fought for him at the Boyne, and was soon after killed. He was attainted, but his brother obtained a reversal of the attainder. The latter leaving no issue, the lands and titles passed to the Captain Hamilton who had assisted in relieving Londonderry. I have not space to mention the various civil, military, and ecclesiastical offices subsequently held by this branch of the Hamilton family. One of them, by the way, held no less than six rectories and vicarages in the diocese of Armagh. About the year 1745 the Earl of Abercorn purchased the estate of Duddingston, in the county of Edinburgh, which had passed by marriage from the Lauderdale to the Argyll family, and erected a mansion thereon at a cost of £30,000. In 1790 the ninth Earl was created a Marquis, and his grandson was in 1868 created a Duke. In addition to the above there are ten other Hamiltons, who own between them about 140,000 acres more, chiefly in Ireland and Scotland, and of most of whose acquisitions I have no doubt an equally satisfactory account may be given. I shall certainly be quite safe in affirming that nearly the whole of the 367,000 acres possessed by this fortunate clan has been at some time or other obtained by lavish grants from the Crown.

XCII.
The Nevilles.
(BRAYBROOKE BRANCH.)

IN dealing with the Russell, Manners, Paulet, Cecil, and other families, I have shown how largely their present prosperity is due to the confiscation of ecclesiastical property, at, or subsequent to, the Reformation; but many of the chief spoliators have no legitimate male descendants, and their shares of the plunder are now inherited by their descendants in the female line, who of course have other names, or have passed by bequest or inheritance to other families. There is a Lord Audley still, but he is not descended from the Chancellor of Henry VIII.; the inheritor of the greater part of Lord Chancellor Audley's lands is Lord Braybrooke. The barony is not quite 100 years old, but its possessor is descended from the great house of Neville. Lord Braybrooke owns in

Essex	9,684 acres.
Berks	3,590 ,,
Total	13,274 ,,

With a rentroll of £18,984.

His chief seat, at Audley End, near Saffron Walden, in Essex, is one of the finest mansions in the country. We have to consider how the land was obtained, and how the mansion was built.

Lord Chancellor Audley is fitly described by Lord Campbell as "a sordid slave," who further declares that "no eunuch in a seraglio was ever a more submissive tool to the caprice and vengeance of a passionate and remorseless master." This judgment is not at all an exaggerated one; his whole ignoble career is unrelieved by any touch of uprightness or manliness. He was born to poverty, and he rose to wealth and power by the basest means. His first places were earned by defending, in the House of Commons, the worst abuses of the Royal Prerogative, and supporting Wolsey's demand for extortionate subsidies. When Sir Thomas More was disgraced Audley was appointed Lord Keeper, and subsequently Lord Chancellor. This pliant, servile tool of tyranny never shrank from the basest deeds in order to please his master. It was he who presided at the shameful trial of More, and at the still more shameful trial of Bishop Fisher, in which his conduct as a judge was simply infamous. It was he, too, who presided at the trials of Queen Anne Boleyn and the Marquis of Exeter and Lord Montagu. It was he, too, who took an active part not only in the spoliation of the ecclesiastical houses, but in "the division of the plunder among those who planned the robbery." It was he, too, who was one of Henry's chief instruments in raising money by illegal expedients, the commissions being issued under the Great Seal; in short, he was a willing tool in executing all the worst measures of that evil reign. And he had his reward. His own repeated applications to Cromwell are still extant, his chief desire being to secure for himself the lands of the rich Abbey of Saffron Walden. He had sold himself to the devil apparently without remorse, and he was not slow in claiming whatever gain he could hope from the bargain. "I have," he writes, "in this world sustained great damage and infamy in serving the King's Highness, which this grant (Walden Abbey) shall recompense." He obtained his desire, and was also further rewarded with a priory at Aldgate, where he built a mansion, and with four or five other confiscated monastic houses. Thus the lands were gained.

Audley is mentioned by Sir Henry Spelman as one of the persons who were punished for sacrilege by having no male heirs. If the failure of male heirs is a mark of Divine displeasure, it is clear that not a few royal and noble houses must have been exceedingly wicked. Be that as it may, Audley left behind him only one daughter, who lived to mature years; and she married the unfortunate Duke of Norfolk who was beheaded for treason in the reign of Elizabeth. One could almost wish that Audley had lived long enough to see the daughter of the Queen upon whom he had pronounced sentence of death sign the death-warrant of his own daughter's husband. The eldest son of the marriage, Thomas Howard, was subsequently restored in blood, and inherited from his mother the Barony of Walden which had been obtained by Lord Chancellor Audley. One of his daughters married William Cecil, the first Earl of Salisbury; another the Earl of Essex, and subsequently Carr, Earl of Somerset, the favourite of James I. It is not at all surprising, then, to find that, soon after the accession of James, he was created Earl of Suffolk, and that he held for some years the lucrative post of Lord High Treasurer. In the first years of that reign he was Lord Chamberlain; and, in company with Lord Monteagle, who had received a warning of the Gunpowder Plot, he inspected the cellars beneath the Houses of Parliament, where he discovered Guy Fawkes, with his stores of gunpowder. After the fall of the favourite Somerset, whose connection with the Countess of Essex is known to every reader of English history, the Earl of Suffolk fell into disgrace. According to Rapin, his Countess "made no scruple of taking bribes with both hands." According to the same authority, "It was discovered that the Treasurer has converted to his own uses part of the money received for the cautionary towns from Holland." This was an old claim which we had upon the Dutch, which was settled by the payment of 2,728,000 florins, and eighteen years' interest. The Earl was fined £30,000, and sentenced to be imprisoned in the Tower during the King's pleasure. Whether the fine was paid I know not; but, after a short confinement, he was released. But, in the meantime, he had erected the magnificent mansion of Audley End, which he named after the Lord Chancellor, and which is said to have cost £190,000—an enormous sum in those days. Thus the house was built.

The third Earl of Suffolk sold the mansion and park to Charles II. for £50,000, two-fifths of the purchase money being allowed to stand over. After the Revolution of 1688 he was allowed to re-purchase it at the same price which he had actually received from Charles. This nobleman having no male heirs, the Earldom of Suffolk devolved upon his next brother. The Barony of Walden, which for a time fell into abeyance between his daughters and their heirs, is now held by the present Lord Howard de Walden, who is descended from his younger daughter. His elder daughter, however, married Lord Griffin of Braybrooke, in Northamptonsh re, and her descendant, John Griffin Whitwell, inherited her share of the Saffron Walden estates, and for his lifetime the Barony of Walden. He, having no issue, obtained during his lifetime a new patent of peerage as Lord Braybrooke, with remainder to his relative, Richard Aldworth Neville, of Billingbere, in Berkshire, who, after his death, became the second Lord Braybrooke.

These Nevilles are an offshoot of the Abergavenny Nevilles. I have been unable to discover how they obtained Billingbere, in Berks, which is still held by Lord Braybrooke. The first who is spoken of as possessed of it was Sir Henry Neville, who is several times mentioned by Burnet as a courtier in the latter part of the reign of Henry VIII., and, according to a MS. written by the father of Sir Thomas Overbury, he was a bastard son of that monarch. He married the daughter and heiress of Sir John Gresham, by whom he had a son, Sir Henry Neville, who narrowly escaped becoming a prominent statesman. That Sir Henry was employed by Elizabeth as Ambassador to France, but, being implicated in the conspiracy of Essex, he was fined £5,000, the penalty being rigorously exacted. In the following reign he filled some subordinate posts, and his further progress was retarded by the hostility of the favourite Carr.

The Richard Aldworth Neville before spoken of was the son of a Mr. Aldworth, by a Neville heiress, and assumed the maternal name. It is worth notice that the Lords Braybrooke are Hereditary Visitors of Magdalene College, Cambridge, and that younger sons of the second and third lord both became masters of the College. The first of these, the Rev. George Neville, was also Dean of Windsor and Chaplain in Ordinary to the Queen. Of his sons, one became Prebendary of Wells and Vicar of Butleigh, another Vicar of Wyrardisbury. The other, the Hon. and Rev. Latimer Neville, Master of Magdalene College, is also Vicar of Haydon (£681 and a house), a family living, and a Bishop's Chaplain. The third Lord Braybrooke is best known as the editor of "The Diary of Samuel Pepys."

XCIII.

The Butlers.

THE great House of Butler has for centuries played an important part in Irish history. At the present time there are no less than five Irish Peers who bear the name, four of whom are descended from one common Norman ancestor. These are the Marquis of Ormonde, the Earl of Carrick, Viscount Mountgarret, and Baron Dunboyne. The Marquis of Ormonde owns 31,873 acres in Kilkenny and Tipperary, with a rent-roll of £17,457; Viscount Mountgarret 14,823 acres, nearly all in Kilkenny, with a rent-roll of £9,090. The landed possessions of the other two appear to be but small.

The first of the family in Ireland was Theobald Walter, son of one of the followers of William the Conqueror, who accompanied Henry II. in his expedition to Ireland, and, after the partial conquest made by that monarch, became possessed of the Baronies of Upper and Lower Ormond and other territories. Henry II. also conferred upon him the office of Chief Butler of Ireland, on account of which the surname Butler was assumed by his son. The son married the heiress of another Norman Baron, John de Marisco, who brought him considerable additions to his estates. The next heir followed his father's example by marrying a De Burg heiress. From a younger son of the next heir Lord Dunboyne is descended. This heir, Theobald Butler, obtained from Edward I. a grant of the prizage of wines in Ireland towards the close of the thirteenth century. This grant was more or less in force down to 1810, or more than 500 years. How much the Butlers obtained from it during that period it is, of course, impossible to say; but in 1810 it was repurchased by the Crown for the sum of £216,000. This is certainly one of the most remarkable instances of the power of the dead hand on record in our history, especially as the head of the house was attainted, and his lands and dignities forfeited for treason, in 1715. But towards the close of last century it was decided by the House

The Butlers.

of Lords that no act of the English Legislature could affect Irish dignities, and this ancient grant of the "prizage" of wines was still held to stand. I suppose we must be thankful that, with such enormous powers of taxing posterity to all time, the kings of former centuries were considerate enough not to dispose of the whole of the fruits of our industry.

The next heir but one of the Butlers obtained the title of Earl of Carrick. The second Earl of Carrick, who received during his lifetime valuable grants from the Crown, was created Earl of Ormonde. The third Earl of Ormonde purchased of the Despencers the ancient castle of Kilkenny, which has since been the chief seat of the family. The fourth Earl, who, like several of the others, held the office of Lord Justice of Ireland, was one of the first Irish nobles to enrich himself from the Church, for he obtained a grant of lands of the See of Cashel for ten years after the death of the Archbishop. The next Earl, who was Lord-Lieutenant of Ireland and Lord High Treasurer of England, was beheaded by the victorious Yorkists after the Battle of Towton. His brother was attainted, but Edward IV. regranted him the title and estates. This nobleman had two daughters, one of whom was the mother of Queen Anne Boleyn. At his death without male issue, the next heir was compelled to forego the title in favour of Anne Boleyn's father, and, as a compensation, was created Earl of Ossory, but after his death, the rightful heir again resumed it. At the death of the tenth Earl the title passed to a grandson of the ninth, but Lord Dingwall, who had married the tenth Earl's daughter, contrived to secure the estates. The injustice was happily rectified by the marriage of Lord Dingwall's heiress with the twelfth Earl.

This nobleman, an ardent Royalist, was created Marquis of Ormonde soon after the outbreak of the Civil War in 1642, and at the Restoration he was elevated to a Dukedom. Macaulay speaks of him as the most illustrious of all the Cavaliers, who, though an ardent supporter of Monarchy, was no friend to Popery and arbitrary power. He was supposed to be one of the richest subjects in the kingdom, his income being £22,000 a-year, at a time when the average income of noblemen was but £3,000. The eldest son of the Duke, "the gallant Ossory," died in his father's lifetime, and the grandson therefore succeeded to the Dukedom. This young nobleman, who had fought at Sedgmoor, like Marlborough and others in high command, deserted James for William. He fought at the battle of the Boyne, and in the reign of Anne commanded the force which sank the Spanish galleons in Vigo Bay. In the latter part of the reign of Queen Anne it was proposed to bestow upon the Duke all the forfeited estates in Tipperary, but, this being objected to, another course was adopted. He happened to owe very large sums of money to persons whose estates had been forfeited, and the Crown had therefore become his creditor. The House of Commons actually made him a present of the whole of the debt, a proceeding which Macaulay rightly denounces as indefensible. In 1715 there were not a few nobles tainted with Jacobitism besides those actually engaged in the Rebellion. Chief among them were Oxford, Bolingbroke, and Ormonde. The impeachment of the latter was carried with some difficulty; but as, instead of standing his ground, he fled to France, there was less difficulty in following it up with an Act of Attainder. Soon after Ormonde made an unsuccessful attempt at rebellion by landing on the coast of Devon. He escaped once more, but, all his honours and estates being forfeited, he not only had to eat the exile's bitter bread, but to subsist on a pension from Spain, against whom he had formerly successfully fought. He left no heir; neither did his brother, the Earl of Arran. In 1791 Mr. John Butler, descendant from the eleventh Earl of Ormonde, was declared to be heir to the titles, except the Dukedom and Marquisate, on the grounds before mentioned. This nobleman married the heiress of the last Earl of Wandesford, who appears to have had some property in Kilkenny. His son obtained the title of Marquis, as did also his brother, who succeeded him.

There is another Butler in the Peerage of Ireland beside the four above-mentioned, viz., Butler-Danvers, Earl of Lanesborough, who owns in

Cavan	.	.	.	.	7,526 acres.
Fermanagh	.	.	.	.	6,119 ,,
Leicester .	.	.	.	.	1,854 ,,
				Total	15,499

With a rentroll of £15,297.

He is descended from the younger son of a Huntingdonshire squire, who settled in Ulster in the reign of James I. Sir

Stephen Butler was one of the "undertakers" who received from James a grant of a few thousand acres, to which he afterwards added by purchases. The chief seat of the family for a time was at Newtown Butler, afterwards at Belturbet, which town, returning two members to the Irish Parliament, gave to the Butlers a cheap, safe and regular seat. By the way, they appear to have sold their Parliamentary influence, shortly before the Act of Union, to the Earl of Belmore, who obtained £15,000 for his bargain. The Parliamentary influence of the Butlers, of course, obtained for them a good share of Irish offices; and the grandson of Sir Stephen Butler, in particular, held the Clerkship of the Pells and of the Court of Exchequer. In 1715 he was created Baron Newtown-Butler, and in 1728 his son was advanced a step in the Peerage, with the title of Viscount Lanesborough. The second Viscount was elevated to an Earldom. The second son of the second Earl, whose descendant now inherits the Lanesborough title and estates, married the daughter and heiress of Sir John Danvers, a Leicestershire baronet. The Danvers family had played an active part in politics. By successive marriages, Swithland, in Leicestershire, an estate valuable for its slate-quarries (Swith is an old Northern word for slate), had passed from its Norman possessors into the hands of the Danvers family. One of this house, the Earl of Danby, was an active Cavalier; another, Sir John Danvers, an equally active Parliamentarian. Fortunately for himself, Danvers the Regicide died before the Restoration; but, as it stands recorded on his tomb, his infant son was despoiled of estates in Oxfordshire and elsewhere amounting to £10,000 a year, and only Swithland was left to him. Swithland being bequeathed by the last Baronet to his daughter's husband. The Earls of Lanesborough have since borne the name of Butler-Danvers.

XCIV.
The Campbells.
(BREADALBANE AND CAWDOR BRANCHES.)

AN estate a hundred miles long cannot be passed by unnoticed. A man able to walk along a tract of his own land as lengthy as the distance between London and Warwick must have enormous power —power of depopulation and expatriation over a large number of people. And in the case before us that power has been exercised.

Although the Duke of Argyll is the head of the Campbells, the Earl of Breadalbane has an equal income, and more than double the number of acres. In Argyll alone he owns more land than the Duke, no less than 179,225 acres, and in Perth 193,504 acres—total, 372,729, with a rental of £49,931. The trustees of the late Marquis of Breadalbane also hold 65,629 acres in these two counties, rental £8,662.

These Campbells are descended from Colin, younger son of Sir Duncan Campbell of Lochow, upon whom his father settled the estate of Glenorchy, in Argyll. How Glenorchy came to the Campbells I cannot say with certainty. According to one account it was acquired by a marriage, according to another it was anciently held by the Chief of the McGregors, and was acquired by the Campbells either through confiscation or conquest. Somewhat later the King granted to Colin the Barony of Lawers. His second wife was a kinswoman, daughter and co-heir of Lord Lorne, through whom he acquired a third part of that lordship, which, as my readers will remember, had been legitimately obtained by a previous marriage. One of his descendants, who was created a baronet by James VI., also was made by that monarch hereditary keeper of the forests of Mamlorn, Bendaskerlie, &c. The third baronet, Laird of Glenfalloch, married the daughter of Sir Lachlan Mackintosh, captain of the Clan Chattan. The fifth baronet, being chief creditor of the Earl of Caithness, obtained a disposition of his whole titles and estates, and at his death was created Earl of Caithness; but, it having been decided that the dignity in question belonged to the rightful heir, he obtained, in 1681, the title of Earl of Breadalbane. At the death of the third Earl in 1782 the title and estates passed to a distant kinsman, who was subsequently created Marquis of Breadalbane. At the death of his son the Marquisate expired, and the Earldom and estates passed to another distant kinsman.

Let us look at the manner in which the Campbells of Breadalbane have treated their hundred-mile-long estate. In the Statistical Account of Scotland I find allusions to the depopulation of the lands to convert them into sheep farms, but, of course, in cautious and guarded terms. About five-and-twenty years ago, however, a Perthshire laird with whom I am personally acquainted, wrote a book on "The Barriers to the National Prosperity of Scotland," in which passing reference was made to the Breadalbane evictions. The second Marquis of Breadalbane wrote a lame answer in a local paper, which happily provoked from his antagonist a more detailed statement, in regard to which no answer at all appeared. The principal facts therein brought out I now repeat. As late as 1793 the Breadalbane estates furnished 1,600 soldiers; sixty years after they could not have produced more than 150. At a time when the highest military authorities express their regret as to the number of boys we have to send into the field, we may well lament the loss of those stalwart Highlanders, whose forefathers so freely shed their blood in fighting the battles of England. But Mr. Alister goes into detail. He states that in Glenqueich, where the same families had been tenants for 400 years, almost all were swept away, the 60 families having been reduced to four or five; that the 40 or 50 families inhabiting the braes of Taymouth and Tullochyoule were all expatriated; that in Glenetive, where were formerly 16 tenants, not one was left; that in the island of Ling 25 families had given place to one; that the population of Glenorchy had been reduced by one half; that in three other places, which formerly were tenanted by 50 families in all, only one family was left; and that several other "toons" had been cleared of from 10 to 14 families each. In twenty years from 1834 no less than 500 families had been cleared off the soil. He further states that the land in front of Kenmore, the land around Drummond Hill, and Black Mount had all been converted into deer forests. The latter alone contained nearly 100,000 acres of fine pasture-land capable of grazing 70,000 sheep, instead of the 3,000 which were there on a portion of it. Well might Sir Walter Scott write: "In too many cases the Highlands have been drained, not of their superfluity of population, but of the whole mass of the inhabitants, dispossessed by an unrelenting avarice, which will be one day found to have been as short-sighted as it is unjust and selfish." Of the selfishness of the policy which drove men out to make room for sheep and deer there can be no question; of its injustice I have already spoken when dealing with the Leveson-Gowers. The ancestors of these poor people had been living industrious lives in these glens for ages; it was only by what Mr. Hill Burton calls "iniquitous legal jugglery," that the lords obtained the right to dispossess them. Their expatriation was spoliation of the worst kind. Their descendants in the American Glenorchy, which was named after the old home, might well say with Nicol,

> "We sow the corn and hold the plough,
> We all work for our living;
> We gather nought but what we've sown,
> All else we reckon thieving."

The lords of Breadalbane held a different opinion. By the way, I presume that the rentals furnished for the Landowners' Return do not include the rent of deer forests, but it would be desirable that the matter should be made clear by those who are able to give definite information.

The Earl of Cawdor is descended from a cadet of the great house of Campbell. The property he possesses has been acquired by successive fortunate marriages. He owns in

Nairn	46,176 acres.
Carmarthen	33,782 ,,
Pembroke	17,935 ,,
Inverness	3,943 ,,
Cardigan	21 ,,
Total	101,857

With a rentroll of £44,644.

A younger son of the Earl of Argyll married the daughter and heiress of Sir John Calder of Calder, or Cawdor, in

The Campbells.

Nairnshire. At Cawdor Castle they used to show the very room in which King Duncan was murdered. Considering that Duncan was not murdered at all, and that the Castle was not built till some hundreds of years after his death, this must have been a valuable relic of antiquity. They even showed the bed on which the King slept, but unfortunately that was burned. Later, one of these Campbells married the sister and heiress of Sir Gilbert Lort, of Stackpole Court, Pembrokeshire. It is uncertain how the Lorts acquired the estate. The eldest son of this marriage contracted an alliance with another Welsh heiress, Mary Pryse. His grandson was created Baron Cawdor, and the second Baron obtained an Earldom.

The Earl of Cawdor is one of those Welsh Tory landowners who, in virtue of the acres they possess, have hitherto managed to secure, in several of the Welsh Counties, Members who vote in direct opposition to the principles of the majority of the voters. His eldest son is one of the two Tory Members for Carmarthenshire, and Pembrokeshire also returns a Tory Member. The county voters of these two counties are just as Liberal as the borough voters. The only difference is that the screw cannot be used in the boroughs as in the counties. If voting was absolutely free, and no canvassing was allowed, the landlords know full well that in all Wales no Tory candidate would have a chance. Under such circumstances, I, for one, should have no more scruple in promising to vote one way and voting another, than in breaking a promise not to prosecute a burglar when it was made with a pistol at my head.

It is worthy of notice that there are no less than twenty-eight other Campbells, each owning 5,000 acres and upwards, for the most part in Scotland—the total amount being 538,861 acres. The Campbells, therefore, hold between them no less than 1,253,989 acres. At the time of the passing of the first Reform Bill, sixteen Campbell placemen and pensioners divided £24,000 between them annually.

XCV.

The St. Maurs.

THE Duke of Somerset stands next in order of precedence to the Duke of Norfolk, his title dating as far back as 1547, but he possesses but a fragment of the great domains acquired by the first holder of the title, the Protector Somerset. In modern times the family have reverted to the ancient manner of spelling their name, derived either from St. Maur in France, or from a place once called St. Maur, in Monmouthshire. However, as history knows them as Seymours, it will be more convenient to use the latter name only.

As I have previously stated when sketching the history of the Hereford branch of the house, the Seymours were a Norman family of no great note, who were anciently settled at Undy or Woundy, in Monmouth. By two advantageous marriages with an heiress of the great house of Beauchamp and with an heiress of the Sturmys of Wiltshire, their fortunes were greatly improved. As a result of the latter marriage Wiltshire became their home. In the reign of Henry VIII., John Seymour, having suppressed a Cornish insurrection, and having served in the French wars, was knighted by the King, who afterwards married his daughter Jane, mother of Edward VI. One of his younger sons, afterwards Lord Seymour of Sudeley, married Henry's widow, Queen Katharine Parr. Sir John's eldest son was created Viscount Beauchamp and Earl of Hertford by Henry. From the same Monarch he also received large grants of land. At Henry's death he, having been appointed one of the King's executors, seized the reins of Government, and was appointed—we might almost say appointed himself—Lord Treasurer of England. He next created himself Duke of Somerset and Protector and Governor of the young King, with a salary of 9,000 marks per annum. A little later Edward VI. was made to settle upon him lands of the value of £500 a-year. He obtained numerous grants beside, amongst others the episcopal palace at Wells, and certain lands belonging to that See, and Covent Garden, which was afterwards granted to the Russells. Somerset House still marks the spot where he commenced building a palace for himself, with practices which showed contempt alike for the rights of the Church or of private property, or even for the graves of the dead. Though rapacious himself, his fall was mainly occasioned by his efforts to save the common people from the rapacity of the new nobility. The extent of his possessions may be to some extent gathered from the fact that, though at his fall he was fined £2,000 a-year of land, yet he had subsequently licence granted to him to retain two hundred persons in his service, beside household servants. Much of his property was confiscated, but a portion was restored, and, in regard to a part of the rest, an exchange with the Crown was effected by which he acquired a considerable estate at Glastonbury, in Somerset. On attempting to regain his lost power he was arrested, condemned, and beheaded, much to the grief of the common people, whose gratitude he had fairly earned.

The Protector Somerset had obtained his patent of peerage, with remainder to the children of the second marriage, he having repudiated his first wife on account of her alleged incest with her own father, but his honours became forfeited at his execution. The eldest son of his second marriage was, however, created Earl of Hertford by Queen Elizabeth. This unfortunate nobleman, having secretly married the sister of Lady Jane Grey (a lady of Royal blood), was immured for nine years in the Tower, and fined £15,000. His grandson was almost equally unfortunate in matrimony, for, having privately married Lady Arabella Stuart, he had to fly the kingdom to avoid the wrath of James I. At the outbreak of the Civil War, after some indecision, he took the Royalist side, and at the Restoration was rewarded by obtaining the reversal of the attainder of the first Duke in his favour. He only enjoyed the Dukedom but a few months, and left two grandsons, each of whom in turn succeeded him, but died without issue. He left also a granddaughter, by whose marriage with the Earl of Ailesbury the great estates of Savernake Forest and Tottenham Park were carried out of the family.

The title and remaining estates then devolved upon a cousin of the last Duke, who, having been assassinated in Italy, was succeeded by his brother, "the proud Duke of Somerset, and founder of the celebrated Kit Cat Club, who married the heiress of the Percies. Whatever his faults, it must be admitted that he twice rendered distinguished services to the nation. At the Revolution of 1688, and at the Accession of the House of Hanover, his great influence was thrown into the scale of Constitutional Government. When Queen Anne died, his attendance at the Privy Council, unsummoned, at the critical moment, contributed largely to the discomfiture of the Jacobite Tories, who desired to restore the Stuarts. His son, who succeeded him, left a daughter, who carried the vast estates of the Percies to the Smithsons on her marriage; but, the male line of the Protector Somerset's second marriage having failed, the ducal title was claimed by the eldest male descendant of the first marriage.

This branch of the family was seated at Berry Pomeroy, in Devonshire, an estate which the Protector Somerset had acquired by purchase in the early days of his prosperity, and had settled upon one of his sons by his first wife. After the Protector's attainder, Edward Seymour had also obtained from the Crown certain of his father's forfeited lands in Somersetshire. The Seymours of Berry Pomeroy, during the Civil War, were staunch Royalists, and suffered considerably in the cause, their mansion at that place having been destroyed. The Sir Edward Seymour of the Restoration was a man who possessed the ancestral pride which characterised the Seymours. When he was first presented to William III., that Monarch happened to remark that he believed Sir Edward was of the Duke of Somerset's family, whereupon the proud commoner corrected the King by informing him that the Duke was of his (Sir Edward's) family. He was for a time Speaker of the House of Commons, and, proud as he was, yet did not scruple to take bribes from the East India Company under the guise of a contract for saltpetre. His character is summed up by Macaulay in one short sentence—"He was licentious, profane, corrupt, too proud to behave with common politeness, yet not too proud to pocket illicit gain." It was the grandson of this Sir Edward who succeeded to the Dukedom, and who also obtained a lucrative sinecure. The subsequent history of the Dukes of Somerset is uneventful.

The present Duke owns in

Devon	8,138	acres.
Somerset	6,553	,,
Wilts	5,824	,,
Lincoln	2,685	,,
Bucks	1,640	,,
Elsewhere	367	,,
Total	25,207	,,

With a rentroll of £37,580.

The derivation of the Devonshire and Somersetshire property has been already sufficiently indicated. As to Wiltshire, the Manor of Maiden Bradley, where the Dukes of Somerset have long had a seat, was formerly monastic property, and was granted by Henry VIII. to the first Duke. The ninth Duke, who died in 1792, and who held the title and estates for thirty-five years, was a wretched miser, whose parsimony seems to have greatly conduced to the prosperity of his house, for between 1783 and 1803 I find that the Wiltshire estates were greatly enlarged by the purchase of lands at Deptford Tithing, Bathampton, Knook, Hill Deverill, and Fisherton-de-la-Mere, all in the same county.

Bulstrode-park, near Gerrard's Cross, in Bucks, consisting of 800 acres, with lands adjoining, was purchased of the Bulstrodes by that eminent Tory Judge, Jeffreys, who rebuilt, or greatly enlarged, the mansion. It was subsequently sold by the son-in-law of Jeffreys to the Duke of Portland, from whom it was purchased by one of the Dukes of Somerset.

The present Duke of Somerset, who was formerly First Lord of the Admiralty in a Liberal Administration, and who is the author of a theological work with freethought tendencies, has survived both his sons. The younger died in India from the effects of an encounter with a tiger; the elder, who was a Volunteer under Garibaldi, died in 1869.

XCVI.

The Sidneys.

THE De L'Isle and Dudley Peerage only dates from 1835, but its holder has a right to rank among "Our Old Nobility," as being the representative of one of the most distinguished and popular families in England. Its patronymic has become a common Christian name. One of its members has become renowned as the Bayard of England; another has had his memory enshrined in the celebrated toast of the Whig Party, and in one of the most stirring of Campbell's shorter poems. Lord De L'Isle and Dudley not only bears the honoured name of Sidney, but is the owner of the ancestral mansion, around which are clustered so many names dear to poetry and history.

The County of Kent can boast of "many an ancient hall," but of none equal in interest to Penshurst. Knole, Leeds Castle, Ightham Moat, must all yield the palm to the mansion of the Sidneys. Bedford and Gloucester; the ill-starred Stafford-Buckinghams; the Sidney of Flodden; the Sidney who was Elizabeth's Lord Deputy in Ireland; Sir Philip and his friend Edmund Spenser; "Sidney's sister, Pembroke's mother," and the Countess of Sussex who founded Sidney-Sussex College, Cambridge; Waller and his Sacharissa; and last, not least, that stout Republican, Colonel Algernon Sidney, are all more or less associated with the stately house at Penshurst. The mansion on certain days is open to the inspection of the public; were it not so, the exterior and the village itself would be well worth a visit. I was particularly struck with the air of comfort which seemed to pervade the place, and the good taste with which the more modern houses had been erected, in keeping with the stately mansion hard by. Though knowing many of the villages of England, and of Kent in particular, I should find it hard to name one whose exterior is so satisfactory to a stranger's eye as Penshurst. Whether it is, like some others I know, a show village, which has to be considered in contrast with the remainder of the estate, I know not. I simply speak of it as I saw it.

The Manor of Penshurst was purchased by the Duke of Bedford, one of the younger sons of Henry IV. This Duke, and the Duke of Gloucester, his brother, who inherited it, both died without issue, and it passed to Henry VI., as next heir. By this monarch it was granted to Stafford, Duke of Buckingham, whose grandson was beheaded by Richard III. His son succeeded to the estates, but became one of the earliest victims of Henry VIII., when Penshurst reverted to the Crown. Edward VI. bestowed it on Sir Ralph Vane; and, after his execution, re-granted it to Sir William Sidney.

The Sidneys are a family of Angevin extraction, whose ancestors came over with Henry II. Sir William, who had been Steward of the Household of Henry VIII., and who afterwards was one of the English commanders at Flodden, had a grant from Edward, as an inscription on the house itself records, of "Pencester, with the manors, lands, and appurtenances thereto belonging." His son and heir, Sir Henry Sidney, who obtained from Elizabeth a grant of the advowson of Penshurst, was Lord Deputy of Ireland, and played a prominent part in the Irish Wars of her long and eventful reign. Sir Philip, the son of Sir Henry, who fell on the field of Zutphen in the lifetime of his father, was the friend and patron of Spenser; and there is a tradition that the author of "The Faerie Queen" sojourned for a time at Penshurst, and there wrote his early poem, "The Shepherd's Calendar." At Sir Henry's death, his eldest surviving son succeeded him, and was successively created Baron Sidney, Viscount De L'Isle, and Earl of Leicester, by James I. The Earldom of Leicester had been held by several great families—the Bellamonts, De Montforts, the Dudleys. Elizabeth's Earl of Leicester was the last of the Dudleys who held it; but the wife of Sir Henry Sidney was the eldest daughter of Dudley, Duke of Northumberland. The reader will see at once that, in the modern Peerage, an old title and an old family alliance have been kept in view.

The second Earl of Leicester of the new line was father, beside his successor, of "little Sid for simile renowned," of. the patriot Algernon Sidney, and of Dorothy, afterwards Countess of Sunderland (the Sacharissa of Waller's poems).

In earlier days Ben Jonson, alluding to Sir Philip, had sung of
> "That taller tree which of a nut was set
> At his great birth, when all the Muses met."

A tree, by the way, which no longer exists. But we may still wander in "the sacred shade" of "the lofty beeches" which Waller immortalised in verse when he vainly paid his court to the proud beauties whom he called Sacharissa and Amoret.

The seventh Earl died apparently without legitimate issue, and left his estates to a natural daughter. The result was prolonged litigation, which was terminated by a compromise. The daughter in question obtained an allowance, and the estates were divided between the daughters and co-heiresses of the third son of the fourth Earl. The park at Penshurst was then curtailed to less than half its former dimensions.

The daughter of one of these ladies was the second wife of Sir Bysshe Shelley, Bart., and she became the owner of Penshurst. Another attempt was made to wrest the estates from the Shelley-Sidneys. The wife of the seventh Earl of Leicester, from whom he was never divorced, although they had long been separated, appears to have had a son, who sought to gain Penshurst by an action at law, but failed.

The Shelleys are an ancient Kentish family, whose name is derived from a manor in that county. They formerly held Hall Place, in Kent, now the seat of Mr. Samuel Morley, M.P. John Shelley, who married a Sussex heiress, and who died in 1526, had three sons, from the eldest of whom was descended Sir John Shelley, Bart., who a few years ago was one of the Members for Westminster. From the second is descended Sir Percy Shelley of Castle Goring, Sussex, and Lord De L'Isle and Dudley. As before stated, a Sidney heiress was the second wife of Sir Bysshe Shelley. By his first wife Sir Bysshe had a son, Percy Bysshe Shelley, the poet, whose son by his [wife Mary Wollstoncroft Godwin, is the present holder of the baronetage. By his second wife Sir Bysshe had a son, Sir John Shelley Sidney, who inherited the Sidney estates, and whose son was created Lord De L'Isle and Dudley in 1835. It looks as though the peerage was due to his matrimonial connections, for in 1825 he married Lady Sophia Fitzclarence, and his peerage was obtained when his father-in-law was King. Be this as it may, the sternest

Republican will hardly complain that the illustrious house of Sidney is still represented in the Peerage of England. As the present Lord is the son of the Fitzclarence marriage, he can boast not merely that he has Royal blood in his veins, but that he had a King of England for grandfather.

Lord De L'Isle and Dudley owns in

Kent	4,356 acres.
Yorkshire	4,896 ,,
Total	9,252 ,,

The Yorkshire estates appear to have been derived by his marriage with the only child of the late Sir William Foulis, Baronet, of Ingleby Manor, in Cleveland. The baronetcy was obtained by Sir David Foulis, one of the Scotch favourites of James I., who became in succession Cofferer to Prince Henry and Prince Charles, and held divers other appointments. His emoluments as a courtier enabled him to purchase Ingleby, an ancient baronial seat. In 1633 he became a victim to the tyranny of Strafford, and for speaking plainly concerning the illegal exactions of that Minister he was haled before the Court of Star Chamber, was deprived of all his offices, committed to the Fleet, and fined £5,000 to the King and £3,000 to Strafford. To defray these ruinous fines he was compelled to sell a portion of his estate. The son of Sir David, at the same time, was also committed to the Fleet, and fined £500. The subsequent history of the Foulis family has been uneventful.

The connection of the Sidneys with English history, that is from the day when Sir William fought at Flodden to the day when Algernon died upon the scaffold, only occupies a space of about 170 years; since that time the ancient energy seems to have died out. We might spare, perhaps, the memory of "Flodden's fatal hill," and of the fierce rigour of Lord Deputy Sidney's government of Ireland; but we could ill spare from our national annals the pathetic story of the field of Zutphen, and the stoical fortitude with which Algernon met a not less glorious death. At the same time, we cannot forget that it was as courtiers the Sidneys gained their possessions. On the gateway at Penshurst, in the records of the Foulis family, in the date of the modern peerage, the same fact is recorded.·

It remains only to be added that Lord Lisle, the defendant in the Brompton County Court case, who is said to have set up his privileges as a Peer when sued for a paltry coal merchant's bill, is not in any way related to the Sidneys. He is an Irish peer, whose family name is Lysaght, and whose ancestors distinguished themselves in the Irish wars of 1641 and 1699. This nobleman is, or rather was, owner of 10,376 acres in the counties of Cork and Tipperary, with a rent-roll of £6,558. A "Friend of the Family" says that he is an upright and honourable man, though the victim of most adverse circumstances, and that, through the extravagance of his predecessors and the unavoidable expenses of Chancery, he finds himself, as an old man, penniless, having even sold his life interest in all his property for the benefit of his creditors. I am sorry for his misfortunes, but as he has several grown-up sons he ought not to be left destitute. As for the coal bill, a penny subscription among all the Peers would suffice.

XCVII.
The Fitzgeralds.

O family has occupied a more prominent place in the history of Ireland than the Geraldines. Until it pleased Disraeli to reward the faithful support of the Abercorn Hamiltons with a dukedom, the Duke of Leinster was Ireland's only Duke. One of his ancestors was created Baron of Offaley in 1205, and another Earl of Kildare in 1316. The dukedom dates from 1766. Its present holder is the twenty-seventh Baron and twenty-second Earl. It so happens, too, that by marriage a cadet of the house of Fitzgerald acquired the ancient English barony of De Ros—the baronies of De Ros and Le Despencer, the two of the oldest English peerages, dating from 1264. The Duke owns in—

Kildare	. . . . .	70,462 acres.
Meath	. . . . .	1,119 ,,
	Total	71,581 ,,

With a rentroll of £48,841.

His family motto is "Crom a boo"—Crom (the ancient seat of the house) to victory. His crest, singularly enough, is a monkey, said to be derived from an old tradition that an heir of the house, when an infant, was carried to the top of the castle and brought safely down by a baboon.

The Fitzgeralds profess to be descended from a Florentine family, one of whom settled in Normandy, and thence passed over to England, where he became one of the favourites of Edward the Confessor. The Norman Conquest was rather favourable to their fortunes than otherwise. Maurice, the great grandson of the original settler in England, in the reign of Henry II., went on an expedition to Ireland, in which he was afterwards joined by Strongbow. The conquest then made laid the foundation of the Geraldines as a great Irish house. Maurice, brother of the ancestor of the Fitzmaurices, obtained as his share of the plunder the Baronies of Offaley and Wicklow, and other estates, including Maynooth. The son of Maurice, who built the Castles of Armagh and Athlone, was created Baron Offaley, and appointed Lord Justice of Ireland. One might almost say that the history of this powerful family is the history of Ireland for several centuries. Successively they held the highest judicial and other offices, and down to the reign of Elizabeth they did more to extend and consolidate the rule of English Kings in the sister island than any other noble house. In the almost incessant rebellions that occurred the Geraldines were constantly at the front whenever there was any fighting to be done. Parenthetically I may here note that the son of the sixth Lord Offaley had two sons, the younger of whom was created Earl of Desmond. Both these branches of the Geraldines from time to time augmented their fortunes by matrimonial alliances, but the Earls of Desmond for a time seem to have eclipsed the elder branch. Like other of the Norman-Irish nobility, they seem in process of time to have become thoroughly Irish, and were followed with passionate loyalty by the people. In the reign of Elizabeth the sixteenth Earl of Desmond was half dragged, half goaded into rebellion. Being defeated, he became a hunted fugitive, and was slain; his head was sent to London, and his vast estates, 110 miles in length, and comprising nearly 600,000 acres, the greater part of four counties, were confiscated. My business, however, is more particularly with the Kildare branch of the Geraldines.

It is impossible to compress within a reasonable compass an outline of their eventful history; I can but glance at the principal facts. The sixth Lord Offaley had a deadly quarrel with Lord de Vesci in 1291, who at that time held the government of that part of Ireland which was subject to the English King. The result was that both were summoned to England, where the cause was heard by Edward I. According to the illogical fashion of those times, Offaley challenged his antagonist to single combat. De Vesci accepted the challenge, but before the appointed day he absconded to France, and the King thereupon conferred De Vesci's lordships and manors of Kildare, Rathangan, &c., upon Offaley, who, in the following reign, was advanced to the Earldom of Kildare. For a lengthened period the Fitzgeralds appear to have been almost continuously occupied in governing Ireland, in waging war upon the chieftains beyond the Pale, and in carrying on private conflicts with the Butlers and other great houses. Their fortunes were further advanced by fresh grants from the Crown, and by marriages with various Irish heiresses.

Within a hundred years from the accession of Edward IV. the Earls of Kildare had several very narrow escapes from total ruin. In 1467 the Earl of Kildare was attainted at the same time as the Earl of Desmond. Desmond was executed, but Kildare was pardoned, and his estates restored. In the reign of Henry VII. the Earl of Kildare, then Lord Deputy, with his brother, who was Lord Chancellor, was deceived by the impostor, Lambert Simnel, and assisted at his coronation at Dublin. The Chancellor fell in the fight in which Simnel's forces were routed, but Kildare was fortunate enough to have his rebellion condoned by Henry VII. In the following reign another Earl of Kildare was accused of disloyalty and incarcerated in the Tower of London by Henry VIII. His eldest son, Lord Thomas, broke out into open revolt, and waged for a time an unsuccessful war, in which his Castles of Maynooth and Rathangan were besieged and taken. Ultimately he and his uncles were compelled to surrender, and were afterwards executed, the old Earl having in the meantime died in captivity. By the act of attainder which followed, all the Kildare estates were forfeited, but the next eldest son to Lord Thomas, having introduced himself at the Court of Edward VI., was fortunate enough to obtain the restoration of the lordships and manors of Maynooth, Moylaugh, Rathangan, Portlester (which was originally obtained by the marriage of the eighth Earl with the heiress of Lord Portlester), Kilkea, &c. He continued in favour with Mary, who not only restored to him his father's earldom, and all such honours, castles, and manors, which the Crown still retained of the confiscated property, but also conferred upon him lands, chiefly ecclesiastical, in Down, Meath, Westmeath, Dublin, Kildare, and Louth. Again in 1580 the Geraldines were in great peril. The Earl of Kildare's loyalty being suspected by Elizabeth, he was imprisoned and his estates seized. Subsequently he was liberated and his property restored. At the Revolution of 1688 the Fitzgeralds were fortunate enough to take the winning side, and contributed in a large degree to the triumph of William III. The nineteenth Earl, who was a prominent statesman in the reigns of Anne, George I., and George II., purchased Carton House, Kildare, which was formerly the seat of the Ingoldsby family. He greatly improved this mansion, which now extends 400 feet from wing to wing, and is the chief seat of the Duke of Leinster. His son, the twentieth Earl, distinguished himself by addressing a memorial to George II., denouncing Stone, the Irish Primate, as "a greedy Churchman, investing himself with temporal power, and affecting to be a second Wolsey in the State." "Your memorialist," he concluded, "has nothing to ask of your Majesty, neither place, civil or military, neither employment or preferment for himself or his friends; and begs leave to add that nothing but his duty to your Majesty, and his natural hatred to such detestable monopoly, could have induced your memorialist to this presumption." This Earl was subsequently elevated to the Dukedom of Leinster. One of his younger sons was the brave and unfortunate Lord Edward Fitzgerald, whom Cobbett (himself once a common soldier) described as the only really honest officer he ever knew. Lord Edward, who had previously served with credit in the British Army, became deeply imbued with the spirit which animated the French Revolution of 1789, the result being that he was engaged in revolutionary movements in Ireland. When arrested he made a desperate resistance, in which he killed an officer, and was himself fatally wounded.

The Fitzgeralds have been almost uniformly faithful to their generous and liberal traditions, and their conduct has generally manifested their deep attachment to the interests of the race with which they have been for so many centuries connected. Of late they seem to have receded somewhat from the prominent position they once occupied; but there are few great Irish houses upon which rests so little odium.

XCVIII.

The Molyneux.

TO obtain another conspicuous case of the unearned increase of the rent of land we cannot do better than turn to Lancashire. We have already seen what it has done for the Stanleys; let us glance at their neighbours, once their rivals in Liverpool, the Molyneux family. Their wealth has advanced by leaps and bounds with the prosperity of Lancashire, and they have but very narrowly missed being to Liverpool what the Duke of Westminster is to Westminster, or the Marquis of Bute to Cardiff, or the Duke of Norfolk to Sheffield. As it is, the Earl of Sefton owns in Lancashire 18,769 acres, with a rent-roll of £42,997—these figures being probably but an inadequate representation of his actual income, and no representation at all of his prospective wealth. Our most powerful landowners have one foot upon the country and the other upon the town. The rural squire will feel terribly the pinch of agricultural distress. To him a fall in rents means a great deal more than a nominal 10 or 20 per cent. Mortgages and any family burdens with which the land may be charged are a fixed quantity. The 10 or 20 per cent. reduction falls in its entirety upon the nominal owner, after he has paid all other claims. Commercial depression falls but lightly on the landlords, who draw most of their wealth from great towns. The rents of their leaseholds are secure, or, at worst, they can seize upon valuable property which neither they nor their fathers built.

The first Molyneux came over at the Conquest, his name appearing eighteenth on the roll of Battle Abbey. My readers will consequently be prepared to learn that the Molyneux family have obtained everything they possess for nothing at all. A grant made by one of the chief followers of the Conqueror, and other grants made by Yorkist and Lancastrian Kings, have given them the right to all time to take tithe and toll of the industry of South-West Lancashire, always bearing in mind that the feudal obligations under which these grants were held have been shifted on to the shoulders of the general body of the people. When I think of the burdens which the land bore for ages; of the easy terms on which it was obtained by those who were eager to acquire it subject to those burdens; of the immense growth in the value of land, especially urban land, due alone to the industry and enterprise of the common people—I am lost in astonishment to find rational men listening to the absurd nonsense of those who complain of the unfair burdens put upon the land.

To return to the Molyneux. William de Molines came over with the Conqueror. He is said to have been a Norman noble, who derived his name from the town of Moulins. Considering that William I. was accompanied by half the scum of Europe it is as likely as not that he was no noble at all. However, William De Molines, or his son Vivian, obtained a grant of land from De Poictou, Lord of Lancaster, to whom William I. had granted all the lands between the Ribble and the Mersey. The De Molines grant consisted of Sefton and two other manors, one of which passed to another family by marriage. Sefton Manor has been held in unbroken succession by the Molyneux family ever since the Conquest. Toxteth, however, was exchanged by them for other lands in the reign of King John. We shall see that it afterwards again came into their possession. In process of time their estates were somewhat augmented by successive marriages with Lancashire heiresses.

In the days of the Lancastrian and Yorkist kings Liverpool was beginning to acquire some little importance, and between the Stanleys and the Molyneux there was a rivalry which at times almost broke out into private war. Sir Richard Molyneux was with Henry V. at Agincourt, and from that King he obtained a grant of the Chief Forestership of the Royal Forests and Parks in West Derby, and the office of Constable of Liverpool Castle. The Stanleys, however, managed to obtain Toxteth-park from the Crown. After a time that property was sold by an Earl of Derby to the head of the Molyneux family for £1,100. It consisted of 2,000 acres. It is now covered with villas, houses, factories, and docks, and has a population of more than 70,000 persons.

With the office of Governor of Liverpool Castle, a building

which was partially demolished in the Civil War, and entirely removed in 1721, Sir Richard Molyneux had a salary equal to £100 of our money. By a subsequent grant the office was made hereditary in his family. Sir Richard afterwards held an office in the Court of Henry VI., and from that monarch he obtained a grant of Croxteth, near Liverpool, to him and his heirs. This was confirmed by Edward IV., and the herbage and agistment of Croxteth-park was given to the Molyneux for an annual rent of £100. An Act of Resumption was passed in the latter part of the reign of Henry VI., but the son of Sir Richard was able to obtain the insertion of a clause therein providing that it should not apply to the Molyneux grants. Richard III. confirmed them in their possessions, but the accession of Henry VII. still further advanced their fortunes. That King let Croxteth and Simmonds' Wood to William Molyneux for a perpetual rent of £16 per annum (equal to £100 of our money). They were then mere wastes. Croxteth has long been the seat of the family. It is interesting to note what was the value of property in Liverpool itself about this time. In the reign of Henry VIII. the Corporation of Liverpool demised to Sir William Molyneux a parcel of building land in the town at a rent of sixpence per acre, and as late as 1565 a house in the town let for four shillings per annum, and ten other houses were sold outright for £10.

The Molyneux were for some time lessees of the Crown customs and dues, Liverpool being Royal property. In the reign of Mary, Sir R. Molyneux, being a zealous Catholic, obtained a renewal of the lease for 44 years. The Corporation of Liverpool, which had been growing in strength and independence, threw his collector into prison; but, after an ineffectual struggle, it had to give way. In the reign of Henry VIII. a Molyneux, who was a Royal Commissioner, had become acquainted with the extent of the Crown Rights, and this knowledge seems to have been kept in remembrance by the family for a favourable opportunity. At the accession of James I. Sir Richard Molyneux was created a baronet; and Charles I. created his son an Irish Viscount.

When Charles had got into almost inextricable financial difficulties through attempting to govern without a Parliament, he determined to clear off his liabilities to the City of London by a wholesale alienation of nearly three hundred manors and estates belonging to the Crown. Included among these was the lordship of Liverpool. The trustees on behalf of the City were, of course, anxious to realise, and the year 1635 was a fine time for land jobbers. The lordship of Liverpool was purchased by Lord Molyneux for the trifling sum of £450, though this did not include the payment to the Crown of a fixed sum of £14 6s. 8d., which was also bought up by Lord Molyneux. The second Viscount was an ardent Royalist, and took an active part in the storming of Liverpool by Prince Rupert; he afterwards fought at Worcester, and, dying soon after, was succeeded by his brother, also a Royalist, who had to redeem his estates by the payment of a heavy fine.

Soon after the Restoration this nobleman began to assert some of the ancient Crown rights which had been so recently purchased. The Corporation of Liverpool, however, contended that these alleged rights belonged to them, and not to Lord Molyneux. His lordship contended that the purchase included all the waste lands within the borough, and he put his views into practice by commencing to build on what he called Lord Molyneux Street, now Lord Street, and by proceeding to erect a bridge at the end of it. The Corporation *vi et armis* stopped the builders, and Lord Molyneux then commenced an action against them. Ultimately a compromise was agreed upon, by which his lordship agreed to grant a lease of the property for a thousand years to the Corporation, at a fixed annual rental of £30. That property consisted of 1,000 acres of building land, which was worth £50,000 a year half a century ago, and probably is worth now double that amount.

This example of the unearned increase of the rent of urban land is one of the most striking that I know. Had not the municipal authorities of Liverpool in the reign of Charles II. been enlightened and able men, they would have allowed Lord Molyneux to have his own way. The whole story is most instructive. A tyrant King, in order to enable himself to govern without a Parliament, conveys away nearly 300 of the manors and estates which were intended to keep up the dignity and power of the Monarchy. The City of London, being anxious to realise, flood the market, and land and feudal privileges are to be bought up at ridiculously low prices. Among the properties sold is the lordship of Liverpool, which is obtained by a Molyneux for £450. This occurs less than 250 years ago. Half a century after, Lord Molyneux, finding his claims disputed, lets the waste lands in the borough of Liverpool on what is practically a perpetual lease, for the fixed rent of £30 per annum. These lands consist of 1,000 acres, and are now worth nearly £100,000 a year.

Suppose that Lord Molyneux had granted no lease, but had established his rights in a law court. What would he or his descendants have done to give value to that which then was comparatively worthless? They would have done absolutely nothing except sign their names to leases. And thus that which was only a part of the property of which £450 was the purchase money would have grown in value to £100,000 a year. Yet there are men who talk glibly about the burdens on land. The chief burden on the land is the landlord. You and I, perhaps, would not grumble at having to support him, but it is really too bad that the produce of our hands and brains should be heavily taxed by the Government to relieve him of the onerous conditions under which he obtained his lavish grants.

XCIX.

The Wellesleys.

HAVING already noticed every English dukedom save one, I now turn to our latest military dukedom—that of Wellington. To sketch the military and political career of Arthur, first Duke of Wellington, would be quite superfluous, even if I had sufficient space at my disposal. My business is with his rewards rather than his work. Suffice it to say that I am one of those who regard the great French War as avoidable in its inception, but unavoidable when Napoleon had made himself master of France. The Allies, and especially England, made Bonaparte almost a necessity to the French nation; but when once he had seized supreme power and embarked upon his career of conquest, resistance to the death became necessary. I hold, therefore, that Wellington was engaged in a war wherein the independence of Europe was at stake, that his victories were of vital importance to Europe at large and to England in particular. I consider, too, that it would have been all the better for the Duke's reputation if he had never meddled in politics—that he was a good soldier, but a bad statesman. Successful generals have often proved wise administrators of dependencies like our Indian Empire, but the atmosphere of militarism is not that in which wise governors of free peoples are nurtured. Since the days of Marlborough we have usually kept the professions of the soldier and the statesman far apart. The solitary exception is that of the Duke of Wellington, and the results are not such as to induce us to repeat the experiment.

The Wellesleys were formerly Cowleys, or Colleys, and appear to have been office holders in Ireland almost uninterruptedly from the days of Henry VIII. to the middle of the last century. A daughter of the house married into the family of Wesley, or Wellesley, whose ancestor had accompanied

Henry II. to Ireland, and received from that monarch considerable grants of confiscated lands in Meath and Kildare. The Wesley estates ultimately reverted to Richard Colley, who assumed the name of Wesley, and was created Lord Mornington. His son was advanced to an Earldom. The eldest son of the Earl became Governor-General of India, and, under his administration, the empire of Mysore, ruled by Tippoo Sahib, was conquered. Thus it was that he was created Marquis Wellesley. At his death the Marquisate expired, but the Earldom of Mornington passed from him to his next brother, thence to that brother's son and grandson, and, at the death of the latter, it passed to the second and present Duke of Wellington. The first Duke of Wellington was the third son of the first Earl of Mornington.

I have found it somewhat difficult to sum up the pecuniary rewards of the great Duke of Wellington, and can only pretend to approximate accuracy. We need not trouble ourselves about presentations of services of plate, of jewelled swords, gold vases, and such showy but unprofitable rewards. In the year 1810, shortly after the battle of Talavera, the Duke was awarded an annual pension of £2,000 by vote of the House of Commons. In 1812 he was voted another annual pension of £2,000. After the close of the great war in 1814, Parliament voted £300,000 for the purchase of an estate for him, and such further sum as would make up his income to £17,000 per annum. Besides this, he had a grant of an estate in Spain, of the estimated value of £10,000 a year. After the battle of Waterloo, Parliament voted him an additional £200,000 for the purchase of an estate and mansion; and he also obtained the grant of an estate in the Netherlands, of the estimated annual value of £2,000. With the Parliamentary grants the estate of Strathfieldsaye, in Hampshire, was purchased—a bargain of which the Iron Duke had no favourable opinion, for he declared that it would have ruined any other man than himself. How far his estimate of the folly of the trustees was well founded I cannot say; but, if it was a bad bargain, unquestionably a grateful nation did its best to repair any deficiency in that respect. I find that, in 1830, the various pensions which the Duke received from the Consolidated Fund amounted to no less than £8,296 a year. He also drew, as Constable of the Tower, £950; as Colonel of the Rifle Brigade, £238; as

Colonel of the 1st Regiment of Foot Guards, £2,695; and as Lord Warden of the Cinque Ports, £295 annually. Subsequently, he held the offices of Chief Ranger and Keeper of Hyde Park and St. James's Park.

Leaving out of sight the Duke's military pay, his emoluments during the time when he held civil offices, as Prime Minister, &c., and his salary during the many years that he held the post of Commander-in-Chief, the Duke of Wellington must have received from the public purse, in one way or another, upwards of a million of money; and, if he retained the estates in Spain and the Netherlands, and their actual value proved to be equal to the estimate, he must have received from these sources nearly half a million more. Nor must we forget that the two Parliamentary pensions of £4,000 per annum descended to the two next inheritors of the title.

It was not merely the Duke of Wellington himself who was rewarded by a grateful nation, the whole family participated in his success and in that of the Marquis Wellesley. It was estimated in the year 1823 that the Wellesleys obtained no less than £99,000 annually, either from Church or State. The Marquis Wellesley had a pension of £5,000 from the East India Company, held a place as Lord Steward of the Household, with a salary of £1,540, and another as Joint Remembrancer of the Court of Exchequer in Ireland, with a salary of £5,387. The Marquis had no legitimate issue, but it was stated by an Irish newspaper in his lifetime that his numerous family were all provided for in the public service. The mother of the Duke of Wellington—the Countess of Mornington—had a pension of £600 per annum, dating from 1813. A brother of the Duke, the Rev. G. V. Wellesley, went into the Church, where, beside a Royal Chaplaincy, he held a Prebendary in Durham Cathedral, value £2,000; the rectory of Bishop Wearmouth, value £2,000 and a residence; the rectory of Chelsea, value £1,400 and a residence; and the rectory of Therfield, value £937 and a residence. Besides these, there were other relatives, who were provided for in an almost equally lavish manner. The Duke's youngest brother, Lord Cowley, for instance, held in succession a number of lucrative diplomatic appointments, and one of his sons, who went into the Church, became Dean of Windsor and Lord High Almoner of the Queen, offices which he still continues to hold. The first Lord Cowley, who at one time held the post of Ambassador at Vienna, with a salary of £12,000, retired on a pension of £2,500. The Duke of Wellington also had another brother, Lord Maryborough, who for a great number of years was a place-holder, and seems to have been under the special care of his yet more fortunate brother, the Duke. He began in 1802 with the office of Clerk of the Ordnance. Successively he held the places of Chief Secretary for Ireland, Master of the Mint, Master of the King's Buckhounds, and Postmaster-General. Leaving the less important relatives of the great Duke, I think, from the examples I have given, that the estimate that the family must at one time have drawn nearly a hundred thousand pounds a year from the public revenue is not far from correct.

At the death of the Great Duke, in 1852, he was succeeded by his eldest son, who is a lieutenant-general in the Army (though his military achievements are *nil*), and Lord-Lieutenant of Middlesex. The present Duke of Wellington owns in—

Hants	.	.	.	.	.	15,847 acres
Herts	.	.	.	.	.	2,246 ,,
Somerset	.	.	.	.	.	529 ,,
Essex	.	.	.	.	.	337 ,,
					Total	18,999 ,,

With a rental of £31,233.

The present Duke is over seventy years of age, and has no children. His nephew is presumptive heir to the dukedom and to the pension of £4,000.

How far the prodigious rewards of the Marlboroughs, Nelsons, and Wellingtons serve as an incentive to those who are engaged in the profession of arms it would be difficult to say; but there can be no comparison between the material prizes of the soldier and those which are offered to those who serve the nation by other than destructive arts. In literature our mightiest Englishmen—Shakespeare and Milton, and others of later time—have met with scanty recognition from the State. Our greatest inventors—Arkwright, and Watt, and Stephenson—died commoners. Even our greatest statesmen met with scant reward. Since the accession of the House of Hanover, not one of them has climbed from the House of

Commons to the highest rank in the Peerage. It is only the successful general who, commencing at the lowest round of the ladder, can hope to aspire to the position of a Duke. In future times, our children may reach a more just estimate of the value of the services rendered by men to their fellows.

C.
The Power of the Landed.

MY work having extended to double the length which I had at first projected, I consider that I may now bring the inquiry to a close. It would not be difficult to continue it for another year, but having sketched the agrarian history of most of our leading families, including every English ducal house, I think I have travelled over sufficient ground for all practical purposes. Before finally closing this series of articles, however, I deem it useful to sum up the results of this inquiry, and to supplement it by a few general observations which could hardly find a place when dealing with particular families. I am not conscious of having done any man an injustice. That the corrections I have had to make have been so few and so trivial is to me ample proof that there is hardly anything for which I need offer an apology. I have a strong conviction that, if the whole truth could only be ascertained, the only thing that I should have to apologise for would be that my record of the misdeeds of our great houses has been so incomplete. I have had to use such materials as lay ready to hand, chiefly peerages of ancient date and county histories, the compilers of which found a market for their wares among the great houses or those connected with them. Such writers almost invariably represent everything in the most favourable light, and it is only by carefully observing their unguarded admissions that it is possible to get at the truth. From historians like Macaulay, Froude, Burton, Green, Massey, and even Lord Stanhope, I have derived much valuable information, and that able, but now almost forgotten, writer, Mr. William Carpenter, has been often useful in putting me on the right track.

We must never forget that, while in France and other Continental countries an aristocratic title involves nothing more than the right of its owner to use a certain style in denominating himself, in England it means that the owner thereof shall have the right of sitting in the Upper House, and of helping to mar or put an actual veto upon the legislative work of the representatives of the people. Since 1832 these powers have rarely been exercised in a direct manner. Indirectly, however, they are of great importance. The fact that such powers exist continually has a strong influence in shaping legislation. At the same time, I cannot but admit that so long as a landed aristocracy exists it does less mischief sitting apart, for it cannot hope successfully to contend against the clearly-expressed will of the House of Commons.

Even as it is, the landed interest dominates to such an extent in that House, that only in a qualified sense can we call it the House of the People. No less than 176 of its members are connected with the Peerage by birth or marriage, and beside these there is a very large number who represent the landowners who are commoners. The state of our county representation is truly lamentable, not so much on account of the party politics of the great majority of county members, but because of the legislative qualifications of a large proportion of them. It would puzzle the most ardent Conservative to discover the senatorial merits of Lords Burghley, Bective, Emlyn, Dalkeith, Holmesdale, Percy, Newport, March, Stafford, Yarmouth, the Hon. W. Egerton, and the Marquis of Hamilton. They sit for counties as representatives of land, not of men. If they were not their fathers' sons no one would have thought of nominating them. There are sons of peers like Lord Hartington, Lord E. Fitzmaurice, Lord George Hamilton, and Lord Sandon, who stand in quite another category, but these are brilliant exceptions. As a rule the aristocratic county members represent not even the Conservatism of the bucolic mind, but simply themselves and their fathers. Could anything be more humiliating than the present position in South Warwickshire? The farmers very properly insist upon a direct representative; one of the two sitting members is obliged to retire; but the man who is forced to retire is the best of the two. There can be no comparison between Sir J. Eardley Wilmot and Lord Yarmouth in point of ability or usefulness; yet the former has to withdraw, and the latter, with no qualification save that he is the son of the Marquis of Hertford, remains. Rural superstitions are proverbially tenacious of life, and the electoral superstitions are perhaps the most tenacious of all. Until adversity forced men to think, agricultural tenants, as a rule, seemed to regard it to be as much their duty to vote in accordance with their landlords' wishes as to pay their rents and rates. If the landlords or their fathers before them had created the land, they could not have been more docile. It probably never occurred to them to consider how the land had been acquired. As these articles of mine have been extensively quoted in provincial papers, they probably have set not a few thinking upon the subject; and if the result has been that some agricultural tenants have been led to take a more accurate view of their position, I shall not have written in vain. Alike to the urban population, to the tenant-farmers, and to the agricultural labourers, there is nothing more pernicious, from a political point of view, than the agrarian electoral superstition. Intrinsically there is little to fear from the Conservative instincts of Englishmen; it is only as those instincts are made subservient to landlordism that they become a grave national peril.

Lord Beaconsfield has told us in one of his novels that " we owe the English Peerage to three sources: the spoliation of the Church, the open and flagrant sale of its honours by the elder Stuarts, and the boroughmongering of our own times. These are the three main sources of the existing Peerage of England, and, in my opinion, disgraceful ones." For once I agree with his Lordship, both in his statements and in his inferences. Of course there are exceptions, though not of great importance. That which strikes me most forcibly is that almost all of these great houses, whether ancient or modern, seem to have run to seed. "With such a vantage-ground for nobleness," how few distinguish themselves. Even the Dukes, the *duces*, are no longer leaders of the people. "What are they doing?" asked Carlyle a generation ago; and he gave the scornful answer, "Preserving their game." That is just what the great majority of them are doing at the present hour. Consider the advantages these men possess. Ample wealth, complete leisure, the highest education, full publicity if they have anything worth saying, influence out of all proportion to their intrinsic merits. The nation has heaped upon them all possible advantages. What are the services they render in return? Who are those who have distinguished themselves in statesmanship or in literature? You can count them on your fingers. As for those who have made a name as philanthropists you may count them on your thumbs. Thus much for living lords; let us go back a little, and take the Settlement of the House of Hanover as a starting point. Who among our statesmen of the first rank was a member of the House of Lords, or could hope to reach there by right of primogeniture? Not Walpole, nor either of the Pitts, nor Fox, nor Burke, nor Canning, nor Palmerston, nor Russell, nor Gladstone. Among living peers, born to a peerage, only Earl Granville, the Duke of Argyll, the Earl of Carnarvon, the Earl of Derby, and the Marquis of Salisbury, rise above the level of respectable mediocrity, and the last was born a younger son. Considering the splendid traditions of many of the noble houses, we might have expected greater things. With their large acres, their vast wealth, their exalted position, how much might the peers of the United Kingdom achieve! how small are their actual performances! With but very few exceptions, their translation of the phrase " Noblesse oblige" seems to be, "Nobility obliges us to do nothing."

CI.
Modern Peerages.

I HAVE dealt almost exclusively with our older nobility, but much might have been said of the wholesale creations of the four last reigns. Mr. Disraeli's phrase, "the borough-mongering of our own times," is almost obsolete now; but it is still true that the exercise of electoral influence is the surest road to the House of Lords. When the present Premier was last in office several peers were created who owe their titles to political partisanship, among the number being Lords Penrhyn, Kesteven and O'Neil. But, during the last six years of power, the large-acred and steady-voting Tories have had a rare time of it, while superannuated or incompetent colleagues of the Minister have been lifted into the House of Lords when offices could not be found for them. For nearly forty years Sir John Pakington sat for what was once the pocket-borough of Droitwich; in 1874 the people of Droitwich asserted their independence, and rejected Sir John. At once he was created Lord Hampton. Colonel Wilson Patten, another old colleague, had to be provided for, so he was created Lord Winmarleigh. Then there was the heir of "My dear Grey de Wilton," whom the electors of Bath placed at the bottom of the poll in 1874; he, too, was consoled with a seat in the Upper House. The Ormsby-Gores had done much for the Tories in Shropshire and other counties, and the late Lord Harlech had his reward in his elevation to the Upper House in 1876. The Sturts had been equally useful in Dorsetshire, and in the same year Mr. H. G. Sturt became Lord Alington. Mr. John Tollemache had long served the Tories well in Cheshire and Suffolk; he had his reward the same year by being created Lord Tollemache. Mr. Gerard had helped to secure South Lancashire; he became Lord Gerard. Lord Wharncliffe had served the Tories equally well in South Yorkshire; his reward was an earldom. The late Lord Ravensworth and his son, Lord Eslington, had fought hard for Conservatism in Northumberland and Durham; his lordship was created an earl. The Homes, hitherto Scotch peers, were rewarded for the use of their great territorial influence with an English barony. Mr. Hylton Joliffe, whose seat for Wells was abolished by the last Reform Bill, was consoled with the title of Lord Hylton. Sir Charles Adderley conveniently retired from the Ministry not long ago, and became Lord Norton. The Government has certainly been mindful of its friends, but its own principal members have not been lost sight of. Mr. Disraeli has become Earl of Beaconsfield, Lord Cairns has become Earl Cairns, Mr. Gathorne Hardy has become Viscount Cranbrook, and Sir Stafford Northcote is generally supposed to be only within a few months of his peerage. Perhaps before the Government abandons office Earl Ulundi and Lord Smith will be added to the number.

These instances, drawn from the history of the last six years, will suffice to show how unscrupulously the House of Lords is used at the present time. The first step for a wealthy *parvenu* is to buy up land right and left; the second is to keep a steady pressure upon his agricultural tenants at each election; in due time he or his heir may hope for the coveted reward. Since the accession of the House of Hanover a very large proportion of the modern aristocracy—probably half of them—owe one or more titles to the exercise of electoral intimidation. We deal in a very curious manner with offences against the free exercise of the franchise. The bribed electors are temporarily disfranchised, the briber obtains an office or a judgeship. The ruffian who tramples on a voter's head is sent to gaol; the landlord who tramples on a voter's conscience is created a peer.

There have been not a few modern Peers who have gained their titles by the possession of land alone, as well as a yet larger number who have gained them by the exercise of such influence as the possession of land carried with it. We must never lose sight of the fact that the House of Lords is not only a legislative body, but also a great agrarian institution. We hear much, at the present time, of the artificial causes which tend to the aggregation of estates. We may do much by destroying such of these artificial causes as are due to class legislation, or to the permission by the law of practices which are inimical to the public interest. But the House of

Modern Peerages.

Lords itself is the most powerful of all these artificial causes. I am not pleading for its abolition, but I bring the fact forward to show that those who dread Free Trade in Land will still have a powerful conservative force on which to rely, and to serve as an argument against the degradation of the Peerage, to which we are growing accustomed. We are constantly told that great modern estates which have been acquired by purchase are only the results of natural causes; but in England wealthy buyers have constantly been induced to accumulate land, no matter at what price purchased, as a road to the House of Lords. Thus, out of one great manufacturing establishment in South Wales, during the present century, two Peerages and a Baronetcy have been produced; but, as a necessary preliminary, the wealthy ironmasters bought up land right and left. The first Mr. Loyd who came to London owned no land at all; the first Lord Overstone has 30,849 acres of land in eleven different counties. The Barings, Caringtons, Foleys, Denisons, and other modern families, have travelled to the Peerage by the same road; and I might name a multitude who have already reached the half-way house of the Baronetage. Even when a coronet has been obtained, the earth-hunger is unappeased. There are steps in the Peerage to be gained, and the noble who has not sufficient brains to become a statesman can still continue to buy up land. It is a common complaint against farmers that they have been too eager to farm more land than their capital allows them to manage properly. Unfortunately, a great many landowners have set them the example. A generation ago, the most conspicuous instance of this tendency was found in the case of one who had already reached the highest rank in the Peerage—the Duke of Buckingham. Though the family was already embarrassed, the Duke went on buying up land which paid him two per cent. with money borrowed at four per cent., until at last the inevitable crash came. There are not a few landlords who have recently been playing the same game, though more circumspectly. It is simply impossible for them to do justice to the land, or to make provision for the depression that has overtaken agriculture. For my part, I am not all surprised at the gradual extinction of the yeoman class, when we offer the highest prizes in the State to the men who will accumulate the most land in their own hands.

There are some Peers who are not suffering from family

greed of aggrandisement, but from past family extravagance. I pity them. They must make no sign of distress, while the teeth of the fox concealed beneath the cloak are fixed in their flesh. Honest poverty is not hard to bear so long as it does not verge on destitution ; but to a good man, assumed wealth masking actual poverty must be a constant torture. But if I pity such men, still more do I pity their lands and all that dwell thereon. If an ordinary trader cannot meet his bills, we wind up his affairs in the Bankruptcy Court; if a Duke of Newcastle, with 34,000 acres of land in a single county, is in the same position, another measure is dealt out to him. From a sentimental point of view, it may be well that life-ownership should save an old family from destruction ; but what of the interests of those who live upon the estates of a bankrupt lord?

Yet another point must not be overlooked. The rent-rolls given in the preceding chapters must only be regarded as giving an approximate idea of the incomes of their owners. In some cases I believe they are greatly under the mark; in others the owners would be only too glad to put into their pockets the amounts put down. There are not a few estates, even where earth-hunger and extravagance have had but little influence—where "the dead hand" controls the living much more than most people are aware ; and just now landowners are beginning to feel this most acutely. Family encumbrances are a fixed sum; rents fluctuate. It was all very well so long as rentals had an upward tendency ; it is otherwise now. One of the most beneficent results of the great uprising of the farm labourers was to quicken the zeal for improvement in the housing of the men. In some counties the expenditure must have been very large, and has been, doubtless, owing largely to the facilities afforded by Land Improvement Companies. These Companies have also done not a little in the way of agricultural improvement generally, though the inquiries of Lord Salisbury's Commission showed that the cost to landowners was burdensome even in prosperous times. What must it be now, when rents are fallen on all sides?

Of legal Peerages of recent date nothing adverse could be reasonably advanced if only they were but Life Peerages. Such men as Lords Selborne, Penzance, O'Hagan, and Coleridge, would be ornaments to any Legislative Assembly. The same may be said of what may be called the Civil Service

Peerages. The matured wisdom and experience of such men as Lords Blachford, Hammond and Cottesloe, should not be lost to the country, or left to find vent in magazine articles, when age has necessitated their retirement from active duty in the less obtrusive, but none the less eminent duties of Statesmanship. As to our modern military peerages, I fear they are quite numerous enough to make the Service impatient of long-continued peace. Since the outbreak of the Crimean War, we have had Lords Raglan, Clyde, Strathnairn, Sandhurst, Napier of Magdala, and Airey. Against these, Literature can only place two novelists and one historian, and these would have never sat in the House of Lords had they not been also politicians.

CII.
The Growth of the Landed Interest.

IN a hundred chapters I have briefly sketched the agrarian history of the majority of our most notable aristocratic houses. In my selection I have not been guided mainly by the greatness of their possessions, but rather by their historic interest or present prominence. Thus I have included some like the Erskines and Fanes, whose estates are small, and have altogether omitted peers like Lord Tredegar, with over 100,000 acres, and Lord Penrhyn, with a rentroll of £66,000. I have dealt in all with 122 nobles, owning in round numbers nearly 5½ millions of acres, with a rentroll of nearly 5¾ millions, an average ownership of 45,000 acres, and an average rentroll of over £46,000.

It certainly has not been my object to seek out examples of what, for want of a better word, I will call the illegitimate acquisition of landed property. When once I have selected a house for inquiry, I have never desisted from completing its story because I found that it had a clear record. Yet the result is that those who can claim that they have obtained their lands by money solely acquired in commercial or professional pursuits, are singularly few—perhaps about a dozen in all.

Compared with other people we are a landless nation, and we are a landless nation in consequence of continual encroachments upon the rights our ancient forefathers possessed. On this point let me quote Mr. Freeman, who says in his Norman Conquest:—"In the realities of History, the king and the lord—that is, the lord on a great scale, and the lord on a small one—are each something which has crept in unawares, something which has grown up at the expense of rights more ancient than its own. Each alike, king and lord, grew to his full dimensions by a series of gradual and stealthy encroachments on the rights of the people. As the king swallowed up the powers and possessions of the nation, so the lord swallowed up the rights and possessions of 'the mark.'" That which was true in ancient times is also true in modern days. Throughout the reigns of the Hanoverian Kings landowners' Parliaments were constantly passing enclosure Acts, desirable, for the most part, with a view to increased production, but resulting in the appropriation of between seven and eight millions of acres of common land, of which the common people retained but a very small proportion—not more than threequarters of a million acres in all. Occasionally I have been able to point out where vast estates have been increased by these Acts; but generally it has been impossible to obtain exact information. Whenever the agricultural labourers are sufficiently powerful to press their claim to the cultivation of "public lands," especially to charity lands, they will find in the injustice with which their fathers were treated a powerful argument for the equity of their demands.

It is worthy of notice that anciently the lavish grants of the Crown were checked by the power of Resumption. Most of the vast estates seized and retained by William the Conqueror were dissipated by William Rufus, who was compelled subsequently to resume the grants which he had made. Henry IV. was called upon by his Parliament to resume the grants, parcel of the ancient inheritance of the Crown, which had been alienated by Edward III. and Richard II. Similar demands were made and acted upon in the reigns of Henry VI., Edward IV., and Henry VII. In fact, from Henry III. to Henry VIII. there was only one reign in which one or more Bills of Resumption were not passed. Had it been impossible for English monarchs to alienate the estates appropriated to the support of the dignity of the Crown, we should have had no occasion in modern times for Royal grants or dowries. Repeated attempts were, indeed, made to restrain the Crown from alienating its lands, but they were generally opposed by crafty and greedy Ministers. The latest instance of a successful Resumption Bill was in the reign of William III. About the middle of last century the grasping avarice of one of the Lowthers, in attempting to obtain for himself a large tract of Crown lands, which had been previously granted to the Bentincks, occasioned the passing of what is known as the Nullus Tempus Act, which secured the grantees of Crown lands against any resumption of their properties.

It is obviously impossible to reckon up acre by acre the

quantity of land which has at various times been obtained otherwise than by purchase. The agrarian history of many of the great houses is complicated by the acquisition of property by marriage. I have, however, traced the previous history of such lands in a sufficient number of cases to show that we may safely presume that as a rule they have been acquired in much the same way as the rest. After a careful consideration of all the houses I have noticed, bearing in mind modern Enclosure Acts, and the increased value of lands due to the improvements of tenants, I cannot but arrive at the conclusion that not one-tenth of the estates in question have been acquired for value received. All the rest, in one way or another, has been obtained for nothing.

In Ireland the great majority of the landlords owe their possessions to successive confiscation. In the North of Scotland, where the so-called rights of property have been put into force with almost unexampled cruelty and injustice, the landlords owe their position to the iniquity of law. Let me quote Mr. Freeman once more:—"When, as in the Celtic parts of the British Islands, the old constitution of the gens or clan went on longer than it did amongst ourselves, we can see the actual process by which, under the influence of an alien jurisprudence, the chief of the clan changed into the lord of the soil. The land of the clan was held to be the land of the chief, and the body of the clansmen, *in truth his fellow-owners*, came to be looked on as tenants holding of him."

With regard to Irish landowners it ought to be borne in mind that in a very large number of cases it is the labour of successive generations of tenants which has given to the land almost all the value it possesses, and that not a few landlords have improved their properties by the aid of the State. When the Corn Laws were repealed a sop was given to the landowners. In the darkest days of commercial distress no statesman ever proposed to find out of the public revenue capital for manufacturers or shopkeepers; yet this was what was done for landlords after the repeal of the Corn Laws. Acts were passed which declared, "Whereas it is desirable that works of drainage should be encouraged in order to promote the increased productiveness of the land and the healthiness of the districts when it is required, and to supply the demand for agricultural labour, especially at that season of the year when other sources are expanded, &c.," £2,000,000 were allotted to English landowners, and £1,000,000 to Irish landowners, in order to make advances to them, to be gradually repaid at a low interest. Nor was the accommodation of the State Loan office resorted to by comparatively small proprietors. Among the Irish recipients was the wealthy Marquis of Waterford. For the most part, too, the landlords were content that the farmers should do the work of improvement, and we have the authority of Mr. Caird for stating that sometimes they borrowed of the Government for their permanent advantage, and charged the farmer, who had only a temporary advantage, one and one and a half per cent. more than they themselves paid.

The popular theory that in England and Scotland all permanent improvements have been effected by the landlords is only very partially true. Take, for instance, the great reclamations of land in the Eastern Counties. Anciently, when the embankments gave way, the sheriff had full authority to impress the labour of the county. At different times Acts of Parliament were passed authorising the construction of drainage works, and tenants as well as owners were made contributories. I know I shall be met with the theory that it is the landlord who pays rates in the end, because the tenant would take them into consideration in making his bargain. But until very recent times the tenant brought up to agriculture had no choice in the matter but to submit to the terms of the owner of that natural monopoly—land. We, who live in days when the large farmer has many opportunities of employing his capital profitably at home, and can with comparative ease take it to the very ends of the earth, must not make him the standard of measurement for the ancient farmer who lived when he was practically shut up to one employment and one locality.

If we turn from the lowlands to the hills, the same truth holds good that the cultivator has done the greater part of the work of reclamation. Had I but the space I could give multitudinous examples. Only give a young and energetic man a nineteen years' lease of an uncultivated waste contiguous to his farm, and he will work miracles. In a multitude of cases it has needed not even that small security, the landlord's or agent's word was enough. But when the lease expired, or the old landlord or the old tenant died, the permanent gain at once became the property of the owner of the bare soil. I have walked on land, not more than a long day's walk from London, which is now paying its owner three times what it did a generation ago, and the owner has not laid out a single sixpence upon it. Landowners may try to throw dust in the eyes of the public by complaining that they cannot just now get three per cent. interest on the present purchase-money of agricultural land; but when I read that a little farm in Carmarthenshire, which in the middle of the last century only brought in £10 a year to its owner, now pay his descendant ten times that amount every year, I laugh them to scorn.

CII.
Conclusions.

DURING the next few years we may expect two demands in regard to the land to be put forward, the demand of the landowners to be relieved of burdens at the expense of the public, and the demand of the public that property in land shall not be used to the general disadvantage. I trust that I have put not a few weapons into the hands of those who will resist the former and insist upon the latter.

The favourite panacea of the landed interest for the alleviation of agricultural distress is the remission of local burdens. The tendency of Tory legislation is shown by the Prisons Act, the Scotch Roads and Bridges Act, and the relief of the counties from the charge of lunatics. We shall, probably, have further demands in the same direction, particularly as regards Education and the Poor Law. Already some Conservative members are demanding that half the cost of the in-door poor shall be thrown upon the Consolidated Fund and the other half spread over the whole country. This means nothing more nor less than that the landlords shall be relieved of present burdens, for, save where farmers have leases, and then they obtain only a temporary advantage, rates remitted go into the pocket of the landlord. There are not a few country members, too, who declare their readiness to vote for Protection, if they can only find fools enough in the towns to follow the Reciprocity craze. The latter only want to use Protection as a temporary weapon by which to force a more liberal tariff for their manufactured goods; but the former desire a permanent Bread Tax, so that their rents may be kept up by the enforced contributions of every mechanic and labourer in the kingdom. Whether they want us to keep up the dignity of their station by the remission of burdens or the imposition of a tax for their support, it will be quite sufficient answer to point them to the means by which their estates have been acquired and have grown to their present value.

Their enormous incomes are of comparatively modern growth. We have it on established evidence that, shortly after the Restoration, the revenue of the greatest estates in the kingdom was only about £20,000 per annum; and this applies only to such men as the Dukes of Ormond, Buckingham and Albermarle. Compare these with the Dukes of Westminster and Portland, or the Marquis of Bute or Lord Derby, or a score of others mentioned in the preceding chapters. The wages of agricultural labourers are from three times to four times what they were then, but in those times agricultural labourers had opportunities of adding to their resources of which most of their descendants have been long since deprived, mainly through the grasping policy of the landlords.

At the same time, land-reformers must remember that on many estates much capital has been laid out during the last generation or two, and especially within the last few years, in improved buildings, cottages, drainage, &c. How partially the work of drainage has been accomplished may be seen from the report of Lord Salisbury's Commission in 1870, that out of 20,000,000 acres requiring drainage, only 3,000,000 had been drained.

We must never lose sight of the root idea that property in land is a trust rather than a right. "Land," says John Stuart Mill, "is the gift of Nature to the whole human race . . . it is a necessary of life . . . it is limited in quantity." Even though we might derive our whole consumption of agricultural produce from foreign countries, it is not to our national advantage that we should do so. Considering the means by which land has been usually acquired, I ask what right have the rent-owners to cripple or ruin agriculture? What right has the Marquis of Salisbury, whose ancestors obtained all they had as gifts from the Monarch, to hinder the application of capital to the soil by contracting himself out of the Agricultural Holdings Act? What right has the Duke of Rutland, who owes not a little to Enclosure Acts, passed with the declared object of increasing the agricultural produce of the country, to keep game on his estates to devour the crops that other men have reared? What right has any landowner to provide against the consequences of family improvidence by tying up his land in the hands of men who cannot discharge a landowner's duties? I know the cant of such men as Lord Elcho about "freedom of contract." There should be no freedom of contract detrimental to the public interest, and that is, I believe, an established principle of law. Behind the right of the landowner is the right of the nation—a right which it has never lost, and which it will, ere long, have to again exercise. Parliament, which has passed Resumption Bills, Enclosure Acts, Nullus Tempus Acts—which recognises the ultimate right of the nation in the Irish Encumbered Estates and Land Acts, the Artisans' Dwellings Act, in every Public Improvement Bill, and every Railway Bill, may and will exercise its powers still further.

I refrain from arguing for or against any particular scheme of land reform. I am content to lay down one principle—that the right of the nation is superior to every other right, and that the rights of a class who have acquired landed property in all kinds of sinister ways must always be subordinated thereto. When the fathers of this generation of landowners asked, "Cannot we do what we like with our own?" Thomas Carlyle scornfully replied, "Yes, indeed! If I could melt Gneiss Rock, and create Law of Gravitation; if I could stride out to the Doggerbank some morning, and, striking down my trident there into the mud-waves, say, 'Be land, be fields, meadows, mountains, and fresh rolling streams!' by Heaven, I should incline to have the letting of *that* land in perpetuity, and sell the wheat of it, or burn the wheat of it, according to my own good judgment."

My lords and gentlemen, you have no right to do what you will with land. You have no right whatever to prevent it producing as much as possible. None. Your conquests, your confiscations, your Royal grants, your Enclosure Acts must all be subordinated to the right of the nation to support itself and the right of the people to live. I have shown you how you have obtained possession; it is for you to prove, if you can, that you have any right whatever to exceptional privileges. You have farms on your hands, have you? Then go back to the rents of your great-great-great-great-grandfathers, or else hand them back to the State. It is not our business to keep up your rents to a certain figure. You always preached the law of supply and demand to the labourer; now take it for your own comfort. You always denounced any trade union rules in restraint of trade; we shall apply the same principle to yourselves. You keep upon your lands vermin that eat up very often a fourth of the farmer's crops, you claim to be a preferential creditor, you tie the farmer down to cultivate as you please, you refuse the farmer compensation for improvement. All these things are in restraint of the trade of agriculture. You fence round your great estates with artificial legal restrictions, which keep vast estates in the hands of men whose interest is to get all they can out of the land for the benefit of their younger children, and which prevent the golden stream of capital from fertilising the soil—all this is in restraint of trade.

All this you do in the prostituted name of Freedom. It is the freedom of one man to injure another, the freedom of the few to gratify their selfishness at the expense of the whole community. It cannot stand. Ignorance and corruption and servility may avail you for a little time longer, but cannot avert the inevitable end. The longer you delay reform the more drastic will it be when it comes. At the present moment you have the opportunity to secure yourselves and even to check the fall in your rents by allowing to the food-producers the same legal rights which every other manufacturer enjoys. —if you are wise you will use the opportunity. We are on the eve of great changes. Hitherto, British agriculture has been very much subordinated to family aggrandisement, selfish pleasures, and aristocratic assumptions. Those who are the competitors of your tenants know nothing of these disadvantages. You must yield to the moderate demands now made, and the sooner the better for yourselves, and your tenants, and the nation at large.

THE END.

LONDON:
BRADLEY AND COMPANY, PRINTERS, 12, 13, AND 14, FETTER LANE, E.C.